PETERSON'S

ULTIMATE GRE TOOL KIT

Drew Johnson

THOMSON

PETERSON'S

Australia • Canada • Mexico • Singapore • Spain • United Kingdom • United States

About Thomson Peterson's

Thomson Peterson's (www.petersons.com) is a leading provider of education information and advice, with books and online resources focusing on education search, test preparation, and financial aid. Its Web site offers searchable databases and interactive tools for contacting educational institutions, online practice tests and instruction, and planning tools for securing financial aid. Thomson Peterson's serves 110 million education consumers annually.

Petersons.com/publishing

Check out our Web site at www.petersons.com/publishing to see if there is any new information regarding the test and any revisions or corrections to the content of this book. We've made sure the information in this book is accurate and up-to-date; however, the test format or content may have changed since the time of publication.

For more information, contact Thomson Peterson's, 2000 Lenox Drive, Lawrenceville, NJ 08648; 800-338-3282; or find us on the World Wide Web at www.petersons.com/about.

© 2004 Thomson Peterson's, a part of The Thomson Corporation
Thomson Learning™ is a trademark used herein under license.

Chapter 5: GRE Word List is excerpted from *The Insider's Guide to the GRE CAT*. 2nd Edition, by Karl Weber. © Petersons, 2002.

Editor: Mandie Rosenberg; Production Editor: Megan Hellerman; Manufacturing Manager: Ray Golaszewski; Composition Manager: Gary Rozmierski; Cover and Interior Design: Allison Sullivan; CD Producer: Carol Aickley; CD Quality Assurance: Jeff Pagano.

Contributing Writer: Keith Cox

ISBN 0-7689-1432-9

Printed in the United States of America

10 9 8 7 6 5 4 3 2 1   06 05 04

First Edition

Contents

PART V: APPENDIX

About This Tool Kit

Your Tools

Peterson's Ultimate GRE Tool Kit provides the complete package you need to score your personal best on the GRE and get into your top-choice program. Unlike any book previously published, this tool kit contains many features that used to be available *only* to those who purchased expensive test-prep classes.

e-Tutoring

Use the CD to go on line to register for one-on-one math help from a live expert whenever you need it. Tutoring is offered using an on-line whiteboard shared by you and the tutor, which allows you to communicate with one another in real time. However, if you prefer, you can submit your math question in writing instead and receive a written answer within 24 hours.

The free tutoring offered with this product is limited to 30 minutes, although you may purchase more time if you need it. A written response to a submitted question counts as 20 minutes. The tutoring service is available for six months from the date you register on line. *Note:* The e-tutoring service offered to purchasers of this 2005 edition will expire on January 1, 2006.

This service is available 24 hours a day, seven days a week for most of the year. During the summer the service is available from 9 a.m. to 1 a.m. Eastern Standard Time. Due to low demand, the service is not available during several holiday periods, including Thanksgiving, Christmas, Easter, Labor Day, and Memorial Day.

Remember, to register for this service, you will need the CD that accompanies this book. You will also need to refer to this book to provide the access code when prompted.

Essay Scoring

The CD that accompanies this book allows you to write 2 practice test essays on line and receive a score for each of them, which approximates your performance on the essays in the actual GRE. In addition to a score, you will also receive constructive feedback on your essays, including tips to improve your score.

With this tool kit, you get scoring for 2 practice test essays—one analysis of an issue and one analysis of an argument. If you wish, for a fee, you may obtain scoring information and feedback for additional practice essays you write on line.

Note: Your practice test essays will be scored by a computer, but on the actual GRE test, the essays are scored by a combination of a computer program and a human reader.

To register for the essay-scoring service you need the CD that accompanies this book. In addition, you will need to refer to this book to provide the access code when prompted. Note: The scoring of 2 essays is offered *free* to purchasers of the 2005 edition and this offer will expire on December 31, 2005.

Computer-Adaptive Tests on CD

The actual GRE is a computer-adaptive test (CAT)—the test questions you see depend on your performance on previous questions. On the CD-ROM, which accompanies this book, you receive 3 practice GMAT CATs that carefully reproduce the experience you can expect on test day. The additional 3 practice tests in the book can be used for further practice.

STRUCTURE OF THE GRE CAT		
Test Section	Number of Questions	Time Allotted
Computer-Based General Test		
Analytical Writing	2 writing tasks	75-minute section
	Present Your Perspective on an Issue	45 minutes
	Analyze an Argument	30 minutes
Verbal	30 questions	30-minute section
Quantitative	28 questions	45-minute section
Paper-Based General Test		
Analytical Writing	2 writing tasks	75-minute section
	Present Your Perspective on an Issue	45 minutes
	Analyze an Argument	30 minutes
Verbal	30 questions	30-minute section
Quantitative	28 questions	45-minute section

PETERSON'S
getting you there

Introduction

Does This CAT Have Claws?

Unless you've been living as a hermit in a hut for the past twenty years, chances are good you have already taken at least one standardized test in your lifetime. And we bet the list of tests you might have taken reads like a bowl of alphabet soup: SAT, ACT, ITBS, TAAS, MAT, and the PSAT/NMSQT, to name just a few. Standardized tests such as these have become a fixture of America's educational system, and like them or not, they are not going away anytime soon. Students encounter them at every stage of their education—like toll booths on the academic highway. Students in grade school get the ITBS or a similar exam. Teenagers hoping to enter college must pass through the SAT or ACT Assessment toll booth. For those brave folks who wish to enter graduate school, the exit is labeled GRE (Graduate Record Examination).

If you have taken the SAT, you will already be somewhat familiar with the GRE. Both tests are administered by the same company. Each test is a timed, multiple-choice exam that schools use as a factor when making enrollment decisions. Like the SAT, the GRE has a Quantitative (math) section and a Verbal section, and many of the questions in these SAT and GRE sections are similar in style. For example, there are analogy, sentence completions, and reading comprehension problems in the Verbal section of both tests. Many of the math topics covered on the SAT—geometry, algebra, understanding charts and graphs—make an encore appearance on the GRE.

While these similarities exist, don't be fooled into thinking the GRE is simply another SAT. The GRE is more like the SAT's weird older brother. Although you can see some family resemblance, some big differences are pretty obvious as well. For example, both tests have analogy and sentence completions problems, but GRE questions are typically much harder, since they employ a more advanced vocabulary. This is because the GRE problems assume a college-level vocabulary, while the SAT questions are set at a lower, high school level. This is just one reason why the GRE can be

1

seen as an *older* brother, since it is geared toward an older, college-educated audience. The GRE's weirdness comes from its unusual format. The SAT remains a pencil-and-paper test, meaning students across the country are still using chewed-up number 2 pencils to fiercely darken ovals on a score sheet. In contrast, the GRE is now primarily a Computer Adaptive Test (CAT), so all questions appear onscreen and are answered by using a mouse to click on an answer choice.

> There are still some places, mostly outside of the United States, that offer pencil-and-paper versions of the GRE. For more information about these exams, and about registering for the GRE in general, turn to the Appendix.

X-Ref

The GRE CAT is more than just a pencil-and-paper test transposed onto a computer screen, and unless you have taken the GRE previously, it is unlikely you have ever experienced an exam like it. For one thing, the method used to score the GRE CAT is radically different from most tests. Most exams start with easy questions, and then gradually progress to medium and harder problems. People taking this type of test might get the easiest problem wrong but still manage to answer the toughest problem correctly. In the end, the number of right answers is added up (regardless of which question was answered right or wrong), and a score is eventually determined.

On the GRE CAT, things are a bit different. How well (or not well) you answer each question determines the next question. In each section of the test, you start off with a question that has a medium difficulty rating. If you get it right, the computer says, "Okay, Brainiac, you handled that one, now try this tougher problem." If you get the next problem right, you get a harder question, and if you get that one correct, an even tougher question comes next. Depending on how you answer each question, the computer *adapts* the next question to make it either harder or easier than the next one. The way the computer adapts *your* GRE experience will be different from what other GRE test-takers experience, so even though you're all taking the same GRE CAT, you're not seeing the same problems as everyone else. In the same way, if you get the first question wrong, you'll get an easier one. And if you get the easier questions wrong, you'll see an easier question.

One consequence of the computer adaptive format is that getting a high score means handling only medium and hard questions. The more difficult your questions are, the higher your score potential, and vice versa. And there are no easy questions at the start of a section to help you get your feet

2

wet. The first question will be somewhat difficult, and it may well be the easiest problem you see on that section. In terms of your score, seeing only medium and tough questions tells you that you are getting problems right, which is good news. However, having to answer one challenging question after another makes the testing experience a really nerve-wracking, unpleasant affair, kind of like visiting a dentist who holds a personal grudge against your gums.

The Unique Peterson's Approach—Adaptive Preparation for an Adaptive Test

Test preparation is not a "one-size-fits-all" proposition. Each person has different strengths and weaknesses, different quirks and anxieties. We designed *Peterson's Ultimate GRE Tool Kit* with those differences in mind. We provide a two-tiered approach that lets you decide how best to organize your program of study to suit your needs. The first tier is the general instruction in this book, and it provides skills and strategies you will need to handle medium-level questions on each section. You then have an opportunity to *Take It to the Next Level,* and learn skills and strategies for the hardest questions on the GRE. No other GRE test-preparation book does this. It's the next best thing to having a personal tutor.

PETERSON'S
getting you there

How to Use This Book

How do you know where to begin? We give you a roadmap. After you read Chapters 1 and 2— required reading for all GRE CAT takers, no matter what—take the diagnostic pretest in Chapter 3. Use the scoring discussion provided on pages 32–33 to assess your current GRE CAT testing level. You can then either follow the suggested course of study we provide, or design your own.

Your personalized *Peterson's GRE* course of study will help you accomplish four things:

1. You will become thoroughly familiar with the computer adaptive test format.

2. You will be comfortable with all question types you will encounter on the three sections of the test.

3. You will brush up on any weak subject areas.

4. You will learn and practice specific test-taking strategies to help you achieve your target score.

If you give yourself enough time to work through your personalized course of study at a measured pace, you will accomplish all of these things.

Combining relevant factual knowledge with a sound strategic approach is the best way to score well on any standardized test, not just the GRE. This book will provide you with the facts and strategies you need to succeed on the GRE. The first step is to learn about the computer adaptive format, covered in the next chapter. So, let's get started.

Understanding the GRE

Chapter 1

Everything You Need to Know about the GRE CAT

Once upon a time, people who wanted to take the GRE (Graduate Record Examination) and go to graduate school had to take a paper-and-pencil test much like the SAT they had to take to get into college. They had to show up at a test center early on a Saturday morning with dozens of other prospective grad students, all with their number 2 pencils sharpened, ready to fill in a lot of answer sheet bubbles and spend pretty much the entire morning slogging through the test.

That was before the CAT (Computer Adaptive Test) came along and changed everything. . . .

No more number 2 pencils, no more answer bubbles; the GRE world changed. Like anything new, of course, the GRE CAT takes some getting used to. Most students have taken countless paper-and-pencil tests, but few have taken a high-stakes standardized test in a computerized format. In this chapter, we'll help you get a grip on the world of computer adaptive testing.

Why the GRE CAT Rocks!

No one likes taking a big test and having to wait, and wait, and wait for the results. The time between finishing the test and getting your score fills you with conflicting emotions. You might be confident one moment and filled with despair the next. The doubt and uncertainty won't go away until you finally get your scores in the mail, so the issue goes unresolved for about a month.

With the GRE CAT, waiting for your score is a thing of the past. Once you finish your test, you have the option to cancel your score. If you decide not to cancel, your Quantitative and Verbal scores appear on the screen. Voila! A wait of six weeks reduced to the time it takes to click one button.

Note

You don't receive your Analytical writing score immediately, since the two essays must be graded by professional readers. You should get your Analytical results back in about three to four weeks.

This immediacy is the prime advantage of the GRE CAT. It lets you know where you stand in terms of the application process and allows you to plan accordingly. Most schools release information about the average GRE scores of their incoming graduate students, and some also include an idea about the range of scores by releasing factoids like, "Over 90% of the incoming class of psychiatry students scored more than 600 on the GRE." If you wanted to go to that school, and you just received a combined Quantitative and Verbal score of 750, then you know your GRE score is good enough to get into that program.

If your GRE scores are not as high as you wanted, the immediate feedback gives you a chance to shift to Plan B right then and there. You might decide to take the exam again, although you won't be able to do so for at least one calendar month. (You can take the GRE up to five times in a single year.) If you were only considering extremely competitive schools, you might decide to broaden your search and look at some schools with more inclusive admissions standards. When your Analytical scores arrive, you will also receive a form you can use to report your scores to additional schools. (You can download this from the GRE Web site.) Knowing your scores right away gives you a chance to react to them right away.

The second big advantage to the GRE CAT is that you can schedule it for a convenient time. Other big standardized tests, like the business school exam (GMAT) and the law school entrance exam (LSAT), are given at fixed times on fixed dates at fixed locations. If any one of these three factors poses a problem for you, tough luck.

This rigidity is not a problem for the GRE CAT. Most test centers are open during regular business hours, and all you have to do is call one up and decide on a time that works well for you.

Tip

Before you schedule your actual GRE CAT, make sure you complete your personalized course of study with this book and take all the practice exams we provide. At that point, schedule an exam for two weeks in the future. Use the two-week interval to take practice CAT exams and write practice esays using the CD-ROM included. Your skills will stay fresh and you will be accustomed to taking the test on a computer.

In addition to the flexible schedule and immediacy of the test results, you can also send your scores to schools automatically by filling out the proper computer form before the test.

Why the GRE CAT Doesn't Rock

No matter what the standardized test is, one fundamental truth always holds true: The more familiar you are with the test format, the better your score will be. Familiarity with the test design allows you to focus more attention on the questions themselves and expend less mental effort just figuring out the test itself. This axiom holds true whether you are taking the MCAT (medical school exam) or a third grade math and reading exam.

Now, answer this question: How many computer adaptive tests have you taken in your lifetime?

Most people would answer "none" or "one or two" to the above question, but the real answer is, "not enough to be comfortable with them." The adaptive format is unusual, and this can work against your score. Most people are already a little nervous about taking the GRE, and the added stress of having to tap dance with the three-legged wonder that is the GRE CAT only makes matters worse.

In addition to being stranger than a paper-and-pencil test, the GRE CAT is riskier. Here's why:

Typical Test	GRE CAT	What It Means
Every question counts the same toward your score.	Earlier questions are "weighted" more than later ones.	Minor mistakes at the beginning have greater negative impact.
You can skip a question that you don't understand.	Must answer each question presented. You can't proceed to the next question until you have submitted an answer to the current one.	Limits your options regarding a tough problem you don't understand—you must guess.
Can go back and check work for careless errors.	Once the question is answered and verified, it's out of your hands.	Adaptive format eliminates the ability to go back and catch any mistakes.

If the GRE CAT were a pencil-and-paper test, you could begin with the easy questions and skip over any questions that were too tough for you on the first pass. On a second pass, you could review your work to catch any careless mistakes, and devote time on those problems you skipped. This sound strategy is no longer available to you, because of the adaptive nature of the test. Instead, you are thrown into the middle of the fray, and how well you answer the first half of the questions posed to you goes a long way toward determining your score.

This doesn't mean the adaptive nature will invariably lead to an unfairly low score. You could be given an initial set of questions that plays right into your hands, like a hard antonym that you just happen to know the definition of or a particular type of math problem you've always been good at. If that's the case, the weighted nature of the GRE CAT works to your advantage. Either way, the GRE CAT is a *riskier* test because many of the fail-safes you have on other standardized tests—getting easy problems first, being able to go back over the entire section and not just one question—are not present on the GRE CAT.

So, yes, you get your score back super early, but if you're not ready for the adaptive format, it might not be the kind of score you want to get back super early.

Learning about the computer adaptive format will give you the opportunity to eliminate many of the negative aspects of the CAT while keeping the good ones, so the rest of this chapter is devoted to just that.

Putting the "Computer" into the Computer Adaptive Test

Take a moment and give an honest answer to the following question:

How would you describe your comfort level with computers?

In other words, do you feel your trusty laptop is like an extension of your body, or do you believe that computers are little more than mutant typewriters determined to destroy the world? Take your time.

Whichever category you start out in, by the time you take the GRE CAT you need to be completely comfortable navigating through a computer test. If you start out already feeling good about computers, then it won't take much time to get used to the commands used when taking the GRE CAT. If you're closer to the "mutant typewriter" faction, then the amount of time needed to acclimate yourself will probably be much longer. Even if that is the case, it will be time well spent, since the day you need to take the

PETERSON'S

getting you there

test should be exclusively about answering GRE questions correctly and not about learning how to move through a computer adaptive test.

Before starting the GRE CAT, you go through a computer tutorial, which goes over every facet of the onscreen instructions in excruciating detail. You could wait until test day and then spend 15–45 minutes in the tutorial familiarizing yourself with all the different instructions, but wouldn't you rather learn the instructions beforehand so you can skip the boring tutorial and get right to the actual test? The goal on that day is to use all your brainpower to take a GRE CAT, not waste time and mental energy learning about how to take a GRE CAT.

Be sure you go over this tutorial before taking any tests on that disk. Learning about the computer commands ahead of time is a valuable skill. A tutorial similar to the one you'll see on test day is contained on the CD that came with this book. Or, check out the Appendix on page 332, which goes over all the major screen commands, what they look like, what each command means, and when they will appear. Be sure you understand all the different commands before you take the actual GRE CAT.

Now that we've talked about the instructions you'll see on the computer, let's talk about the computers themselves. You know those computers you see on every TV show, the ones with monstrous flat screens, dynamic graphics, and blazing computing speed? Those are NOT the computers you will use to take the GRE CAT. Instead, the computer you will probably use resembles the kind you find in a public library. It will be a no-frills, functional PC with an average keyboard, average mouse, average screen, average everything, really.

Many people who work on computers for a long time make modifications to their computers to maximize comfort. They might replace the regular mouse with a wireless trackball version designed to reduce carpal tunnel problems and place ultra-fine netting over their screen to reduce the glare. None of these modifications will be in place on the GRE computer, so if you are someone who uses modified accessories, you have two options:

1. You can replace your nice gear with the basic equipment in order to simulate the real GRE experience.

2. You can use your nice gear at home but be aware that during the real test none of it will be there for you.

Both options have advantages. Option 1 gives you greater verisimilitude (a good GRE vocabulary word, by the way). If you want your computer practice to be as close to the real thing as possible, this is the plan for you. On the other hand, if you understand ahead of time what the real thing will be like, there's no reason not to practice in a way that's more physically or aesthetically comfortable. Ultimately, the type of computer mouse you use won't be the deciding factor in your score, so this is not a major point, but every little thing counts. Knowing what to expect and planning for it is a good way to boost your confidence level going into the exam.

Alert!

Before you register for the test by phone or computer, try to visit the actual testing site ahead of time—before you plunk down your money. Most testing sites are fine, but what if the testing site gives you a bad vibe or something? Don't go there! You need to be at your best on test day, so make sure the site is adequate before you sign up. Once you call and get a time, you're locked in, and even if you cancel the appointment, you lose a large chunk of change.

The "Adaptive"

To get a taste of what the computer adaptive format is like (without taking a test), rent a movie you know nothing about. Don't look at the cover or read any summary of the events of the film. Fast forward to the middle of the film and begin watching at that point. After a few minutes, if you think you understand what's going on, keep watching. If you start watching the middle of the film and have no idea what's going on, go back about 20 minutes and start watching from that point. Move forward when the movie makes sense, and rewind when it doesn't. Keep watching until you reach the end of the film.

You have just watched your first adaptive movie. Was it fun? How was the popcorn?

You probably don't watch movies this way on a regular basis, and you don't take computer adaptive tests like the GRE every day, either. The danger is that the unusual format leads you to take the wrong approach to the test. The chart on the following page lists some common mistakes people make when taking the CAT.

PETERSON'S
getting you there

Common Thinking	But Really . . .
Tests go from easy to hard problems.	GRE CAT problems start in the middle, and then go all over the place from there depending on how you score.
Work at a consistent pace to have a chance to answer every problem.	Early problems on the GRE play a greater role in determining your score than later ones, so you should make sure to spend more time on the first 10–15 problems. Even if this means you end up guessing on the last five problems in a section because you have no time left, your score will still be better than if you rushed through the first questions. Remember, even if you don't have time for the last few problems, be sure to guess.
If I study hard enough, the test should be easy.	If you have the necessary knowledge, then you'll quickly find yourself mired in the hardest math and verbal questions the computer can dredge up. This means you're heading toward a good score, but it doesn't mean the test will be easy. Unlike a pencil-and-paper test with set easy, medium, and hard problems, the computer will adapt to throw you the nastiest, toughest, most convoluted questions it has to offer.

On many standardized tests, people rush through the initial easy questions because they want to answer every problem. This impatience often leads to careless errors at the beginning. This impatience is harmful on a regular test, but it's deadly on the GRE CAT. The first 10–15 questions you face on each section are the most crucial, and you should slow down and take as much as 2 minutes apiece if it will help you answer them correctly. As for the last 5 questions? If you don't have time for them, just guess. They are not as critical to your score. If you can get to them, it's a bonus, but the real way to improve your score is to focus on the earlier questions to the best of your ability.

Now that the "Slow down and get the early question right" mantra has been beaten into your skull yet again, it might be a good time to clarify just what an easy, medium, and hard question looks like. Officially, a hard problem is one that previous test-takers have seen and found to be very difficult to answer correctly. The official derivation of "easy" and "medium" also comes from how well previous test-takers did when trying to answer these problems.

Yet these labels are all subjective, since everyone carries around a unique knowledge set. You might have a knack for geometry, so a medium geometry problem appears easy to you. The best way to get a feel for a problem's difficulty level is to look over samples of easy, medium, and hard questions. You can find these throughout this book, and you can also go right to the source and purchase *The Official Guide to the GRE, 10th Edition,* by the Educational Testing Service. This roughly $20 book contains a host of old pencil-and-paper GREs with questions arranged in old-timey easy/medium/hard order of difficulty. The exams are all over a decade old, but they do give you an idea of what constitutes an easy, medium, and hard problem.

X-Ref

The Official Guide is a good place to work on sample problems, but the format has changed a lot since these test were issued, so don't bother working the sections under timed conditions. Use the sample tests at the back of this book for that, as they are geared toward the new exam.

The ability to determine easy, medium, and hard problems is a nice skill to have on the CAT, but it is not a crucial one. Don't spend any amount of time looking at a problem and debating whether or not it's a medium or hard one. Either way, it's in front of you, so you have to work it one way or another. But understanding what kind of problem you are looking at can help you avoid incorrect answer choices. For example, if you are taking the math section and doing pretty well, you'll notice the problems are getting more difficult. Suddenly, you get the following probability question:

There are seven tokens in a bag, labeled 8 through 14 consecutively. The first number pulled out of the bag is 10. What are the odds that the next two numbers pulled out of the bag will BOTH be less than 10?

A. $\dfrac{1}{15}$

B. $\dfrac{3}{14}$

C. $\dfrac{2}{7}$

D. $\dfrac{1}{3}$

E. $\dfrac{2}{5}$

PETERSON'S
getting you there

On the CAT exam, letters will not be used to designate choices, as each choice will simply appear on the screen with a hollow oval next to it. Obviously, the test-maker did not care that this lack of lettering would make it hard on the poor souls who make a living writing test-prep material. Throughout this book, all answer choices will have letters next to them so that they can be discussed without having to resort to phrases like "the second oval from the top" or "you know, the answer that's got the word 'hamster' in it."

Note

This is a medium → difficult problem, something to keep in mind when you look over the answer choices. If you try to figure this problem in your head, you might think that there are two numbers less than 10 (8 and 9) and 7 tokens total, or 6 tokens now that the 10 has been removed. Choice (C) is $\frac{2}{7}$ (which is two tokens over 7 tokens, right), while choice (D) has $\frac{2 \text{ tokens}}{6 \text{ tokens}} = \frac{2}{6} = \frac{1}{3}$.

Both of these answers use the wrong math, but they are *also* too easy. If you know it is a medium → difficult problem, how could the answer be so simple that you could just do the math in your head? Finding choice (C) takes only 15 seconds and choice (D) takes only a bit longer than that. When you find the answer to a tough problem that easily, your GRE "sixth sense" should start tingling wildly, telling you that you are picking an answer that is so easy it is probably incorrect.

For this particular problem, eliminating incorrect answers is just as important as finding the correct choice. If you don't know how to do the math, eliminate choices (C) and (D) and take a guess. This gives you a 1 in 3 shot of choosing the right answer, which happens to be choice (A). Even if you guessed wrong that time, you gave yourself a fighting chance by understanding the GRE CAT well enough to know which answer choices were traps.

The math regarding this problem is covered on pages 100–101, the section on probabilities.

X-Ref

The "Test"

Use the following checklist to prepare for the day you take the actual GRE:

Items to Bring to the GRE:

1. Good old picture I.D., preferably something legitimate like a driver's license and not a badly laminated "Honorary Member of the Justice League" card.

2. Fruit snack or something light, yet filling, like nuts. You don't want to eat something so heavy you find yourself dying for a nap.

3. A bottle of water. Some would rather drown out the entire experience, but this practice is frowned upon for a multitude of reasons.

4. Overshirt of some kind. When you check out the site initially, you should get an idea of what the ambient temperature is like. Dress accordingly. The testing room is often rather small, just a cubicle farm of 6–10 spaces. Depending on how many people are taking tests next to you, the room can be either cold or warm, so the best advice is to start with light clothing with the option of bundling up.

5. A positive attitude. If that's asking too much, just don't bring a negative one. Shoot for feeling relaxed and confident, since this disposition will help you stay sharp and focused on the task at hand.

Note

Many test centers have a set of lockers just inside the testing room for you to keep valuables and whatever else you want. This is another thing you should look for when you are scouting out a GRE location.

The test's sign-up process is a mixture of registering for a seminar and getting arrested. You have to write out a mini-essay claiming you'll be a good person and not sell your GRE secrets to a cheesy newspaper tabloid—or anyone else for that matter. Then you sign in again, have your identification checked, and get a mug shot taken . . . just in case. In many locations, you are also filmed throughout the testing procedure. These actions are all part of the underlying theme of, "Don't try anything funny, bub."

You have the option of wearing noise-blocking headphones while taking the GRE, which we don't recommended unless you studied for the GRE

PETERSON'S
getting you there

wearing noise-blocking headphones. A little sound—the whir of the computer's fans, the hum of air-conditioning—should be the type of background noise you're used to, and total silence can be a little freaky. Unless there's someone trying to cough up a lung next to you in the room, skip the 'phones.

At long last, you get in front of the computer, ready to get your GRE groove on. Unfortunately, the meaty portions of the GRE, i.e., the sections that count, are still a long way off. First you have to fill out a basic form for what seems like the umpteenth time, then you get a market research section where the computer asks you a lot of basic questions like, "Why are you taking this test?" and "Have you taken other standardized tests before?" Is the computer trying to hit on you, or is it just being nosy? It's up to you to decide, but the fact is, you're stuck in that chair and you have to answer all the questions before you can start taking the exam.

After the market research section, you get another section asking you where you want the scores sent. You should have an idea of where you want to send your scores. If not, this section can take a while. Even if you do know where you want scores sent, scrolling around takes awhile, so be prepared to spend about 5–10 minutes futzing around in this section.

Once you finish leaping through these hoops, the GRE begins . . . almost. You now get a chance to go through the tutorial showing how to navigate the GRE CAT. Hopefully, you will already be very familiar with these commands, so you can just skip this section. Go through one of the tutorial lessons if you feel like it to reassure yourself, but this should not be necessary. Ideally, you can skip this entirely and get to what's important, the test itself.

> The GRE is like an awards show. Most people who watch awards shows are primarily interested in who the big winners will be. To find this out, though, they have to endure endless music performances, skits, sentimental retrospectives, and all sorts of other fodder before the big payoff. For the GRE, these distractions come in the form of market research questions, tutorials, and basic questions about who you are, and so on. All you really want to do is take the sections that count toward your score, but to do so you have to endure the GRE equivalent of a dance medley.

Alert!

The test begins! It starts with the Analytical Writing portion, and you have 75 minutes to respond to 2 essay questions. For many test-takers, the wait is over and it's time to get cracking. However, some people apply to programs that do not "care" about the Analytical score. If this is the case

16

for you—and *be sure this is the case before following the next piece of advice*—then you can be more relaxed in your approach to the essays. You have to answer them, since a zero might raise eyebrows, but if the schools aren't going to give the Analytical score any weight, why should you? Save your brainpower for the sections of the test that do matter.

Once you've finished clacking out your essays, the computer adaptive part of the GRE kicks in. You will see a Quantitative section, a Verbal section, and an Experimental section. ETS, the company that administers the GRE, uses your answers on the Experimental section to fashion future GRE CATs. In this way, ETS seeks to guarantee that future GRE CATs are similar to current GRE CATs in terms of question similarity. This is all well and good in terms of fairness, but what it boils down to is that you have to take an entire test section that doesn't count toward your score. For obvious reasons, you won't know which section is the Experimental section ahead of time.

However, you can sometimes get an *idea* which section is the experimental one. It all depends on how adept you get at understanding the difference between easy, medium, and hard problems. Let's say you've taken one Quantitative section and one Verbal Section. The third section is another Quantitative section, so you know that either this section or the previous Quant one is the experimental. You start off the third section with four questions that you *know* you got correct. You're certain you nailed them. Yet the questions never seem to change in difficulty level, not like they did on the previous Quant section. There are two explanations for this:

1. You botched those questions and just don't realize it.

2. You are working on the experimental section.

There is no way to be 100 percent certain which section is Experimental, so the smart move is to treat all sections as if they count. If you guess wrong about a section, your score goes down the drain, and you would have achieved nothing. Still, it can be reassuring to have a *feeling* about which section is Experimental. If you get this feeling, then you should realize that you are pretty GRE savvy, and that the intricacies of the test are not so mysterious after all.

. . . And Then Some

You should have an idea from this chapter that the GRE CAT is a kind of odd test. It is unlike most of the major tests in another way, and that is overall disposition of the proctors. On most big tests (standardized exams or final exams in the college class), the proctors giving tests have a serious,

PETERSON'S
getting you there

formal air about them. Students are hushed, people avoid eye contact, everyone is a little nervous. It's sort of an "I'm a 9-year-old sitting with my entire adult family at the Thanksgiving dinner table" kind of vibe, nervousness and seriousness and formality all rolled into one. The proctors are the same way, acting officious and ever-diligent in order to make sure that nothing goes wrong.

The GRE CAT is, as you might expect, different. Here the test is given all the time, every day and sometimes even at night during most of the week. There's nothing exceptional about a single GRE administration. It means a lot to you, but the people at the test centers see people like you every day of the week. For them it's just a day's work.

This does not mean to imply that the proctors are lazy, uncaring, or anything bad. Nothing of the sort is true. It's just that they aren't going to have that same "Thanksgiving dinner table" attitude, since they are just doing a routine day of work. They will do it well and be courteous and helpful, but they won't have the sense of "Wow, this is an important moment" that *you* will.

They also won't be at the front of the classroom eagerly scanning the room to see if anyone's cheating or if anyone needs help. The former is not needed because you can't look at another person's GRE since it won't have the same questions. If you tried to bring something in to cheat with it would be spotted on camera. If you need help you can raise your hand, but there's no guarantee that it will be spotted immediately. There's no person watching the testing room with eagle eyes since that mindset is just not prevalent. The overall point is that you should not expect the proctor to come rapidly if you need something during the middle of the section. Therefore, make sure you have all the scratch paper you need during a break and that you have enough pencils as well. There's no way to guarantee someone will come speedily to your aid while the test is in progress.

There! You now have a host of strategies to help you comprehend the computer adaptive aspect of the GRE. For some additional test-taking strategies on how to handle each section of the GRE—Quantitative, Verbal, and Analytical—all you have to do is turn the page.

Chapter 2

Section Strategies

In the last chapter, we familiarized you with the computerized aspect of the GRE. In this chapter, we'll acquaint you with the three GRE sections. Our goal is to eliminate any element of surprise you might have while taking the test, since unexpected problem-types lead to confusion, uncertainty, and an overall negativity that can hinder your exam performance. We'll tell you about the makeup of the GRE and how it is administered, and your anxiety will diminish as the test becomes less of a mystery. While you might still run across some individual problems that throw you for a loop, we'll make sure you won't run into any question *types* that leave you befuddled.

Quantitative

The GRE section devoted to math goes by the mouthy word "Quantitative." Half of the problems in this section are regular multiple-choice problems, but the other half are presented in a format known as Quantitative Comparison (QC for short).

QC Problems

The directions for Quantitative Comparisons look something like this:

Directions: Column A and Column B will have one quantity each. Your goal is to compare the quantities in each column and choose

A   if the quantity in Column A is greater
B   if the quantity in Column B is greater
C   if the two quantities are equal
D   if the relationship between the two quantities cannot be determined from the information given

Here's a wildly simple example of a QC problem.

Column A	Column B
$h = 2$	
h	1

You have two columns, A and B, and there is a "quantity" underneath each one. This quantity might be a variable (like Column A), a number (like Column B), or some mixture of the two with a little extra thrown in for good measure. On occasion, floating above this columnar stew is some additional information that applies to the quantity in both columns, like "$h = 2$."

Like the example above, the items in the two columns often can't be compared to one another, because they are in different formats. In our example, one column has a variable while the other has a number. You would need to convert the variable into a number in order to compare them. Since the centered information states $h = 2$, you know that the quantity, or value, of the letter h in Column A is 2. Under Column B, the value is 1. There are no other possible interpretations or solutions using the centered information. We know that 1 is less than 2, so the correct answer must be (A).

> **Note**
>
> Converting the information in both columns into easily comparable forms is a good strategy for many QC problems, especially if you find that you are stuck.

Note the qualifying phrase "There are no other possibile interpretations or solutions" in the previous sentence. Exploring alternate possible answers is critical on QC problems, because there are often hidden outcomes that can affect the answer on a problem. Here's a QC problem that looks similar to the previous one.

Column A	Column B
$h^2 = 4$	
h	1

Again, you want to convert Column A into a number so you can compare it to the number in Column B. The obvious answer is that $h = 2$, since $(2)(2) = 4$. This would mean (A) is the answer . . . if there are no other possibilities, that is. In this case, you should see that h could also equal -2, since $(-2)(-2) = 4$. If you compare -2 with Column B's 1, Column B's quantity is larger, so (B) is the answer in this scenario.

One possible value for h gives you the answer (A), while another gives you an answer of (B). Whenever you have a conflict like this, the correct response is choice (D), "the answer cannot be determined by the information given." A more precise statement for choice (D) would be that "more than one answer can be determined, and there's no way to tell which answer is correct." It's not that you *can't* determine *an* answer, it's just that you don't know *which* answer is correct.

To properly explore all possibilities on QC problems involving variables, don't just use easy numbers like 2, 3, and 4 when giving values to variables. Be sure to insert some weird numbers like those on the following list:

Weird Numbers	
The Number	**Why It's Weird**
0	Any number multiplied by 0 equals zero. Also, any number to the zero power equals 1, or $x^0 = 1$.
1	Any number multiplied by 1 does not change.
Fractions between 0 and 1	Normally, when you multiply two numbers together, the end result is larger. When you multiply two fractions less than one together, the result is less than the original two numbers.
Negative numbers	Two negatives makes a positive when multiplying or dividing, and -2 is greater than -4 even though our minds like to think that 4 is bigger than 2.

On our second sample question, realizing the existence of -2 (the weird negative number) led us to the correct answer of (D).

Many incorrect QC answers are chosen in the name of speed, as people look at a problem and "see" the answer that must be the correct one. If the answer is so obvious, why not pick it quickly and zip on to the next question? The response to this hypothetical question is that *answers that look correct are often traps* designed to catch those who do not actually work the problem. Here's a classic QC trap on a medium-difficulty problem.

PETERSON'S
getting you there

Column A	Column B

$$4(g + i) = 76$$
$$3i = 57$$

6^g	8^g

If *g* is a regular, Joe Schmo kind of number, the answer seems pretty obvious. Column B is going to be greater since 8 is bigger than 6 and both numbers are being taken to the same exponential power, *g*. An experienced GRE taker—which you will be after reading this book—should have internal alarms going off at the sight of this problem. It just looks too simple, and there has to be something more to this problem in order to justify the fact that it's a medium problem.

Take the time to solve for both *g* and *i*, and you'll discover the trap. From the second equation, you will discover that $i = 19$. Placing this value into the first equation, you will find:

$$4(g + i) = 76$$
$$4g + 4i = 76$$
$$4g + (4)(19) = 76$$
$$4g + 76 = 76$$
$$4g + 76 - 76 = 76 - 76$$
$$4g = 0$$
$$g = 0$$

If *g* equals zero, then Column A's $6^g = 6^0 = 1$ and Column B's $8^g = 8^0 = 1$. Both columns are equal, and there's no other possible value for *g*, so the correct answer must be (C).

You will see a lot of QC problems throughout this book, so use the following checklist as a way of remembering the key strategies to use when handling these problems.

QC Approach Check List

1. For the answer choices, the word *always* is critical. You can only pick (A) if the quantity in Column A is *always* greater, and you can only pick (B) if Column B's quantity is *always* greater. Choice (C) is the answer if the two columns are *always* equal, no matter what weird numbers are punched in. Whenever you find a QC problem that has more than one possible outcome, (A), (B) and/or (C), you have (D) as your answer.

2. The goal is to compare the two problems, so you should take information and try to rearrange it in a way that makes comparison easier. If you have a problem with a lot of variables, you should realize the goal will be to get comparable variables into both columns. If one column only has numbers in it, the key to that problem is finding a way to convert the other column into a number than can be compared.

3. When variables are involved, don't be content to plug in one value for the variable and then use that as the result. Use a "weird" number to challenge your initial finding. If you find a weird number that leads to a different result, you know the correct choice on that problem is (D). (See the table on page 21 of this chapter)

4. Many QC problems are designed to look like there is one obvious answer. Never jump to this answer unless you have done all of the actual math that the problem demands. The obvious answer is often an incorrect choice set there to trap hurried test-takers.

How Much Does Your Brain Weigh?

There are several ways you can answer this question. You could take your brain out and place it on a scale, although this is not recommended. You could find out what the average brain weighs by looking it up in a reference book or surfing the Net. You could place both your hands around your head, lean over, and use your arms as a scale.

Or you could just guess. You won't be completely accurate, but you should be pretty close. Look at the following choices, and then take a guess:

Which of the following is the most likely weight of your brain?

A. 1 pound
B. 3 pounds
C. 6 pounds
D. 10 pounds
E. 15 pounds

The correct answer is B. Estimating an answer can sometimes lead you directly to the right answer, but this does not happen very often. More important than determining the correct answer, guessing can often help you eliminate wrong answers, which increases your odds of getting a problem right. If your brain weighed 10 or 15 pounds, you would need metal girders in your neck to help support its weight. So, (D) and (E) can be eliminated, leaving you three choices. Choice (A) is a little light, and although this answer provides a fertile ground for a cutting remark, it's not

PETERSON'S
getting you there

correct. This leaves (B) and (C), and if you thought 6 pounds was a bit portly for a brain, you were right. The answer is (B).

Some problems are hard because the math required to answer them is hard. If you can use your eyeballs and your 3-pound brain to estimate what the answer should be, you will increase your chances of getting a problem correct. It might not lead you directly to the right answer, but it can steer you clear of answer choices that are clearly wrong.

Geometry problems involving angles, lines, figures, or measurements are the most susceptible to estimating, although the fact that the images are displayed on a computer screen makes it a little problematic. Whenever you are given a figure on the screen, redraw it on paper in front of you as accurately as possible, and then work with that figure. For example:

> The shortest side of a triangle is *n* centimeters long. Another side is three times this length, while the third side is 22 centimeters greater than *n*. If this is the case, which of the following is the only possible value of *n*?
>
> **A.** 2 centimeters
> **B.** 4 centimeters
> **C.** 5 centimeters
> **D.** 6 centimeters
> **E.** 8 centimeters

There's an equation you can use to solve this problem, but you can also attack it with just a number 2 pencil and some scratch paper. Start with choice (A), 2 centimeters. The second side would be (2)(3) = 6 cm and the third side is 2 + 22 = 24 cm. Now, try to accurately draw a triangle with sides of 2, 6, and 24. With one side 24 cm, how are the sides of 2 cm and 6 cm actually going to connect?

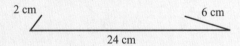

Since (A) fails spectacularly, you might want to head to the larger values like choice (E). If *n* = 8, then the other two sides are 24 cm and 30 cm. If you freehand this, it seems to work. At this point, knowing the math would come in handy, but if you don't know it, guess (E) and move on.

> **Note**
>
> In a triangle, the length of every side must be less than the sum of the other two sides. Choice (E) fulfills this, since even the length of the longest side, 30, is less than the sum of 8 and 24.

24

Techniques, strategy, practice, and factual knowledge can be combined to give you a good score, but it doesn't guarantee a perfect score. Inevitably, there will be one or two questions that seem to defy explanation, and these often appear as time is winding down on the section. If you can't take an educated guess, just take a plain guess and move on to the next problem. On the computer, you must place an answer down on every problem, even if it that means you're simply filling in (E) on the last couple of questions. Keep in mind that these questions are not worth as much as the earliest questions. On a 28-question test, you can randomly fill in the last 6 questions and still get a score in the high 700s. The point is that guessing late in the test won't hurt you as much as you might think. If you have to guess early in the math section, try to use estimating and common sense to eliminate some answers, and then just take your best shot.

Verbal

The Verbal portion of the GRE will be eerily familiar to anyone who took the SAT when applying for college. All four question types have made an appearance on the SAT at one time or another, and they've even starred in other standardized tests as well.

Question Types on the GRE Verbal	
Question Type	Description
1. **Antonyms**	You are given a single word and then must find its opposite in the answer choices.
2. **Analogies**	You'll see two words separated by a colon at the beginning of each problem. These are called the "stem" words, and the stem words have some sort of relationship with each other. Your job is to find the paired words in the answer choices that have the same, analogous relationship as the stem words.
3. **Sentence Completions**	A good old fill-in-the-blank exercise where you must add the correct missing word or words to an initial sentence.
4. **Reading Comprehension (RC)**	Read some text and then answer questions about it. The staple of standardized verbal exams everywhere.

There are 30 problems on the Verbal section and four different question types, so you might think that there will about 7–8 of each question type on the test. It rarely works out that way. Although every CAT is different, for the most part, Sentence Completion problems get short shrift on the GRE CAT, and this is especially true if you are answering a majority of the questions correctly. If you're doing well, you'll find yourself bombarded by antonyms and analogies. These two question types are very vocabulary-centric, since knowledge of the words used is a large factor in getting the problems right. The better you do on the GRE CAT Verbal, the more the section resembles a vocabulary quiz by the end.

In-depth discussion and suggestions on how to tackle each of the four Verbal question types is covered starting on page 25.

X-Ref

The Verbal section also starts out like a vocabulary quiz, since the first 3–6 questions are usually antonyms and some analogies. This means that on the initial part of the Verbal test (when questions count the most), a lot depends on whether you know the particular word given in a question. This makes the beginning of the Verbal section a little arbitrary. People with large vocabularies might get an unfamiliar word, while someone with a less-developed vocabulary will get a tough word whose meaning they just happen to know. All in all, the start of the section is a bit of a crap shoot. Getting the right word or words can help your score, especially if you don't consider yourself someone with a large vocabulary.

The Verbal section might seem less fair than the Math, but there's no real difference. If you're strong in geometry, and your first two math questions concern geometry, then you're in luck. If geometry is your worst subject, then you're out of luck. The adaptive format, with early questions counting for more, is the culprit (or helper) in both cases.

In the end, just knowing how the Verbal section will begin gives you a mental advantage over someone who just shows up and starts answering questions blindly.

A reading passage will show up sooner or later, with 2–4 questions attached to it. If you do a lot of Web site reading, then you won't have much problem with the computer format. There's a scroll bar to help you move up and down the text, but the actual text box is ridiculously small. It only holds two or three sentences at a time, so no matter how short the reading passage is, there's always going to be some scrolling to do. To give yourself a preview of what it will be like, open up some text on a computer, and place it in a box about 3 inches by 4 inches. Give yourself some big letters, and allow for a nice amount of space between each line.

Tip

> On RC problems, the passage takes up the upper left portion of the screen, while questions appear on the right side. The bottom of the screen contains a lot of basic instructions like "Time on/off" and "Wanna quit, fraidy cat?" stuff that you will rarely, if ever, use during the exam.

If the above instructions are too tech-savvy for you, don't sweat it. The point is that you will have to move up and down to read some text, so be prepared to do just that.

The last problem type, Sentence Completion, translates very well to the computer. Of the four Verbal question types, these questions are probably the easiest to prepare for and improve on, which might be why they show up the least. Even so, when they do pop up on your screen, lick your chops and dive right in.

. . . **And You're Done**

For most people, time is not as big an issue on the Verbal section as it is on the Math section. Many hard Math problems are complex, multi-step questions that require a lot of computations in order to unravel the right answer. This takes time. In contrast, hard questions on the Verbal section consist mainly of hard vocabulary words. You still need time to go through the answer choices and use some strategies, but this doesn't take as long as

figuring out what the value of $\dfrac{\left(\frac{2}{9}\right)\left(\frac{7}{15}\right)}{\left(\frac{8}{25}\right)\left(\frac{14}{33}\right)}$ is.

There's no need to rush through any questions on the Verbal section, since lack of time is rarely a problem. On average, you have a minute per question, but some questions will take less time. For example, if there's an antonym question with a word that you know, finding the right answer can take under 15 seconds. Don't spend less than 15 seconds, because you want to make sure not to make a careless error by speeding. That gives you a lot of extra time to spend on another problem, such as a RC question. These typically take more time since you want to check your answer with the information in the passage.

If you are running out of time on a practice Verbal section, then you are probably staring at some questions and dredging your brain to come up

PETERSON'S
getting you there

with a definition of a word. This is not a good use of your time. The vocabulary on the GRE can be tough, so there will be some words whose meaning you don't know. Accept this, use any elimination strategies you can on those problems, pick an answer, and move on.

Analytical Writing

The first essay prompt you see poses an issue, and then gives you 45 minutes to analyze and discuss that issue. This is your standard, "There's no right or wrong side, all that matters is how well you present your side of the case" kind of essay. You are often given two topics to choose from, so pick the topic you feel comfortable—um, talking about.

For the second essay, analysis of an argument, you only have 30 minutes to write. This time, you are first given some text, in which someone makes an argument about something. This argument is lame in some way or another. Your goal here is to evaluate the argument, i.e., explain ways in which the argument's lame and ways in which it works.

Combined, the two essays take over an hour to start at the beginning of every GRE CAT. That's a lot of time spent typing, and the key word here is *typing*. How fast do you type? Answering this question will determine your approach to these essays. Many English aficionados will talk gushingly about the standard five-paragraph essay approach that virtually guarantees you a top score of 6 on the Analytical portion. Yet, this approach doesn't work if you're such a slow typist that you can't type five paragraphs in the time allotted.

As stated in the previous chapter, if you're applying for a graduate program in astrophysics, your Analytical score might not be of highest importance. Do your best, but spend your time studying the section that matters most, which is Math.

Alert!

Before anything else, find out how fast you can type. Sit down in front of a computer with some word processing program. Start timing, and then type something like, "The quick brown fox jumps over the lazy dog" over and over again until one minute is up. If you make a mistake while typing, stop and correct your error while the clock is running. Now count up the number of words you typed correctly in one minute. Take this number and use it to answer the following question:

Question	How long should my essays be?
Step 1	Take the amount of time given for an essay. For essay 1, this means 45 minutes.
Step 2	Subtract 5 minutes. This time will be used to decide what you want to write in your essay. You shouldn't just blaze off at the start; it helps to plan out your essay a bit.
Step 3	40 minutes remain. Take the number of words you type per minute and multiply by 40. If you can type 20 words per minute, then $(20)(40) = 800$.
Step 4	This is the number of words you could type if you knew exactly what you were going to say and typed nonstop. Since there will be many points in your essay where you pause for a moment to come up with the right phrase or sentence, 800 is not really achievable. Halve this number for a more realistic assessment, giving you 400 words.
Step 5	If you assume a standard paragraph is around 100 words, you can see that your essay will not make the five-paragraph format due to technical reasons (i.e. your slow typing.) You only have time for four paragraphs. You should therefore state your case clearly in Paragraph 1, back it up with claims in the next two paragraphs, and then wrap things up in Paragraph 4 as time expires on you and your nondexterous fingers.

Unless you practice typing or type a lot, you might be appalled at how slow you are. Even with fast fingers, there's no way to compose a flawless, five-paragraph essay on a previously unknown topic in 45 minutes. Flawless essays require time to map out, draft, and then rewrite. Maybe a professional essay writer—if there are any still around these days—could do it, but folks taking the GRE can't, and it isn't expected of them. What *is* expected is that the thoughts you do punch into the computer are good, and that the overall structure of your essay is sound.

On both essays, don't sacrifice quality for quantity. Two body (middle) paragraphs with 1–3 compelling sentences that back up your initial claim are all that is needed to get a decent score on the Analytical section. Some people have even peppered their essays with jokes—relevant to the discussion, of course—and received a 6, so you don't have to kill yourself to place words on the screen. Just make sure that the words you do put down help support your position in the essay.

If you want to increase your typing skills, get a dictionary, a computer, and get ready to kill two birds with one stone. Purchase a book that lists college-level vocabulary words, and then spend time typing in each word and its definition into a word processing document. By doing this, you will improve your typing skills and create a vocabulary study guide at the same time.

PART II

Diagnosing Strengths and Weaknesses

Diagnostic: Dipping Your Big Toe in the GRE Waters

Now that you have some section-specific techniques, it's time to put them to use. Trying a sample set of math and verbal questions has the following benefits:

1. It gives you an idea of how you might do if you were to take the real GRE this very moment.

2. It lets you see what areas of study you're strongest in, and what areas need improvement. This knowledge can be used to fine-tune your study plans for the GRE.

3. No matter how you do on the diagnostic, *it doesn't count*.

The third point is perhaps the most important. If you answer every sample question correctly, then bellow out a proud "Huzzah!" You can't send that score to universities, but you can feel good about the fact that you've demonstrated the ability to do well on GRE-type questions. On the other hand, if you miss a lot of diagnostic questions, don't sweat it.

Alert! If you waited until the last moment and are taking this diagnostic the night before the real GRE CAT, you can sweat a little. Hopefully, you are taking this diagnostic at least a month in advance of the real test, giving you ample time to go through the rest of the book at a measured pace.

The whole point of the diagnostic is to determine what subjects you're good at and what subjects you need help in. You can then use this information to devise a study plan tailored to your strengths and weaknesses.

Should You Take It to the Next Level?

As stated earlier, the adaptive nature of the GRE makes it likely that someone shooting for a good score will only see medium and hard questions. Since you probably didn't purchase this book to get a lousy score, it makes sense to concentrate on medium and hard GRE questions. The bulk of this book does just that. The first part of each chapter in the subject review section focuses on how medium questions will appear on the math and verbal sections, and it provides you with the facts and strategies needed to tackle these problems. The general instruction for the Analytical section goes over the basic structure of the essay, giving you the knowledge needed to gain a respectable score on the written portion. For most students, starting with the medium-level material is the wisest course of action.

However, suppose you feel very confident about your math abilities. A high score on the math portion of the diagnostic proves that this confidence is well-founded. If that's the case, you *may* choose to skip over the general study material on math and go straight to the *Take It to the Next Level* material. This material focuses on more advanced topics—involved probabilities and number sets, for example—and it shows how these topics appear on hard problems. The *Next Level* Verbal and Analytical sections cover advanced topics and problems in a similar fashion.

So what's the best study plan? Not to get too mystical or anything, but the answer to this question can only be found inside you. By working through the entire book, you give yourself a look at everything this book has to offer. Yet this approach takes time, and time is a scarce commodity in many people's lives. Therefore, you might wish to *Take It to the Next Level* in subjects you feel comfortable with in order to use the time you have to concentrate on your weakest areas.

The requirements of your graduate program might let you tailor your approach in another way. For example, some fine arts programs require students to take the GRE, but these programs are not concerned with a student's Quantitative (math) score. If this is the case for you, you could decide to skip the *Next Level* math, since a high score in math will not help you one way or another. It would still be a good idea to go over the basic study material—you don't want to completely blow the math section—but a high math score is just not a relevant concern.

Before making any decision, take the diagnostic and let the results guide you. There are 28 Quantitative questions, roughly divided so that the first half contains medium questions while the second half contains hard questions. If you ace 20+ Quantitative problems in allotted time, then you are a good candidate for skipping the general material if you want. If you miss questions randomly throughout the section, it would be a good idea to look over both the general and *Next Level* materials, since there's no clear pattern as to why you got some questions right while missing others. It could mean you were weak in a specific subject—like determining mean/median/mode, for instance—in which case a comprehensive review of a wide range of topics would be beneficial. If you miss a bunch of medium questions but get all the harder problems right, chances are your problem lies in pacing. You rushed through the medium questions, making careless errors, in order to spend more time on the harder problems. If this is the case, slow down, Sparky!

PETERSON'S
getting you there

Note In our diagnostic the Quantitative section starts off with 14 QC questions, and then follows with 14 regular math problems. The 14 QC problems are arranged in order of difficulty, and the 14 regular questions are also in their own order of difficulty.

Things are a little different for the Verbal section. There are 30 questions, still divided into half medium/half hard, but there are four distinct question types:

- Antonyms
- Analogies
- Sentence Completions
- Reading Comprehension

Questions within each question type are arranged in order of difficulty, so the first antonym you see is (theoretically) the easiest, while the last is the hardest. After that section, you proceed to analogies, with all analogies arranged in their own order of difficulty. For the Reading Comprehension section, the first passage is easier than the second one.

You can fine-tune your approach depending on how you do within each question type. Suppose you answer every analogy correctly but miss half of the Reading Comprehension problems. If this occurs, a voice inside your head should start hollering, "Focus on Reading Comprehension in both levels, and don't worry about analogies as much."

This book has been designed to give you a variety of study plan options. You want to take charge of the GRE, and a good way to start doing this is to take charge of your study plan.

Optimal Diagnostic-Taking Conditions

As much as you might like to, you should not take the diagnostic while watching television, answering questions only during commercial breaks. Seal yourself away in some solitary location with a heap of scrap paper and a handful of number 2 pencils as your companions. Give yourself 45 minutes for the Quantitative section and 30 minutes for the Verbal section. Take both sections consecutively with a 1-minute break in between. Don't rush, but try to answer as many of the questions as you can.

 Tip You can write your answers in the book, but make sure to do all work on scratch paper since that is what you have to do for the GRE CAT. Afterward, check to see how much scratch paper you used on each section. This will help give you an idea of how much you'll need on the real GRE.

Once finished, give yourself a pat of the back. You will have just finished a GRE-like test. It wasn't a computer adaptive test, but it was a GRE-like test nevertheless.

Good luck!

The Test

Quantitative

General Information

1. The test has 28 questions. You have 45 minutes to complete the section.

2. All numbers used are real numbers.

3. All angle measurements can be assumed to be positive unless otherwise noted.

4. All figures lie in the same plane unless otherwise noted.

5. Drawings that accompany questions are intended to provide information useful in answering the question. The figures are drawn closely to scale unless otherwise noted.

Directions: For questions 1–14, Column A and Column B will have one quantity each. Your goal is to compare the quantities in each column and choose

A if the quantity in Column A is greater
B if the quantity in Column B is greater
C if the two quantities are equal
D if the relationship between the two quantities cannot be determined from the information in the problem

On some questions, information about one or both quantities will be given. This information will be centered above the two columns.

Column A	Column B		Column A	Column B
1. $\dfrac{4}{15}$	$\dfrac{692}{1,781}$			

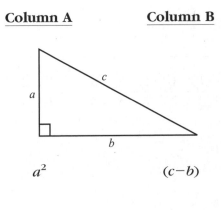

3.

a^2 \qquad\qquad $(c-b)$

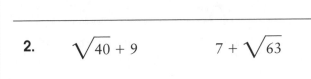

2. $\sqrt{40} + 9$ \qquad $7 + \sqrt{63}$

PETERSON'S
getting you there

	Column A	**Column B**		**Column A**	**Column B**

4. $\left[4(2+3)^2\right]^{\frac{1}{2}}$ $\dfrac{\left[50+2(2+3)^2\right]}{10}$

8. $\theta = x^2 y \quad x \neq 0 \neq y$

$\theta^2 = x^4 y^2$ $\qquad x^3\theta\dfrac{x}{y}$

---

5. A circle has a radius q.

Twice the area of the circle divided by the radius | The circumference of the circle

---

9. x is a positive integer.

$(x^2 - 3x + 2)$ $\qquad x^2 - 4$

---

6. The area of a square with a perimeter of 20 | The area of a rectangle with a perimeter 20

10.

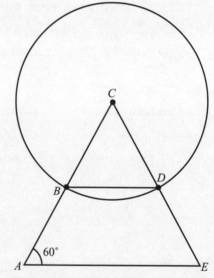

Point C is at the center of the circle.
$\overline{AB} = \overline{DE}$

$\angle CBD$ $\qquad\qquad$ $\angle CEA$

---

7. $\dfrac{1}{3} - \dfrac{1}{2} + \dfrac{1}{7} + \dfrac{2}{5} - \dfrac{3}{4}$ $\qquad -\dfrac{1}{4} + \dfrac{2}{5} + \dfrac{1}{7} - \dfrac{1}{5} + \dfrac{2}{3}$

	Column A	Column B

11. The sum of all even integers one through one hundred | The sum of all odd integers one through one hundred

12. The cube of an even prime number | The square of an odd prime number

13. $x < 0$

$$\frac{x^2 - 12x - 4}{2x - 3 - x + 1}$$ | x^2

14. $x\mu = (x)(x + 1)$

$(3\mu)\mu$ | $(3\mu)(3\mu)$

Directions: Select the best answer for each of the following questions.

15. There are 13 marbles in a bag. One is red, 4 are blue, and 8 are yellow. If a blue marble is drawn from the bag, what is the probability that a red or yellow marble will be drawn next?

A. $\dfrac{1}{4}$

B. $\dfrac{2}{3}$

C. $\dfrac{8}{13}$

D. $\dfrac{3}{4}$

E. $\dfrac{9}{13}$

16. Bananas at Max's Grocer went on sale for 50 percent off. They were then marked down again by 30 percent. If x is the original price of bananas per pound, how much does it cost to buy 2.5 pounds of bananas?

A. $0.15x$
B. $0.375x$
C. $0.42x$
D. $0.50x$
E. $0.875x$

17.

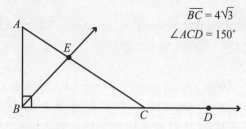

$$\overline{BC} = 4\sqrt{3}$$
$$\angle ACD = 150°$$

If $\overline{BE}$ bisects $\overline{AC}$, what is the length of EC?

A. $2\sqrt{3}$

B. 4

C. $4\sqrt{3}$

D. 8

E. $8\sqrt{3}$

18. If x is an odd integer, in which one of the following expressions must y be even?

A. $x + y = 12$
B. $x^2 + y = 16$
C. $xy = 25$
D. $xy^2 = 49$
E. $xy = 98$

19. Export Auto charges $30 for an oil change and $40 for a brake job. On Tuesday, they charged a total of $320 for all oil changes and brake checks. They performed a fourth as many brake checks as oil changes. How many oil changes did they perform on Tuesday?

A. 2
B. 4
C. 6
D. 8
E. 10

Questions 20–21 refer to the following graphs.

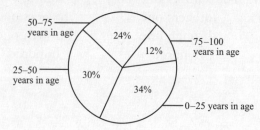

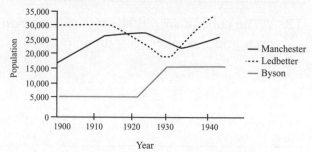

20. Which of the following has the greatest value?

A. Segment of Manchester population 0–25 in 1920
B. Byson population in 1900
C. Byson population in 1915
D. Segment of Manchester population 25–50 in 1920
E. Segment of Manchester population 50–100 in 1920

21. Which town in which decade had the greatest percentage increase in population?

A. Manchester 1900–1910
B. Ledbetter 1920–1930
C. Ledbetter 1930–1940
D. Byson 1920–1930
E. Manchester 1930–1940

22. $\dfrac{[(6a)a - (4a + 7a)]}{a} - 7a + \otimes =$

  A. $\dfrac{6a^2 - 18a}{a} + \otimes$

  B. $\dfrac{6a^2 - 4a}{a} + \otimes$

  C. $7 - a + \otimes$

  D. $-11 - a + \otimes$

  E. $13a - 11 + \otimes$

23.

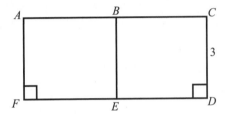

B is the midpoint of $\overline{AC}$, and E is the midpoint of $\overline{FD}$. If the area of rectangle $BCDE$ is 12, what is the perimeter of rectangle $ACDF$?

  A. 18
  B. 20
  C. 22
  D. 24
  E. 26

24.

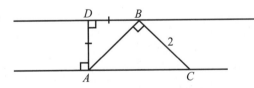

What is the perimeter of $\triangle ABC$?

  A. $2 + \sqrt{2}$
  B. $2 + 2\sqrt{3}$
  C. $4 + 2\sqrt{2}$
  D. $4 + 2\sqrt{3}$
  E. $4 + 4\sqrt{3}$

25. If x is an odd integer, what is the value of half the sum of x and the next three odd integers?

  A. $2(x + 3)$
  B. $3(x + 3)$
  C. $4(x + 3)$
  D. $5(x + 3)$
  E. $6(x + 3)$

Questions 26–28 refer to the following graphs.

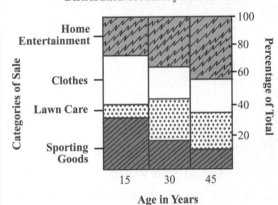

Distribution of Murray Sales in 1995

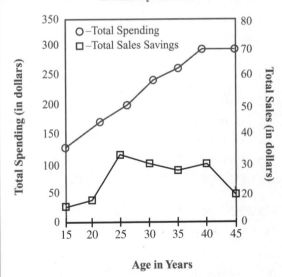

Total Spending Verses Total Sales Savings at Murrays in 1995

PETERSON'S
getting you there

26. Whose annual savings/annual spending ratio was the smallest?

A. 15
B. 20
C. 30
D. 35
E. 45

27. What category of sales had the greatest amount of money spent on it if you only consider 15-, 30-, and 45-year-olds?

A. Home Entertainment
B. Clothes
C. Lawn Care
D. Sporting Goods
E. Apparel

28. Over what 5-year span did percentage of spending increase the most?

A. 15–20
B. 25–30
C. 30–35
D. 35–40
E. 40–45

Verbal

General Information

1. The test has 30 questions. You have 30 minutes to complete the section.

Directions: Each question contains a word printed in capital letters, followed by five answer choices. Choose the answer choice that contains the word or phrase most nearly OPPOSITE in meaning to the word in capital letters.

1. PRISTINE :

A. dull
B. hopeless
C. congested
D. majestic
E. polluted

2. IMPREGNABLE :

A. penetrable
B. tangible
C. intractable
D. tolerable
E. reliable

3. LUCID :

A. translucent
B. myopic
C. putrid
D. luminescent
E. opaque

4. MALLEABLE :

A. brittle
B. ductile
C. pliant
D. flaccid
E. verdant

40

5. CASTIGATE :

   A. criticize
   B. laud
   C. ignore
   D. mollify
   E. obfuscate

6. APPROBATION :

   A. disapproval
   B. fanfare
   C. calamity
   D. enigma
   E. rejoinder

7. MENDACITY :

   A. evil
   B. wisdom
   C. perfidy
   D. honesty
   E. irregularity

8. TRUCULENT :

   A. pugnacious
   B. boorish
   C. gentle
   D. beneficent
   E. altruistic

9. SALUBRIOUS :

   A. salutary
   B. deleterious
   C. beneficial
   D. acrid
   E. ignominious

Directions: In each question, there is an initial pair of words or phrases that are related in some manner. Select the answer choice containing the lettered pair that best expresses a relationship similar to the initial pair.

10. POTTER : CLAY ::

   A. bull : rider
   B. conductor : instrument
   C. poet : words
   D. doctor : patient
   E. lady : gentleman

11. MINISCULE : SMALL ::

   A. large : gigantic
   B. exuberant : happy
   C. downtrodden : unjust
   D. humorless : hapless
   E. tense : relaxed

12. HOMOSAPIEN : MAMMAL ::

   A. lung : organ
   B. beach : ocean
   C. canine : feline
   D. mystery : novel
   E. bovine : husbandry

13. IMMUTABLE : CHANGE ::

   A. political : mastermind
   B. contingent : necessity
   C. ecstatic : joy
   D. imminent : proximity
   E. humble : hubris

14. VITUPERATE : BERATE ::

   A. destroy : rebuild
   B. vacillate : waver
   C. synthesize : raze
   D. confuse : clarify
   E. pacify : enrage

15. BUCOLIC : PASTORAL ::

   A. frigid : lukewarm
   B. basic : advanced
   C. irascible : temperamental
   D. haughty : selfish
   E. pugnacious : optimistic

16. LACONIC : VERBOSE ::

   A. terse : taciturn
   B. delicious : delectable
   C. passive : lethargic
   D. guileless : deceitful
   E. fastidious : studious

17. MALEVOLENT : BONHOMIE ::

   A. hateful : disgust
   B. calm : anxiety
   C. dangerous : peril
   D. hungry : want
   E. facetious : sarcasm

Directions: Each sentence below contains one or two blanks, with each blank corresponding to an omitted word. Find the answer choice that has the word or set or words that best fits the meaning of the sentence as a whole.

18. The mayor's unpopularity was dramatically demonstrated by his _____ performance in the citywide straw poll.

   A. sanguine
   B. dismal
   C. fiery
   D. impoverished
   E. discouraging

19. Country X will never stabilize its economy if it does not _____ its disastrous inflationary spending practices.

   A. exacerbate
   B. curtail
   C. strengthen
   D. maximize
   E. weaken

20. Normally the press secretary is fairly _____, but in today's briefing her face was quite _____ and her responses lively.

   A. peppy..morose
   B. subjugated..active
   C. noxious..expressive
   D. concise..perturbed
   E. subdued..animated

21. A slight _____ of the soil's settling rate caused the building's foundation to _____, which led to the building being deemed unusable.

   A. estimation..settle
   B. deviation..bulge
   C. miscalculation..shift
   D. permutation..stabilize
   E. escalation..liquefy

42

22. Prison reform in Victorian England, though _____, was not far-reaching enough to eliminate all the _____ vestiges of harsher times.

A. appreciable..miscellaneous
B. significant..cruel
C. dogged..basic
D. laudable..benign
E. wrongheaded..base

23. For three centuries, classical mechanics was the _____ paradigm in physics until developments in quantum mechanics began to call _____ assumptions of classical mechanics into question.

A. strongest..tangential
B. supreme..superficial
C. reigning..fundamental
D. secondary..basic
E. unchallenged..facile

Directions: Questions follow each passage. After reading the passage, determine the best answer for each question based on the passage's content.

Passage 1

Line Though the founding myth of the Yamato clan sets the beginning of their dynasty at the dawn of time, the Yamato clan did not unify Japan under their
(5) monarchical rule until the sixth century B.C.E. It is difficult to designate a specific date for the beginning of the Yamato monarchy because the process of political evolution in ancient Japan was not
(10) marked by clearly defined stages. Rather, the political evolution from aristocratic rule centered on a number of clan families; the monarchical rule dominated by one family was a gradual process.
(15) The slow pace of the transformation was mirrored by the means employed to achieve the result. The Yamato clan did not militarily subjugate the competing field of clans, but instead gained ascen-
(20) dancy through political, economic, and diplomatic means. Since such means generally preclude decisive shifts in power, the Yamato clan had to patiently leverage their advantages until they were
(25) able to demand recognition as the imperial family. Even when the Yamato clan had nominally laid claim to the title of the imperial throne, their power was still not as absolute as their titular
(30) pretensions suggested. The aristocratic clan chieftains still maintained significant power bases in the regions historically linked with their clans.

This scenario of power diffusion
(35) under the political rubric of monarchy is not peculiar to ancient Japan. In fact, it is a common theme in the narrative of kingdom formation in Medieval Europe. Many monarchs, with the notable
(40) exception of Charlemagne, had great difficulty consolidating their kingdom's resources under their authority given the prominent and powerful positions of dukes, lords, and wealthy merchants that
(45) populated their lands.

24. In line 34, the word *diffusion* could most reasonably be replaced by which of the following?

    A. Assimilation
    B. Sharing
    C. Hegemony
    D. Mongering
    E. Imbalances

25. What is the main point of the third paragraph?

    A. Ancient Japan's political evolution was dissimilar to Medieval European political evolution.
    B. Charlemagne was a powerful monarch comparable to the great emperors of ancient Japan.
    C. Both Medieval European monarchs and Japanese emperors had difficulties in unifying the lands under their power.
    D. Dukes, lords, wealthy merchants, and clan chieftains were politically obtuse throughout the world.
    E. Clan chieftains of ancient Japan resembled wealthy merchants in Medieval Europe with respect to the political role each played in their respective eras and locales.

26. What is the author's attitude toward the notion of absolute monarchical rule in ancient Japan and Medieval Europe?

    A. Harsh criticism of the weak monarchs
    B. Measured skepticism about the absoluteness of the monarch's rule
    C. Strenuous objection to the monarch's political practices
    D. Moderate praise of the monarch's restraint
    E. Fulsome praise of the monarch's policies

Passage 2

Line   Grasping the interrelationship between structure and function is essential to gaining a basic understanding of molecular biology. All biological entities are
(5)   composed of molecules, and every molecule has a specific shape. A hydrogen molecule, for instance, has a simple linear shape, while DNA, the molecule that stores most of a cell's genetic
(10)   information, has a complex double helix shape. The shape of a molecule, combined with the configuration of its valence electrons (the electrons available for bonding with other molecules),
(15)   determine the structure of a molecule. Since this structure determines the biological functionality of the molecule, it is of paramount importance.

    The chemistry of the brain illustrates
(20)   the interaction between molecular structure and biological function. One nerve cell in the brain communicates with another nerve cell by the emission and uptake of molecular signals. A transmit-
(25)   ting nerve cell initiates the communication with a second nerve cell known as a receiving cell. The transmitting cell releases signal molecules that are structured specifically to bond with
(30)   receptor molecules located at specific sites on the receiving cell. The signal and receptor molecules have complementary molecular structures which allow for their bonding ability. You can say the
(35)   signal molecule functions like a key while the receptor molecule is the lock. In this analogy, the molecular structure can be thought of as the nodes on the key and within the lock that complement each
(40)   other and allow for the key to turn the lock. The bonding of the signal and

receptor molecules sets in motion a series of chemical reactions within the receiving cell. Thus, through the biological (45) mechanism of complementary molecular structure, one brain cell is able to communicate and affect another brain cell.

27. The primary purpose of this passage is to

A. demonstrate the importance of biological functionality regarding brain functioning capacities.

B. criticize the contemporary theory that molecular structure and biological functionality are interrelated.

C. present competing views on the nature of the interrelationship between brain chemistry and molecular structure.

D. explain the contemporary theory of the interrelationship between molecular structure and biological functionality.

E. argue that molecular structure has greater explanatory force than does biological functionality.

28. Why does the author mention a hydrogen molecule and DNA in lines 6–11 in the first paragraph?

A. To contrast a simply shaped molecule with a complexly shaped molecule

B. To demonstrate that DNA is similarly shaped to hydrogen

C. To illustrate that biological functionality is not directly related to molecular shape

D. To give examples of the molecular structure of two different molecules

E. To undermine the assertion that hydrogen is more simply structured than DNA

29. What is the function of the second paragraph in relation to the passage as a whole?

A. It relates an anecdote that demonstrates the principle described in the first paragraph.

B. It gives further explanation to the theoretical hypothesis made in the first paragraph.

C. It provides an example that illustrates the relationship discussed in the first paragraph.

D. It presents a second viewpoint on the issues raised in the first paragraph.

E. It debunks a common misconception about the principle discussed in the first paragraph.

30. Based on the passage, which of the following statements would the author most likely agree with?

A. The study of molecular functionality is an important field in molecular chemistry.

B. The advancement of understanding in molecular biology is contingent upon further research in how molecules are structured.

C. Brain chemistry will not ultimately be understood until neurotransmitters are fully conceptualized.

D. Biological functionality is not dependent on molecular shape.

E. DNA is the most complex molecule known to biology.

Answer Key

Quantitative		Verbal	
1. B	15. D	1. E	16. D
2. A	16. E	2. A	17. B
3. A	17. B	3. E	18. B
4. C	18. E	4. A	19. B
5. C	19. D	5. B	20. E
6. D	20. E	6. A	21. C
7. B	21. D	7. D	22. B
8. D	22. D	8. C	23. C
9. D	23. C	9. D	24. B
10. C	24. C	10. C	25. C
11. A	25. A	11. B	26. B
12. B	26. E	12. A	27. D
13. D	27. A	13. E	28. A
14. A	28. B	14. B	29. C
		15. C	30. B

46

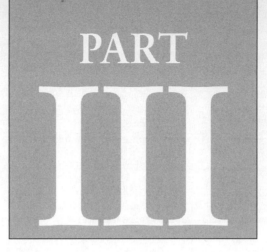

PART III

Section Review

PART III

Chapter
4

Quantitative Review

All the Math You Left Behind

For those who have not seen a triangle since high school geometry, it's scary to think that your graduate school aspirations partially rest on your ability to work with the math concepts of your youth. Those of you who studied math extensively in college aren't off the hook either, since the concepts tested on the GRE are not the ones studied by math majors or engineering students. Brainiacs who are used to working with orthogonal matrices might not remember dividing with remainders.

That's the "half-empty" news. The "half-full" news is that the GRE math section tests a limited number of math concepts, so the math content of the GRE can be mastered. With a little bit—okay, for some of you, a lot—of studying, you can be confident that you will not be tested on an unfamiliar math concept. The reason for this comes partly from the fact that the material covered in the GRE math section is not very difficult. Instead, the difficulty comes when the test demands you apply this basic set of GRE math knowledge in creative ways to solve problems.

Mastering the basic math knowledge of the GRE becomes the first goal, so this is what we'll focus on for now (without such mastery, the math will indeed be difficult). Once this is done, the second step is learning to recognize how and when to apply the basic math knowledge on the GRE. This will take more time than the first part, but you will have more than enough questions to practice on before you have to exercise this skill on test day.

On test day, you can expect to see a lot of math jargon in the Quantitative section. But don't fear; you don't have to be intimidated by math speak. In this section, we will define all the terms that you need to know for the test, and we will work with them so that you can get comfortable with phrases like "positive even integers divisible by 4." As you learn (or refresh your memory about) this math jargon, remember that learning a math term is just like learning a new word. Don't let the jargon-ness (jargonosity?) of it throw you. A math term simply refers to a specific math notion, just like the word *chair* refers to a specific idea we have of "furniture you sit on." When a math term is introduced, read the definition, consider the example, and think of it as your new word for the day.

So, don't let the GRE math section bully you, or your feelings, around. It can be conquered with a little effort. Roll up your sleeves, get to work, and comfort yourself with the thought that once you finish the math section on the GRE, you will probably never have to be concerned about the area of a parallelogram again (unless you decide to go to business school and need to take the GMAT, that is).

Arithmetic, or Fun with Numbers

Most people hear the word *arithmetic* and think "add-subtract-multiply-divide," but arithmetic actually covers many basic math concepts and terms. GRE math loves to pile one math topic on top of another, so there's a lot of arithmetic in the Quant section. Take your time and don't just skim over this portion to get to a juicier topic like Geometry, since Arithmetic covers the fundamental terms that will be prevalent on almost every question, in one form or another.

Integers, or Pretty Much Everything That's Not a Fraction

Integers are the numbers that you count with (1, 2, 3 and so on). They can also be negative (-1, -2, -3 . . .). Zero is also an integer. The numbers -3, -2, -1, 0, 1, 2, and 3 are all integers. Pretty much any whole number you can think of—any number that is not a fraction or a decimal—is an integer, and if you put a negative in front of that number, it also is an integer.

Alert!

In the real world, the terms *integer* and *number* are fairly synonymous, since when any real person says "pick a number," they don't expect you to pick a fraction like $\frac{13}{8}$. However, integer is a more precise term, and since it's also something people are unfamiliar with, it makes many appearances on the GRE.

Besides zero, all integers are positive or negative, and they are also even or odd. Positive integers are greater than zero (like 2, 15, or 309), and

PETERSON'S
getting you there

negative integers are less than zero (-1, -23, -90). Think of the integers as being along a line with zero at the center.

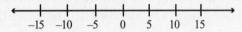

This figure above is called a number line, and seeing it may provoke a jarring flashback to the eighth grade. As you go from left to right on a number line, the value of the number increases. Notice that this means that -5 is greater than -10.

The mathematical definitions for even and odd values use integers, stating that an integer is even if you can divide it by 2 and have no remainder (nothing left over). For example, -4 and 10 are even since two evenly divides into both. 11 and -27, on the other hand, are odd since 2 does not evenly divide into them.

even + even = even	e.g., $12 + 8 = 20$
even + odd = odd	e.g., $6 + 13 = 19$
odd + odd = even	e.g., $7 + 9 = 16$
even $\times$ even = even	e.g., $4 \times 6 = 24$
even $\times$ odd = even	e.g., $3 \times 8 = 24$
odd $\times$ odd = odd	e.g., $1 \times 9 = 9$
(Remember, if you forget one of these, like what an even times an odd is, just pick an even and an odd number and multiply them. Their product will remind you.)	

You might not remember how basic math operations work with that pesky negative sign, so see the quick refresher on the following page.

Working with Negative Numbers

(negative) + *(negative)* = *negative*	e.g., $(-4) + (-5) = -9$
(positive) + *(negative)* = *(positive)* − *(positive)*	e.g., $(10) + (-12) = 10 - 12$ $= -2$ or $(-6) + (8)$ $= 8 - 6$ $= 2$
(positive) − *(negative)* = *positive* + *positive*	e.g., $12 - (-3) = 12 + 3 = 15$
(positive) × *(negative)* = *negative*	e.g., $-6 \times 3 = -18$
(negative) × *(negative)* = *positive*	e.g., $(-7) \times (-4) = 28$
Zero is not negative, but it is good to remember that $0 \times (anything) = 0$	e.g., $0 \times (-10) = 0$

How many integers are there from −5 to 7 inclusive?

A.   14
B.   13
C.   12
D.   2
E.   −12

Here's a simple math question with two well-traveled math terms, *integer* and *inclusive*. You know the first term, so if you figure out what *inclusive* means, you should be able to solve this problem. *Inclusive* means you include −5 and 7 when you are counting the number of integers. How many negative numbers are there from −5 to 7? Five. How many positive numbers are there from −5 to 7? Seven. Test-takers in a hurry may add these numbers, 5 and 7, and then pick choice (C). Yet this would be too hasty, for if you recall, zero is also an integer. That makes the correct answer for this problem 13, choice (B).

This problem typifies the GRE Quant section. The question contains two basic math terms and in many ways looks deceptively simple. You can come up with a quick answer, 12, that's just begging for you to choose it. However, if you take time and use a strong understanding of the basic terms *integer* and *inclusive*, you will not forget the presence of zero.

The terms *divisible* and *product* are often used along with integers. *Divisible* is the math term for when an integer can be divided by another without there being a remainder. For instance, 12 is divisible by 3 since $12 \div 3 = 4$, and there is no remainder. In this instance, 3 also has a name, *divisor*, since it evenly divides into 12. When you multiply two numbers together, the answer is the *product*. So 12 is the product of 3 times 4. In this case, 3 and 4 are called *factors* of 12 because their product is 12.

The factors of 12 are the integers that multiply together to give 12: 1×12, 2×6, 3×4. Notice that the factors of 12 and the divisors of 12 are the same. They just involve using a different math operation. Think of it as going up a set of stairs or heading down a set of stairs. Either way, it's the same set of stairs.

> There is another related term, *multiple*. The multiple of an integer is that integer times counting numbers like 1, 2, 3, and up. So the multiples of 3 are $3(3 \times 1)$, $6(3 \times 2)$, $9(3 \times 3)$, $12(3 \times 4)$, $15(3 \times 5)$, $18(3 \times 6) \ldots$ and so on. The integer $12(3 \times 4)$ is a multiple of 3, and it's also a multiple of 4.

Note

Keeping all these terms in your head can be a bit tricky. It's like having identical triplet cousins whose names are Tad, Todd, and Ted. Don't lose heart in this flurry of terms. None of them individually is difficult to grasp, but they can be a little confusing if they are all heaped together at the same time like in the following problem.

Column A	Column B
The greatest common factor of 18 and 36	The first even integer greater than 4×4

The greatest common factor, or GCF, is the largest number that is a factor of both 18 and 36. You might notice right off the bat that $36 = 2 \times 18$, and so 18 must be the GCF. If you don't catch this, don't sweat it. Just start writing down the factors of 18 and 36.

Factors of 18: 1, 2, 3, 6, 9, 18

Factors of 36: 1, 2, 3, 4, 6, 9, 12, 18, 36

18 is the largest number they share, so the integer value of Column A is 18. Looking at Column B, you just have to unpack the terms. The first integer greater than 16 (4×4) is 17, and the first even integer greater than 16 is 18. Column B also equals 18, so (C) is the correct answer.

Notice that both Columns A and B describe specific numbers that will have a definite relationship. Therefore, (D) cannot be the correct answer.

One final integer-related term to cover concerns prime numbers. *Prime numbers* are divisible by only two integers, themselves and one. Another way of saying this is to state "a prime number only has two multiples: Itself and 1." 11 is a prime number since the only integers that evenly divide into 11 are 11 and 1. Notice that 1 is not a prime number since it has one multiple (1×1) and not two.

It is a good idea to be familiar with the smaller prime numbers because you might need them at your fingertips for a problem. Here's the first ten: 2, 3, 5, 7, 11, 13, 17, 19, 23, and 29. If you want any more, you'll have to figure them out yourself or pay extra.

If n equals the number of prime numbers greater than 10 and less than 20, then $3n =$

- A.   3
- B.   6
- C.   9
- D.   12
- E.   15

Before you can find $3n$, you must figure out what n is. Looking at the list of prime numbers in the paragraph above, you can see that there are four prime numbers between 10 and 20: 11, 13, 17, 19. If $n = 4$, then $3n$ will be $(3)(4) = 12$. Therefore, (D) is the correct answer.

Fractions, or Pretty Much Everything That's Not an Integer

A fraction is a number made up of two integers and it looks like this: $\frac{a}{b}$. The number on top, a, is called the *numerator*. The number on the bottom, b, is called the *denominator*. (If you can come up with a clever way to help yourself remember that the numerator is on top while the denominator is on bottom, you should do so.) A fraction means you are dividing the top by the bottom, so $\frac{a}{b}$ is the same thing as $a \div b$. Since $\frac{a}{b} = a \div b$, b cannot equal zero because mathematicians don't think it makes any sense to divide by 0. I don't have the exact reasons for this, but in general, mathematicians are a serious lot and I don't think they would say this just to pull our leg.

The GRE math section is going to expect you to do things like add and divide fractions, so here is a quick review of how to perform these math operations with fractions.

1. Addition

You can only add fractions that have the same denominator. If you are asked what $\frac{3}{4} + \frac{2}{3}$ equals, you have to make the bottoms look the same. In math speak, this is called "finding a common denominator." The common denominator will be a number that is a multiple of both 4 and 3. 12 is the smallest common multiple (in math speak, the least common multiple or LCM). To get 12 as your denominator for both fractions, you multiply the first denominator by 3 to get 12 and the second denominator by 4 to get 12.

However, you can't just multiply only the denominator by whatever number you please. You must also multiply the numerator by that same number. Multiply the first fraction by $\frac{3}{3}$ and the second one by $\frac{4}{4}$.

This gives you:

$$\frac{3}{4} \times \frac{3}{3} = \frac{9}{12}$$

and

$$\frac{2}{3} \times \frac{4}{4} = \frac{8}{12}$$

$$\frac{3}{4}\left(\frac{3}{3}\right) + \frac{2}{3}\left(\frac{4}{4}\right) = \frac{9}{12} + \frac{8}{12}$$

Now that the denominators are the same you can add the numerators,

$$\frac{9}{12} + \frac{8}{12} = \frac{8+9}{12} = \frac{17}{12}$$

2. Subtraction

Like addition, you have to have the same denominator in order to subtract fractions. Once you have that, just subtract the two numbers on top (the numerators). So,

$$\frac{3}{4} - \frac{2}{3} = \frac{9}{12} - \frac{8}{12} = \frac{9-8}{12} = \frac{1}{12}$$

3. Multiplication

This is a lot easier. Multiply the numerators together and multiply the denominators together. For example,

$$\frac{-10}{4} \times \frac{3}{5} = \frac{-30}{20}$$

Fractions in answer choices on the GRE will usually be in their simplest form, and so $\frac{-30}{20}$ would not be an answer on the GRE. It would be simplified,

$$\frac{-30}{20} = \frac{-3 \times 10}{2 \times 10} = \frac{-3}{2} \times \frac{10}{10} = \frac{-3}{2} \times 1 = -\frac{3}{2} \text{ or } -1\frac{1}{2}$$

4. Division

Dividing two fractions can look like this, $\frac{2}{5} \div \frac{7}{8}$, or it can look like this,

$$\frac{\frac{2}{5}}{\frac{7}{8}}$$

These two expressions are the same. You solve them with a two-step process. First, flip the fraction you are dividing by, so that $\frac{7}{8} \to \frac{8}{7}$. In math speak, this flipping is called "finding the reciprocal." Now multiply the flipped fraction and the other fraction. So,

$$\frac{\frac{2}{5}}{\frac{7}{8}} = \frac{2}{5} \times \frac{8}{7} = \frac{16}{35}$$

A catchy phrase to remember the dividing procedure is, "When dividing, don't ask why; just flip it over and multiply." If you forget it, any 14-year-old kid can remind you of this phrase.

Fractions also come in hybrid form. They're called *mixed fractions*, and they look like $3\frac{2}{7}$, which means $3 + \frac{2}{7}$. In order to do any arithmetic operation like the ones discussed above, mixed fractions should be converted into pure fractions. You might be able to multiply the mixed fractions $3\frac{2}{7}$ with $4\frac{3}{5}$, but it would be pretty messy.

To convert a mixed fraction into a pure fraction, first multiply the integer out front by the denominator, then add that product to the numerator.

$$3\frac{2}{7}$$

$3 \times 7 = 21$ (multiplying the integer 3 with the denominator 7)

$21 + 2 = 23$ (adding the product to the numerator 2)

$$= \frac{23}{7}$$

Voila, you have it.

> All integers can be expressed as a fraction. Place the integer in the numerator and a 1 in the denominator. For instance, 7 in fractional form is $\frac{7}{1}$. If you think about it, $\frac{7}{1} = 7 \div 1 = 7$ should make sense to you.

Note

If $\dfrac{3x}{2} \div \dfrac{3}{8} = 4$ then $\dfrac{2}{3} \times \dfrac{4}{4x} =$

A. $\dfrac{2}{5}$

B. $\dfrac{2}{3}$

C.   1

D. $\dfrac{8}{3}$

E.   4

Here's a basic GRE question that seeks to overwhelm you with a bunch of fractions and arithmetic flitting about. You can't solve the second equation until you learn the value of x, which can be found by solving the first equation:

$$\frac{3x}{2} \div \frac{3}{8} = 4$$

$$\frac{3x}{2} \div \frac{3}{8} = \frac{3x}{2} \times \frac{8}{3} = \frac{24x}{6} = 4x \quad \text{(This solves the left side of the equation.)}$$

$$4x = 4$$

$$x = 1$$

Plugging $x = 1$ into the second equation will get you:

$$\frac{2}{3} \times \frac{4}{4x} =$$

or

$$\frac{2}{3} \times \frac{4}{4(1)} = \frac{8}{12} = \frac{2}{3}$$

You might have noticed that $\frac{4}{4} = 1$, so multiplying out the second equation wasn't necessary. Either way, you end up with (B), the correct answer.

Decimals (Fractions in Disguise!)

Decimal form is another way to write a fraction. Decimals can easily be converted into fractions, since every decimal has a denominator that is a multiple of 10. The decimal 0.7 is the fraction $\frac{7}{10}$, while the decimal 0.765 is $\frac{765}{1,000}$. You take the number and make it the numerator, then you look and count how many spaces there are to the right of the decimal point. This number equals the number of zeroes you need to place after a 1 in the denominator. 0.7 has only one space to the right, so you put only one zero after the 1, giving you 10 in the denominator. The decimal 0.765 has three spaces, so you put three zeroes, giving you 1,000 in the denominator.

All the numbers to the right of the decimal point have place values that end in the suffix "-*th*." The decimal 0.7 is expressed "seven tenths," while 0.25 is "twenty-five hundredths." Place values on either side of the decimal point might crop up, so it's good to have a quick review:

Take the number 934.167:

9 is in the hundreds place, so the 9 means	900
3 is in the tens place, so the 3 means	30
4 is in the units place, so the 4 means	4
1 is in the tenths place, so the 1 means	$\frac{1}{10}$
6 is in the hundredths place, so the 6 means	$\frac{6}{100}$
7 is in the thousands place, so the 7 means	$\frac{7}{1,000}$

A tricky part about place values and decimals is that there is no "unit-*th*s" value. In this example, the 4 is "four units" and the number to the left of it is the tens. However, the number immediately to the right of 4—over the decimal point divide—is the tenths, not unit-*th*s.

When you add and subtract with decimals you need to make sure you line up the decimal points. For instance, 345.4 minus 202.45 is:

$$\begin{array}{r} 345.4 \\ -\ 202.45 \\ \hline \end{array}$$

When multiplying decimals, do the multiplication as if the decimal points weren't there. Just ignore them for starters. Once you have the product, count how many decimal places you have behind the decimal in both factors, and then put the decimal that many places into the product. If that sounds confusing, in application it's not. For instance, $3.5 \times 0.5 \to 175$ (multiplying forgetting the decimals). Or, there are two places behind the decimal in the two factors, one for each factor. Putting two numbers behind the decimal in the product gives you 1.75. If you change the initial numbers to 0.35 and 0.005, you still multiply and get 175 to start. But now there are five spaces to the left of the decimal point (two in 0.35 and three in 0.005), so your final answer will be 0.00175 for that problem.

To divide a decimal by a decimal, first move the decimal in the divisor until it is a whole number, and then move the decimal point as many spaces in the number being divided. The expression $2.3 \div 0.5$ would look like this $5\overline{)23.0}$ in long division form. You would have to move the decimal one space to the left to transform 2.3 into the integer 23, so you must move the divisor one space to the left as well, making 0.5 into 5. Now do the division, and put the decimal in the quotient right where it lies in the number being divided, $5\overline{)23.0}$ with quotient 4.6.

If you need to convert a fraction into a decimal, remember that $\frac{a}{b}$ means $a \div b$. So if you are given a fraction and you need to know its value in decimal form, divide the top by the bottom, and you have it. For example, if you need to know what $\frac{2}{7}$ is in decimal form, divide 2 by 7,

$$
\begin{array}{r}
0.28 \\
7\overline{)2.00} \\
\underline{14} \\
60 \\
\underline{56} \\
4
\end{array}
$$

$\frac{2}{7} \approx 0.28$

Column A	**Column B**

d, c, e are distinct prime numbers and $d + e = c$. They are also part of the six digit number $54de.3c$.

The value in the tens place in the 6-digit number	The value in the tenths place in the 6-digit number

The test is trying to confuse you with math speak. Don't let it. Distinct prime numbers are prime numbers that are different from each other, so $d \neq e \neq c$. You can also infer that d, c, e must be 2, 3, 5, or 7 since those are all the single digit prime numbers.

Let's look at Column A and try to pin it down. The value in the tens place is d. With what you know, $d + e = c$ could be $2 + 3 = 5$ or $2 + 5 = 7$, but there's no way to tell which equation is valid. Therefore, d could be 2, 3, or 5. That narrows it down as much as possible, so it's time to turn to Column B. The tenths place is the one just to the right of the decimal, which is 3.

This gives us three possibilities. Depending on d's value, it could be less than, equal to, or greater than 3. This makes Column A less than, equal to, or greater than Column B, depending on what value you use for d. Therefore, choice (D) is the correct answer.

Exponents^(Those Tiny Raised Numbers) and Roots

Exponents can be a little weird, and that's putting it nicely. A basic exponent looks like 4^2, with the integer 4 called the *base* and the number 2 called the *power*, or exponent. The expression 4^2 is math shorthand for 4×4, which might make you think people have to be in a real hurry to use that shorthand. Exponents come in handy when you deal with numbers like 4^{350}, since writing out 350 fours is a bit time-consuming.

While you might be using some arithmetic—adding, subtracting, fractions, and decimals—in your everyday life, you're usually not walking around raising values to the nth power. Here is a condensed version of how exponents work. Look it over, play with them (plug in numbers and such), and get comfortable with them.

Exponent Refresher

$$x^0 = 1$$
$$x^1 = x$$

$$x^2 = x \times x$$
$$x^3 = x \times x \times x$$

You get the picture. But just for good measure, here's one more:

$$xx^3 = x^4$$

Exponents can also be negative.

$$x^{-1} = \frac{1}{x}$$

$$x^{-2} = \frac{1}{x^2} = \frac{1}{x \times x}$$

You can add and subtract numbers with exponents if they have the same base and are raised to the same power.

$$3x^2 + 2x^2 = 5x^2$$
$$2x^2 - x^2 = x^2$$

but $3x^3 + 3x^2 \neq 6x^3$ since they are not raised to the same power.

You can also multiply and divide numbers if they have the same base.

$$x^a x^b = x^{a+b}$$

For instance, $x^2 \times x^3 = x^5$. This makes sense if you see that $x^2 \times x^3 = (x \times x)(x \times x \times x) = x^5$.

$$\frac{x^a}{x^b} = x^{a-b}$$

For example,

$$\frac{x^3}{x^2} = x^{3-2} = x$$

This also makes sense if you see that

$$\frac{x^3}{x^2} = \frac{xxx}{xx} = x$$

You can also raise a number with an exponent to a power. In gambling terms, this would be like saying, "I'll see your exponent, and raise you another."

$$(x^a)^b = x^{ab}$$

So,

$$(x^2)^3 = x^6 \text{ or } (x^{-3})^3 = x^{-9} = \frac{1}{x^9}$$

Column A	Column B

a and b are positive distinct integers.

$$\frac{(2a^2)^{-2}(4b)}{a^2 b^{-3}} \qquad \frac{10(b^2)^2}{5(2a)^2 a^2 a^2}$$

Here is another problem filled with complex-looking math things, standard issue for the GRE math problem visual. At first, don't worry about the positive distinct integer bit. Just simplify the expressions step by step.

Column A	Column B

$$\frac{(2a^2)^{-2}(4b)}{a^2 b^{-3}} \qquad\qquad \frac{10(b^2)^2}{5(2a)^2 a^2 a^2}$$

$$= \frac{4b(b^3)}{a^2(2a^2)^2} \qquad\qquad = \frac{10b^4}{5(4a^2)a^4}$$

$$= \frac{4b^4}{4a^6} \qquad\qquad = \frac{10b^4}{20a^6}$$

$$= \frac{b^4}{a^6} \qquad\qquad = \frac{b^4}{2a^6}$$

Now that you've done the work, you can go back to the "positive distinct integers" phrase. Since the two variables are positive integers, the denominator in Column A is smaller than the denominator in Column B, while the numerators are equal. Try substituting some small positive integers into the equation if you like. If the denominator in Column B is greater, this means that Column A is greater in value, since $\frac{1}{2} > \frac{1}{8}$. Using these simpler values, you can see how the numerators are equal and the fraction with the smaller denominator is the largest value.

> **Tip**
>
> If the variables weren't "distinct" they could both equal 1, and the two fractions would be equal.

What does $\frac{2^4}{4^2 4^3}$ equal?

A. 2^{-6}
B. 2^{-3}
C. 2^{-1}
D. 4^2
E. 2^5

One way to do this is to raise each number to its power, multiply where needed, and then simplify. You might be able to work this method on this problem, but if the numbers are raised to higher powers, this method becomes very difficult very quickly. The other way is to try to make the numbers in the numerator and the denominator have the same base so that you can simplify directly. Since $4 = (2)(2)$ then

$$4^2 = [(2)(2)]^2 = 2^2 2^2 = 2^4,$$

and

$$4^3 = [(2)(2)]^3 = 2^3 2^3 = 2^6$$

So we can rewrite the fraction like this,

$$\frac{2^4}{4^2 4^3} = \frac{2^4}{2^4 2^6} = \frac{2^4}{2^{10}}$$

This can be simplified straightforwardly,

$$\frac{2^4}{2^{10}} = 2^4 2^{-10} = 2^{-6}$$

You could also have transformed the numerator into a base of 4. Either method would lead to the right answer, although since a majority of the answer choices have a base of 2, transforming everything into that base increases your chances of simply coming up with the right answer without having to do one last conversion.

The annoying relative of the exponent is the square root. It looks like this $\sqrt{}$, and it's the opposite of squaring a number. When you square 4, you multiply it by itself to get 16, but when you take the square root of 4, you get the number that times itself gives 4(2 × 2) = 4, so $\sqrt{4}$ =2. Square roots can also be written as exponents, $\sqrt{x} = x^{\frac{1}{2}}$.

Even more annoying than the square root is the cube root. Just look at it, $\sqrt[3]{}$. Something like this practically screams "convoluted math process up ahead." When you cube something, you multiply it by itself twice (so the cube of 3 is 3^3 = 3 × 3 × 3 = 27). The cube root is the opposite, $\sqrt[3]{27}$ = 3 or $\sqrt[3]{8}$ = 2 because 2 × 2 × 2 = 8. Cube roots are written as exponents like this, $\sqrt[3]{x} = x^{\frac{1}{3}}$.

If $x = 3$ then $\dfrac{\left[\left(2x^2\right)\left(x^{\frac{2}{3}}\right)\left(x^{\frac{25}{12}}\right)\right]}{4\left(x^{\frac{3}{4}}\right)}$

A. 1
B. $\sqrt{3}$
C. 3
D. 27
E. 81

There is good news and bad news about this problem. The good news is that with a problem like this, there are no hidden tricks. The bad news is that you have to work this problem out step by step, but you know everything you need to know to do that. To the solving, then!

$$\frac{\left(2x\right)^2\left(x^{\frac{2}{3}}\right)\left(x^{\frac{25}{12}}\right)}{4\left(x^{\frac{3}{4}}\right)} = x^2 x^{\frac{2}{3}} x^{\frac{25}{12}} x^{-\frac{3}{4}}$$

The four in the denominator is cancelled out by the 2 that gets squared. Now we need to find a common denominator for the exponents in order to add and subtract these fractions. This process was discussed earlier on page 62, and as you can see, straightforward concepts have a way of showing up in odd places on a GRE math question. 12 is an easy choice.

$$x^2 x^{\frac{2}{3}} x^{\frac{25}{12}} x^{-\frac{3}{4}} = x^{\frac{24 + 8 + 25 - 9}{12}} = x^{\frac{48}{12}} = x^4$$

If $x = 3$ then the answer is 81, or (E).

PETERSON'S
getting you there

Common Exponents to Know

$2^3 = 8, 2^4 = 16, 2^5 = 32$
$3^3 = 27, 3^4 = 81$
$4^3 = 64$
$5^3 = 125$

One more tip when dealing with exponents: Always remember that the base can be a negative number. If a problem states, "$x^2 = 36$," it's common to assume that $x = 6$. This is a tried-and-true test trap. Without any more information given in the problem, all you know is that x could be 6 or -6. Any number raised to an even power will yield a positive number, but the base could be positive or negative. When the exponent is odd, the base is the same sign as what it equals.

For instance, if $x^5 = -32$ then $x = -2$.

Percents Are about 4.6% of This Entire Chapter

Percents are not an alien concept, but the GRE expects a greater understanding of percents than what you need to navigate the local grocery store. It isn't a huge amount of additional information that you need to understand, but a few things probably need to be ironed out in your mind about percents. Let's get to ironing.

Percent just means "per hundred" or "divided by one hundred."

So $27\% = \dfrac{27}{100}$, or

$$0.6\% = \frac{0.6}{100} = \frac{6}{1,000}$$

If bananas are 40% off at the store, and their normal price is $3/pound, then their sale price is

$$(100\% - 40\%)(\$3 \text{ } pound) = (60\%)\,(\$3 \text{ } pound)$$
$$= \left(\frac{60}{100}\right)(\$3 \text{ } pound)$$
$$= (0.6)(\$3 \text{ } pound)$$
$$= \$1.80 \text{ } pound$$

Notice that we multiplied the price times 60% because the sales price was 40% off. You could also have found out how much the bananas were discounted due to the sale, and then subtracted that number from the original price. This would give you:

$$(40\ sale)(\$3\ pound) = \left(\frac{40}{100}\right)(\$3\ pound)$$
$$= (0.4)(\$3\ pound)$$
$$= \$1.20\ discount$$

Subtract $1.20, the discount, from the original price of $3/pound and you get $1.80/pound, the same answer as before.

A straightforward use of percent is when you are given two numbers and asked to figure out a percentage value. A simple question of this kind might ask, "What percentage of 33 is 3?" To answer this problem, it helps to travel back in time to the fifth grade and dredge up the skill known as cross-multiplying. Given two fractions equal to each other, you can multiply the numerator of the first fraction with the denominator of the second fraction. Then you can multiply the numerator of the second fraction with the denominator of the first fraction, and set both products equal to each other. Like many basic math concepts, the explanation is tougher than the actual cross-multiplying.

One way to set up this problem is $\frac{3}{33} = \frac{x}{100}$, because you want to know what percentage the original fraction equals. Solving for x by cross-multiplying yields

$$\frac{3}{33} = \frac{x}{100} \rightarrow$$
$$(33)(x) = (3)(100) \rightarrow \quad \text{(the second step is the}$$
$$33x = 300 \rightarrow \quad \text{cross-multiplying one)}$$
$$x = \frac{300}{33} \approx 9$$

With no calculator, 9 is a good estimate. Therefore, 3 is about 9% of 33.

X-Ref

The shortcut on this problem was to see that $\frac{3}{33} = \frac{1}{11}$, and using fraction-decimal conversions, $\frac{1}{11} = 0.09 = 9\%$.

PETERSON'S
getting you there

Those are the user-friendly percent questions. Percent increase and decrease problems are a tad bit trickier. With these problems, the critical point to remember is that any increase or decrease is relative to the original value (what is increasing or decreasing). You need to use the original value if you are trying to find the percent change. Suppose a problem tells you that a certain stock started the year priced at $40/share and ended the year at $56/share. What was the percentage change?

This percentage change is relative to the original value of $40/share. To find the percentage change, you find how much the stock price changed ($16/share) and divide it by the original value, $\dfrac{\$16 \; share}{\$40 \; share} = \dfrac{4}{10} = 0.4$ = 40%. Since the change was an increase, the stock price increased 40%. The same method would be used to find a percentage decrease.

You might see a percentage change problem like this but be given the percentage change and the final value of the item and asked to find the original value. In that case, you are doing the same problem you just did in reverse. Here is the formula you can use to solve either kind of problem, $\dfrac{|x - y|}{x} = z$, where x is the original value, y is the second value, and z is the percentage change. (If the lines around the numerator are like alien scribblings to you, look forward to the section on absolute value for an explanation of them.)

> The price of a house increased 15%, and then decreased 20%. Compared to the original price, the final price was
>
> A.   an 8% decrease.
> B.   a 5% decrease.
> C.   the same.
> D.   a 3% increase.
> E.   a 5% increase.

There's a simple trick that makes this kind of problem a lot easier. If you're not told what the original price of the house is, pick a value and work the problem with it. You want to make things easy, so don't pick a tough number like 17.53. Using the value of 100 is a much better choice, as this makes the first percent change easy to figure. A 15% increase on 100 is 15, and so after the first increase the price of the house is 115.

You now have to calculate a 20% decrease on a house valued at 115. If you recall those fraction-decimal conversions on page 57, 20% = 0.20 = $\frac{1}{5}$. Therefore, to find the value of the 20% decrease, multiply 115 by one fifth, $\frac{1}{5} \times \frac{115}{1} = \frac{115}{5} = 23$. The price of the house decreased 23 from 115, which means the final value of the house is 92(115 − 23). What is the percentage change from 100 to 92? It's an 8% decrease, choice (A).

Ratios, Where You Can Compare Apples to Oranges

Ratio problems on standardized tests are like affable guests on a talk show: They make a lot of appearances. Ratios can be tested in lots of different kinds of problems, which is one reason for their common occurrence. You might see ratios in a word problem or a probability problem, or maybe in just a straightforward ratio problem.

Ratios are a fancy way of writing fractions. There are a couple of different forms of ratios that you might see on a test, but they are all equivalent to each other and they are also all equivalent to the fractional form of the ratio. In a word problem, a ratio would look like this: "9 bananas were sold for every 4 apples that were sold." The ratio of bananas to apples sold is 9 to 4, or 9:4. These three expressions are equivalent, and they are equivalent to the fraction $\frac{9}{4}$ (the first number in the ratio is the numerator and the second the denominator).

Tip

From a precise mathematical standpoint, ratios and fractions are not completely interchangeable. However, the precise distinction between ratios and fractions is not relevant for the GRE, so don't sweat it.

Like fractions, ratios can be reduced to lowest terms. If the ratio had been "9 bananas sold for every 3 apples," the ratio would be 9:3 or 3:1. These ratios are the same, just as $\frac{9}{3}$ is the same thing as $\frac{3}{1}$.

Since you can compare fractions and say that one is greater than another, you can do the same thing with ratios. For instance, which ratio is greater, 4:3 or 5:4? Convert both to fractions and compare. Is $\frac{4}{3}$ greater or smaller

PETERSON'S
getting you there

than $\frac{5}{4}$? It is greater because a third is greater than a fourth (bigger denominator means smaller value, just like earlier), and four thirds is a third greater than one, while five fourths is a fourth greater than one.

Column A	Column B

Before 4 girls entered the class, there were 18 boys and 16 girls in the fourth grade class at Santiago Elementary School.

The original ratio of boys to girls in the class	The final ratio of girls to boys in the class

First, you know that you can determine the two ratios, which means you can compare them. Since there will be a definite relationship between Column A and Column B, choice (D) is out. The original ratio of boys to girls is 18:16 or $\frac{18}{16} = \frac{9}{8}$. The final ratio of girls to boys is 20:18 or $\frac{20}{18} = \frac{10}{9}$. Column A is one eighth greater than one, and Column B is one ninth greater than one, so (A) is greater.

Absolute Value (not a vodka-related concept)

Do you remember the number line on page 50 of this chapter? The concept of absolute value is related to the number line. The absolute value of a number is how many numbers (how far) it is away from zero on the number line. -14 is 14 numbers away from zero on the number line, so the absolute value of -14 is 14. Of course, the powers-that-be came up with a cute little way to denote absolute value. For our example, it's like this: $|-14| = 14$.

Algebra

The word *algebra* usually conjures up memories of numbers and letters mashed together in strings like "$9y + 3x = -\frac{3}{4}$." In simplest terms, algebra uses placeholders, called *variables*, as substitutes for a known value. Using variables in this manner often allows someone to set up an equation and then solve this equation to find the actual value of the variable.

Setting up equations with variables and manipulating these equations are standard fare for all standardized math tests, and the GRE is no exception. Problems filled with variables will be easily recognizable algebra problems, but these are not the only ones you will encounter. On others, the key will be to create the correct equation on your own, although this might not be the most obvious step required. The end point is that you should get comfortable with the idea of using variables and making equations, since this is yet another tool you can use to crack open and solve GRE Quantitative questions.

Alert!

Many algebra problems have a geometry component, and others are filled with the sort of math jargon you just finished studying. As you work through the rest of this chapter, you will see how a firm foundation of arithmetic aids you on all types of problems.

Equations

Equations are like sentences written in math. Unlike sentences written in English, sentences written in math always follow the same form and rules:

1. There is stuff on the right side of the equation, and it equals the stuff on the left side of the equation.

2. If you do something to the right side, you have to do the exact same thing to the left side, and vice versa. (That is how you can keep the equal sign between them. If you do the same thing to each side, they remain equal.)

3. It doesn't matter what you do to one side, so long as you follow Rule #2.

Burn Rules #2 and #3 into your head, since you'll often be given an equation to start with and asked to do something to it. Anything's fair game—multiplying, dividing, raising to a power, cubing the root, adding 43,000,000,000—so long as it's done to both sides.

If $3x - 12 = 33$, then what does x equal?

This is a simple equation. To find out what x equals, you need to get x all by itself on one side of the equation. The variable x will then equal everything on the other side of the equation.

$$3x - 12 = 33$$
$$3x - 12 + 12 = 33 + 12$$
By adding twelve to both sides, we can get rid of the -12 on the left side.

$$3x = 45$$
$$3x \div 3 = 45 \div 3$$
$$x = 15$$
Dividing both sides by three will get rid of the 3 in front of the x.

There you have it.

Notice that in the example there was only one equation and one variable. The next step up is a problem where you are given two equations and two unknowns. It's all still good, because if you have two equations you can solve for two unknowns. It just takes a little bit longer. (The general math rule is that you can solve for as many unknowns as you have distinct equations.)

If $4x + 3y = 13$ and $x + 2y = 2$, then what is the value of $-7xy$?

- A. -24
- B. -4
- C. -1
- D. 4
- E. 28

There are two different ways to try to solve this problem. The first way is the "solve and plug." You solve for one variable in one equation and then plug it into the other equation. It looks like this:

$x + 2y = 2 \rightarrow x = 2 - 2y$ (Plug this in for x in the other equation.)

$4(2 - 2y) + 3y = 13$ (Now we have one equation with one unknown, so we can solve for y.)

$$8 - 8y + 3y = 13$$
$$-5y = 5$$
$$y = -1$$
$$x = 2 - 2y$$
$$= 2 - 2(-1)$$
$$= 4$$

(We can take this information and plug it back into our equation with x.)

Once you have the values for both variables, you can determine what $-7xy$ equals.

$$7xy =$$
$$7(4)(-1) = -28$$

That was the first way. The second way is a little more inventive and can be quicker. To do it, you want to make the coefficients of one of the variables the same in both equations. Then you can subtract one equation from the other and so eliminate one of the variables. In our example, it is easiest to make both of the x's have a coefficient of 4. You can get this by multiplying the second equation by 4:

$$x + 2y = 2 \rightarrow$$
$$4(x + 2y) = 4(2) \rightarrow \text{Rule \#2 at work!}$$
$$4x + 2y = 8$$

Line the two equations up and subtract one from the other:

$$
\begin{aligned}
4x + 3y &= 13 \\
- 4x + 8y &= 8 \\
\hline
-5y &= 5 \\
y &= -1
\end{aligned}
$$

Plugging this back in, you will find that $x = 4$. As you would hope, this is the same result that we got doing the problem the first way.

More Complicated Equations

Equations on the GRE don't get much more complicated than the previous ones. There are, however, quadratic equations occasionally lurking around the test. These sound intimidating, but if you got through high school algebra, you have already mastered these imps once. You'll just need a little refresher so you can master them again.

A quadratic equation means that one variable will be raised to a power like this, x^2. In order to solve these buggers, you often have to factor.

Factor Refresher

$$ab + ac = a(b + c)$$
$$(a + b)(c + d) = ac + ad + bc + bd$$
$$a^2 + 2ab + b^2 = (a + b)^2$$
$$a^2 - 2ab + b^2 = (a - b)^2$$
$$a^2 - b^2 = (a - b)(a + b)$$

PETERSON'S
getting you there

Think back, way back, to Algebra I. You might recall the memory aid called "FOIL." FOIL is used when you are multiplying two groups of two variables that look like this: $(a + b)(c + d)$. The expression stands for, "First, Outside, Inside, Last."

You multiply the First terms $(a \times c)$,

the Outside terms $(a \times d)$,

the Inside terms $(b \times c)$,

the Last terms $(b \times d)$,

and then you add them all together.

If you are asked to "expand"—that's the term often used—the expression, just follow FOIL:

$$(2x + 3)(x - 4) =$$
$$2x^2 - 8x + 3x - 12 =$$
$$2x^2 - 5x - 12 =$$

Factoring is the reverse of FOIL. Factoring is when you make the math expression have parentheses instead of the other way around, so you take something like $2x^2 - 5x - 12$ and must factor it into two parentheses like the $(2x + 3)(x - 4)$ you started with above.

Factoring is often not as straightforward as doing FOIL. Let's use the expression $x^2 - 2x - 15$ as an example of what needs to be factored. First, if there is no coefficient in front of the squared term—x^2 in our example—then you can put an x in the first place of each parentheses, $(x \quad)(x \quad)$. Next, notice that the 15 has a minus in front of it. This could only be the case if one of the last terms in the parentheses is negative and the other last term is positive, which means $(x + \quad)(x - \quad)$.

The product of the last two terms is 15. What factors give fifteen? 1×15 and 3×5 answers this problem. One of these factored pairs is the one needed to complete the parentheses, but figuring out which one is correct can take some trial and error. The difference between the factors must be 2 since that is the coefficient of the x-term, so 3×5 has to be what goes in the blanks of our parentheses. But which goes where? Since the x-term is negative (-2), the larger number, 5, should go in front of the minus sign. This gives us $(x + 3)(x - 5)$.

Note

You can always check to see if you have factored correctly by FOILing to see if you get what you started with:

$$(x + 3)(x - 5) = x^2 - 5x + 3x - 15 = x^2 - 2x - 15$$

You want to be comfortable using FOIL and factoring, since many problems will require these math operations. If this one example of factoring didn't get all those old factoring juices flowing, then it is a good idea to play around with factoring to get more comfortable with it. Make up a few expressions like $(x - 5)(x - 2)$ or $(x + 8)(x + 2)$, expand them, and then factor them. With practice, factoring can become as straightforward as expanding.

Column A	**Column B**

c is a positive integer.

$c^2 - 4$	$2c^2 - c - 6$

When you see a problem like this, you should immediately suspect that you can factor these two expressions and then compare them directly. The GRE isn't going to give a problem where the only way to solve it is just plug in numbers randomly; that's just not how it's designed. Column A is one of the classic factors from the chart, although you may have to look hard to see $a^2 - b^2 = (a - b)(a + b)$. It's there, though, and $c^2 - 4 = (c + 2)(c - 2)$.

Keep these results in mind when factoring Column B. You should be on the look out for a $(c + 2)$ or a $(c - 2)$ since that would make it easier to directly compare Column A and B. In factoring Column B, the first terms can only be: $(2c \quad)(c \quad)$. If you don't see that, play with the numbers and it should become clear. Since there is a negative sign in front of the 6, there must be one plus and one minus sign in the parentheses. The factor pairs of 6 are 1×6 and 2×3. Since the middle c-term has a coefficient of one, 2 and 3 are probably our factors, but with the 2 in front of the first c, we can't be sure.

Play with the numbers to see if 2 and 3 can make it work. After some unavoidable trial and error, you should hit upon $(2c + 3)(c - 2)$. Since both columns have a $(c - 2)$ term in them, you can disregard that term in each column and focus on the other terms. You are now left comparing $(c + 2)$ and $(2c + 3)$. Since c is a positive integer, it seems likely that $(2c + 3)$ is greater, but plug in a few numbers to confirm this if you aren't sure. Make sure to plug in $c = 1$, since 1 is the lowest positive integer and therefore the most likely candidate for making (A) greater or equal to (B). It turns out that (B) is always greater than (A), so the correct answer is (B).

PETERSON'S

getting you there

When factoring quadratic equations, the first thing to be done is to get all the numbers and variables on one side and have the other side of the equation equal zero. Suppose you were given the equation $x^2 + x - 6 = 6$, and asked to determine the value(s) of x. The first step is:

$$x^2 + x - 6 = 6 \rightarrow$$
$$x^2 + x - 6 - 6 = 6 - 6 \rightarrow$$
$$x^2 + x - 12 = 0$$

> **Note**
>
> There is a good reason why you do this, but you don't need to know it because GRE math tests the how's and not the why's of algebra.

Now it's time to factor, and with some work you will get: $x^2 + x - 12 = (x + 4)(x - 3)$. To determine the value(s) of x, look at the two sets of parentheses and remember that any number multiplied by zero is zero. You can deduce that either $(x + 4) = 0$ or $(x - 3) = 0$ equals zero, although at this point you don't know which. When you are dealing with quadratic equations (equations that have squared terms in them), there will often be two answers. In this example, x equals -4 or 3. Keep the "two answers are correct" point in mind when you see quadratic equations, since that's the kind of funky math knowledge that the test-makers love to test.

If $\dfrac{3x^2 + 11x + 6}{x^2 + 6x + 9} = 0$, then $x =$

- A. $-\dfrac{2}{3}$
- B. -1
- C. $\dfrac{3}{5}$
- D. 2
- E. 4

As always, don't be intimidated by how complicated that algebra expression looks. If you see something like this, you should know that the winning strategy on this type of problem is to find a way to simplify it. The denominator looks less intricate, so let's start there:

$$x^2 + 6x + 9 = (x + 3)(x + 3)$$

It is a good bet that in factoring the numerator, you will find a $(x + 3)$ term. Start with that premise and see where it leads you:

$$3x^2 + 11x + 6 = (x + 3)(3x + 2)$$

There it is. It's not a coincidence, either. Putting it all together, you have:

$$\frac{3x^2 + 11x + 6}{x^2 + 6x + 9} = \frac{(x + 3)(3x + 2)}{(x + 3)(x + 3)} = \frac{(3x + 2)}{(x + 3)} = 0$$

Remember that a fraction equals zero if the numerator equals zero, and $(3x + 2) = 0$ if $x = -\frac{2}{3}$, which is the correct answer, choice (A).

Not Equations But Inequalities

Inequalities are like equations except that there is not an equal sign between the left and right side. Instead you might find one of the following:

Various Inequality Signs

$\neq$ not equal to

$<$ less than

$\leq$ less than or equal to

$>$ greater than

$\geq$ greater than or equal to

If $4x + 2 < 12$, then $4x + 2$ is less than 12. If you needed to solve for x in this inequality, the rules are the same as for equations. Whatever you do to one side, you have to do to the other. For example:

$$4x + 2 < 12 \rightarrow$$
$$4x + 2 - 2 < 12 - 2 \rightarrow$$
$$4x < 10 \rightarrow$$
$$4x \div 4 < 10 \div 4 \rightarrow$$
$$x < \frac{5}{2}$$

There is one caveat to working with inequalities. If you multiply or divide by a negative number, the direction of the inequality sign switches. Freaky, eh? Suppose you need to solve the inequality $4 + 2g > 8 - 4g$. First, collect all the g's on one side:

$$4 + 2g > 8 - 4g \rightarrow$$
$$4 - 8 + 2g - 2g > 8 - 8 - 4g - 2g \rightarrow$$
$$-4 > -6g$$

PETERSON'S
getting you there

Divide each side by -6 and remember to switch the inequality. You get $\frac{2}{3} < g$.

Column A	**Column B**
$10 > -2x + 3 > 4$	
x	-3

If $10 > -2x + 3 > 4$ looks a little overwhelming, just think of it as two separate inequalities ($10 > -2x + 3$ and $-2x + 3 > 4$) and solve them separately.

$$-2x + 3 > 4 \rightarrow$$
$$-2x + 3 - 3 > 4 - 3 \rightarrow$$
$$-2x > 1 \rightarrow$$
$$-2x \div -2 > 1 \div -2 \rightarrow$$
$$x < -\frac{1}{2}$$

and

$$10 > -2x + 3 \rightarrow$$
$$10 - 3 > -2x + 3 - 3 \rightarrow$$
$$7 > -2x \rightarrow$$
$$7 \div -2 > -2x \div -2 \rightarrow$$
$$-\frac{7}{2} < x$$

Column B is an actual number, -3. As for Column A, all you know is that x is between negative seven halves (-3.5) and negative one and one half. This means that x could be smaller than, equal to, or greater than -3, depending on where it is within its range. The correct answer is (D).

A Statistics Excursus (Look It Up!)

The next three statistical concepts are kind of like the Marx Brothers. There are three main ones, and then another that's sort of the Zeppo of the bunch. Some combination of mean, median, and mode will make an appearance on your GRE math section. Test-makers like to make questions using these statistical concepts because they test your ability to apply a concept to a math scenario.

Statistics Refresher	
arithmetic mean, mean, or average	*sum of numbers divided by the number of items in set*
median	*middle number when set is lined up in numerical order*
mode	*number that appears most often in a set*
range	*difference between the greatest and smallest values in set*

To compare all the terms, consider the number set, {14, 12, 8, 15, 5, 8}. To determine the mean, you add up the numbers in the set (14 + 12 + 8 + 15 + 5 + 8 = 62), then divide the sum by number of items in set. There are six items, or numbers, total, so $\frac{62}{6} = 10\frac{1}{3}$. This is the average mean of the set.

When people use the word *average* in everyday speech, they are referring to mean. But there are two other ways to find what can be considered an average of a group and these are *median* and *mode*. To find the *median*, you must first line up the numbers in numerical order, {5, 8, 8, 12, 14, 15}. You then pick the one in the middle, and that's the median. This works quickly if there is an odd number of items in the set, but it takes a teensy bit of work if there is an even number of items in the set. If that's the case, the there is not one single number in the middle. Instead, there are two in the middle, 8 and 12. To find the median of this set, you must find the mean of the two middle numbers. $\frac{8 + 12}{2} = \frac{20}{2} = 10$. The median of this group of numbers is 10, even though 10 is not one of the numbers listed in the set.

The *mode* of a set is the number that appears most often. It is 8 for the number set in question, since this is the only number that occurs more than once. To find the *range* (the Zeppo of this group), you subtract the smallest number from the greatest number, 15 − 5 = 10.

The test, though, won't ask you questions as easy as, "What is the average?" It will expect you to be able to find these different values and then work a problem from there. For example, with the number set above, you might be asked a QC question like:

Column A	Column B
{14, 12, 8, 15, 5, 8}	
The median of the set	The range of the set

PETERSON'S
getting you there

You have already found the value of 10 for both these concepts, so the answer to this question would be (C). This problem is easy for anyone knowledgeable with the terms, but to someone who doesn't know what is being asked, it would be time for a one-in-four guess.

> Gina has received the following four scores on tests: 87, 92, 90, and 85. If after a fifth test Gina's test average was 91, what was her score on the fifth test?
>
> A. 85
> B. 88
> C. 95
> D. 98
> E. 101

There are two ways to attack this problem. The first is to set up an equation using the average formula and place a variable for the unknown fifth test score, $\dfrac{87 + 92 + 90 + 85 + x}{5} = 91$. You then solve for x. The second way of attack is to take the likely answer choices and use them as the fifth test score and see if the set averages to 91. With a little mental work, you can guess that neither 85 nor 88 is the correct answer since the fifth test will need to be above 91 to bring the average *up* to that. Proceeding with this approach, you should start with 98, the middle of the three remaining numbers. This way, if 98 is not the answer, you should be able to figure out what the right answer is. Placing 98 as the fifth score, you get $87 + 92 + 90 + 85 + 98 = 452$. However, since $91 \times 5 = 455$, you know this answer choice is 3 points too low. You need a higher score, one preferably higher by three points. Looking at your answer choices, there is only one possible choice that's higher, choice (E). It's the correct answer.

This approach might seem unconventional or non-mathy, but that's good. You don't want to limit yourself to a single method for all problems. The more creative you get in approaching problems, the more flexibility you give yourself to find the right answer.

Word Problems

A train leaves Pittsburgh at 12 p.m. (EST) traveling due east at a speed of 45 mph. A second train leaves San Francisco at 2 p.m. (PST) traveling at 50 mph heading due north. When will the two trains cross paths?

The trains will never meet. The Pittsburgh locomotive will soon run into the Atlantic Ocean, while the San Fran train will take a while before sliding off into the Pacific.

Admittedly, you probably won't see that word problem on test day, but it does illustrate that word problems are questions that contain a set of math conditions in written form. Many word problems on the GRE involve converting a statement in English into an algebra equation, and then solving the equation for the desired variable. Suppose you are told that two doughnuts and three coffees cost $2.70 at the local bakery. At the same bakery, 2 doughnuts and a coffee cost $1.50. You can translate the first sentence into algebra like this:

$$2 \text{ doughnuts} + 3 \text{ coffees} = \$2.70$$
$$2d + 3c = \$2.70$$

With this one equation, you don't have enough information to determine how much a coffee or a doughnut costs. But if you translate the second statement into an equation, then you will have two unknowns and two equations. This will give you the same set-up as seen on page 70 earlier, when you solve for two variables using two equations.

The second equation is $2d + c = \$1.50$. If you subtract the second equation from the first, the $2d$ terms cancels out and you are left with $2c = \$1.20 \rightarrow c = \$0.60$. Plugging in the price for coffee into the second equation, you can solve for d, which is 0.45. Ta da! You used algebra to decipher a word problem and then manipulated two equations to find the values of two unknown variables. You'll be an expert GRE mathematician yet!

The key to translating English into algebra is to do it piece by piece. Suppose a question states, "The difference between Tom and John's age is 13, and Tom is older." The term *difference* means you are subtracting, and the word *is* means "equals," so our translation would be $T - J = 13$ (it is T minus J because T is older).

There are a number of key words and phrases often used when translating English to algebra, as you can see from the chart on the next page.

PETERSON'S
getting you there

Translation Key	
If You See This	**Do This**
sum, plus, added to, combined with, greater than, increased by	Add
difference between, minus, subtracted from, less than, reduced by	Subtract
product, times, multiplied by, twice, doubled, half	Multiply
quotient, divided by, per, ratio of blank to blank, out of	Divide
equals, will be, was, is the same as, costs, adds up to, results in	Equals

A mixture of 14 ounces of water and oil is 50% water (by weight). How many ounces of oil must be added to the mixture to produce a new mixture that is only 25% water?

A. 10
B. 14
C. 16
D. 20
E. 28

This is a little tricky, so we have a little unpacking to do. In the first mixture, 50% of the 14 ounces is water, which we could represent by $\frac{14(0.5)}{14} = 0.5$. The numerator is the number of ounces of water, and the denominator is the total number of ounces. That might seem obvious, but it is helpful for being able to write down the second mixture, which is going to have ounces of oil added to it (added to the denominator in this case) until the percentage equals 0.25. This can be written down as $\frac{14(0.5)}{14 + x} = 0.25$. All that remains is to solve for x, which after some working will get you $x = 14$, choice (B). The alternate way to do this problem is to start with the answer choices and work backward. Always start with the middle value so that if it does not yield the right answer, you will know if you need to go higher or lower (and so eliminate the answer choices in the opposite direction). If you add 16 ounces of oil, then you will have a total of 30 ounces with 7 ounces of water. That is a little under 25% water, so 16 is a little too much to add. 14 then would be a good guess if you are crunched for time.

Geometry

Fortunately, there will be no proofs and no mention of Euclid in the GRE, so you won't have to revisit those painful experiences from high school. There is a limited set of basic geometry that you will be expected to understand and apply to solve problems, so the first order of business is the review of this material.

Lines and Angles

It doesn't get much more basic than the line. Most of the geometric figures that you see on test day will be composed of lines or segments of lines, with circles being the major exception.

The test will use the notation *AB* sometimes to refer to the line segment *AB*. This notation will also refer to the length of the line segment *AB*. You will be able to tell from the context which is intended.

The angle is one step up in complexity. It will include at least two lines.

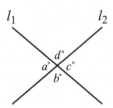

When two lines intersect as in the above figure, the angles across from each other are called *vertical angles*, and they are equal (so $a° = c°$ and $b° = d°$). The sum of the four angles is 360 degrees, while the sum of any of the angles adjacent to each other is 180 degrees ($a° + b°$ or $d° + c°$, for example). The adjacent angles sum to 180 degrees because two adjacent angles in our example define the angle measure of a straight line, and the measure of a straight line is 180 degrees. If $a° = 90$, then you could deduce that all four of the angles are 90 degrees because if $a° = 90$ then $c° = 90$, and if $c° = 90$ then $d° = 90$ because *d* and *c* must sum to 180 degrees, and so on around the diagram. Ninety-degree angles also go by the special name of *right angles*. They have a special symbol as well, the ⌐.

Angles that add up to 180 degrees are called *supplementary angles*. Angles that add up to 90 degrees are called *complementary angles*.

PETERSON'S
getting you there

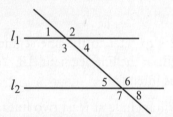

If two lines intersect and the angles formed by their intersection are right angles, the lines are said to be *perpendicular*. In our example, if the angles are right angles then l_1 is perpendicular to l_2, which is denoted as $l_1 \perp l_2$.

Two lines can have one other kind of special relationship, which is known as *parallel* and denoted by two close-together straight lines such as $l_1 \parallel l_2$. Like train tracks, parallel lines never intersect. Two parallel lines are not that interesting, but if you cross two parallel lines with a third line, hoo boy!

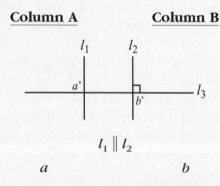

Since they are vertical angles, 1 equals 4, 2 equals 3, 5 equals 8, and 6 equals 7. Also, angles 2 and 4, 1 and 3, 5 and 6, 5 and 7, and a host of others are all supplementary angles. That's just the start. Alternate interior angles are also equal. To unpack that term, consider that *interior* refers to an angle on the inside (3, 4, 5, 6) of the parallel lines. *Alternate* means the angles that are on different sides of the non-parallel line (3 and 6, 4 and 5). So 3 = 6 and 4 = 5. Notice this means we can deduce a lot more about the relationships of the different angles (1 = 8, 2 = 7).

Column A	**Column B**

l_1 l_2

l_3

$l_1 \parallel l_2$

a	b

This looks a little different than the figure we were just working with, but if you rotate it ninety degrees, you can see that it is basically the same. $b = 90$ because it and the right angle must sum to 180 (supplementary angles). At this point there are two ways to get the answer. You could reason, "Two lines that are parallel will intersect a third line at the same angle, which would mean that *a* is a right angle." If you didn't see that, don't worry, since there is another way to get the answer. *b* is equal to the angle across from it (vertical angles), and so *b* is also equal to the angle across from *a* (alternate interior angles). So *a* and *b* are equal since they are equal to the same angle. The correct answer is (C).

Triangles

Triangles are tri-angled geometric figures that have three angles and three sides. There are many different kinds of triangles that all have different names, but we don't need to concern ourselves with those here. The GRE will test some general principles about triangles and will also focus on a few special kinds of triangles. The wisest course of action is to review these general principles and then get really familiar with the triangles that are the GRE's favorites.

A rule that holds true for all triangles is that the three angles sum to 180 degrees. This means that if you know two angles of a triangle, then you can find the third. So if a triangle has two angles that are equal and third angle is 50 degrees, what is the measure of the other two angles?

To answer this, let's go back in this chapter and employ some algebra. Calling the two equal angles *x*, you get

$$2x + 50 = 180 \rightarrow$$
$$2x + 50 - 50 = 180 - 50 \rightarrow$$
$$2x = 130 \rightarrow$$
$$2x \div 2 = 130 \div 2 \rightarrow$$
$$x = 65$$

Another general rule for triangles—referenced earlier in the book—is that any two sides of a triangle must be longer than the third side. Otherwise, the sides would not meet. You might need this information on a QC where one column is the length of the longest side of the triangle and the other column is the maximum length of the other shorter sides combined. In that case, the other two sides must be longer for the figure to actually be a triangle.

Another principle that holds for all triangles is the formula for the area of a triangle, $A = \frac{1}{2}(base)(height)$. Using this formula would be simple if you knew what the base and height of the triangle are, but most problems aren't going to tell you that directly. To find them, you must know that the height is the measure of any line segment that begins at one of the vertices and ends at the opposite side, forming a right angle with that side, and that

PETERSON'S
getting you there

the base is the length of the line that the height forms the right angle with. Look at this figure if that explanation didn't clear everything up for you.

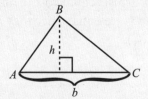

One thing to keep in mind is that the base and the height of a triangle are not fixed values. In the figure above, we could have drawn a line from $\angle C$ and perpendicular with $\overline{AB}$. In that case, the height would be the perpendicular line going from $\angle C$ to $\overline{AB}$, and the base would be $\overline{AB}$. To decide what to make the height and what to make the base, follow this rule of thumb: find the base and height wherever it is easiest. Generally it is harder to find the height—unless you can draw the height so that it is one of the triangle sides—so approach an area problem looking for the easiest way to find the height.

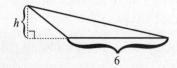

Sometimes you have to get really creative in finding the height of a triangle. That is what the figure above shows. The height doesn't have to be a line inside the triangle. The height is the length of the line from one angle to its opposite side if that line is perpendicular to the opposite side.

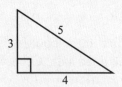

What is the area of the above figure?

A. 3
B. 6
C. 8
D. 9
E. 12

With the triangle-ometry that we have covered thus far, there is only one way to pick the height and base so that you can solve this problem.

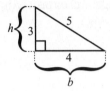

You can pick one of the sides to be the height since it forms a right angle with the side it intersects. So $A = \frac{1}{2}(3)(4) = 6$. Therefore, the correct answer is (B).

Special Triangles

The important thing about special triangles is that the GRE likes to use them. When one pops up on the test, you need to be able to identify it and then use its special properties to solve the problem.

The first kind of special triangle to discuss is usually pretty easy to spot. A *right triangle* is a triangle that has one 90-degree angle in it. Visually, this angle might be denoted by one of those box symbols in it. Recalling that all three angles in a triangle always equal 180, you know that in a right triangle, the other two angles always sum to 90.

The Pythagorean theorem is a special equation that only applies to right triangles. Call it the "Big P," and its equation is $a^2 + b^2 = c^2$, where c is the length of the side opposite the right angle (called the *hypotenuse* by the math establishment) and a and b are the lengths of the other two sides. With this equation, if you know two sides of a right triangle, you can always find the third. That is a basic move the test will expect you to be able to make. A problem won't be that easy, but that will be one necessary step for solving a problem.

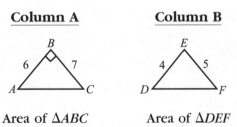

To answer this question, you need to be able to determine the base and the height of each of the triangles. Can you do that? You can with the right triangle, but you can't with ΔDEF. Choice (D) is the correct answer.

A second kind of special triangle is the *isosceles triangle*. It has a funny name but a simple meaning: Two of the sides of the triangle are equal. A problem will either tell you that a triangle is isosceles and expect you to know what that means, or you might see a figure like this:

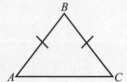

The lines through two of the sides of the triangle mean that those two sides are equal.

Now let's think about triangles for a second. If one angle of a triangle is large—say 120 degrees—will the side opposite that angle be large or small in comparison to the other angles? Draw out a triangle with this angle. The side opposite the big angle will be big in comparison to the other sides. The converse is also true. The side opposite the small angle will be small in comparison to the other sides.

With these illustrations, you can see that the size of an angle in a triangle is related to the length of the side opposite that angle. Again, the converse is true; the length of a side of a triangle is related to the size of the angle opposite it. Now think about an isosceles triangle, where two sides are the same length. Since the sides are equal, the angles opposite those sides are also equal. In the isosceles triangle above, $\angle A = \angle B$.

A wrinkle on the isosceles triangle is the right isosceles triangle. It's nothing more than a right triangle with two sides that are equal. You know one angle equals 90 degrees, and that the other two sum to 90 degrees. Since you also know the other two angles are equal, it can be stated algebraically that

$$x + x = 90$$
$$2x = 90 \quad \text{Here, } x \text{ is the angle for the two equal sides.}$$
$$x = 45$$

The other two angles are 45 degrees. If the right triangle is a special triangle, then the 45-45-90 triangle is a "super special" triangle because it is a special kind of right triangle.

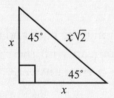

As you can see, the relationships between the sides and angles of a 45-45-90 triangle are all nailed down. The test-makers like this feature of the triangle because they figure that if they give you enough information to identify a triangle as a 45-45-90 triangle, you should be able to determine most everything about that triangle.

If you want to know how the side ratios are determined, just use the Pythagorean theorem on the 45-45-90.

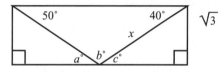

If $a = c$, then $x =$

A. 2
B. $\sqrt{3}$
C. $\sqrt{5}$
D. $\sqrt{6}$
E. 4

This is a busy little diagram, but you'll get some of those. If your test radar is working, you should suspect that there is a special triangle in here somewhere. Notice that b must be 90 for the angles in the top triangle to sum to 180 degrees, and since $a = c$, they both must be 45 because $a + b + c = 180°$ (it is a straight line). This means that the triangle on the right is a 45-45-90 triangle, and since we know the length of one side we can find the length of all sides, including x, which is:

$x =$ (length of one side of the 45-45-90 triangle)$(\sqrt{2})$

$x = \sqrt{3}\sqrt{2} = \sqrt{6}$ or choice (D)

The next kind of super special triangle is the 30-60-90 triangle. There is not a special name for it, but they appear on the test with great frequency for the same reason that the 45-45-90 triangle does. You are expected to identify the 30-60-90 triangle and then use its properties to solve problems.

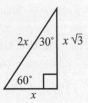

Call the smallest side length x. This will be the side opposite the 30-degree angle. The side opposite the 60-degree angle is $x\sqrt{3}$, and the length of the hypotenuse is always $2x$.

The equilateral triangle, the triangle whose sides are equal, is related to the 30-60-90 triangle. An equilateral triangle is like two 30-60-90 triangles back-to-back.

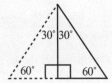

Since the sides of an equilateral triangle are all equal, what must the relationship of the angles be? Equal. This means that 3 sides = 180.

So,

$$3s = 180$$
$$s = 60$$

For every equilateral triangle, each angle is 60 degrees. The lengths of all 3 sides in an equilateral triangle are of equal lengths.

There are two other special right triangles that appear regularly on the GRE. Both are defined by the relationships of the sides.

If you recognize one of these triangles in a problem, and you know two sides of the triangle, you can simply read off the length of the third side.

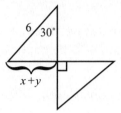

If $y = 3$, then $x =$

A. -1
B. 0
C. 1
D. 2
E. 3

When you see the 30-degree angle, you should immediately start looking to see if you have 30-60-90 triangle. The top triangle is a right triangle since the bottom right angle is vertical with the right angle. This means the top triangle is a 30-60-90 triangle. So $2(x + y) = 6$, which means that if $y = 3$ then $x = 0$.

Triangles: Similar and Congruent

When you say that a Cheeto looks similar to an orange caterpillar, you probably aren't using an exact definition of *similar*. When mathematicians use the term *similar*, they are being much more precise. To a mathematician, two triangles are similar if all corresponding angles are equal and all corresponding sides are proportional. Similar triangles look the same, but one can be bigger than the other.

Triangle *M* has sides that are three times as large as triangle *N*, but all angles are equal. It doesn't matter that triangle *N* is flipped around in relation to *M*. Since the angles are equal and the sides proportional, the two triangles are congruent.

If you were to increase the size of triangle *N*'s sides by a factor of 3, then you would have two triangles with equal sides and angles. This is the definition of congruent triangles.

Other Polygons

Polygon is the fancy geometric word for shapes that have three or more sides. Lots of shapes are polygons like triangles, squares, pentagons, and octagons, to name just a few.

The one general rule to remember about polygons comes in the form of a formula. The interior angles of an *n*-sided polygon sum to $(n - 2)(180)$. You can try this formula out on a triangle and get $(3 - 2)(180) = 180$. This restates the old "all three angles of a triangle sum to 180" rule that should be hammered about halfway into your skull by now. You don't need the $(n - 2)(180)$ formula to find out the sum of the interior angles of a triangle, but you might need it if you need to find the sum of the interior angles of a hexagon.

The rectangle is a polygon. It has four sides, so the sum of its interior angles must be $(4 - 2)(180) = 360$. There are two important properties of rectangle:

1. All interior angles are 90 degrees.

2. Opposite sides are parallel and equal in length.

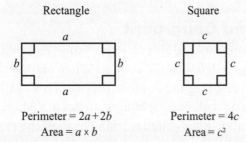

Rectangle

Perimeter $= 2a + 2b$
Area $= a \times b$

Square

Perimeter $= 4c$
Area $= c^2$

Note that only *opposite* sides of a rectangle need to be equal in length. If all sides of a rectangle are equal, you have the figure known as a square.

The perimeter of a rectangle can be found by the formula $P = 2(l + w)$ and its area is $A = l \times w$. For a square, the equations are pretty basic: $P = 4s$ and $A = s^2$.

Note

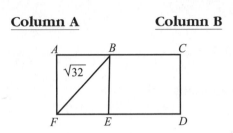

Column A	Column B

In the figure above, *ACDF* is a rectangle,
and *ABEF* and *BCDE* are squares.

32	Area of *ACDF*

You have to find the area of *ACDF* to compare the two columns, which means you need to find the length and the width of the rectangle. The diagonal in the square bisects two right angles, creating your new friend the 45-45-90 triangle. This makes $\sqrt{32}$ the hypotenuse. From this, you can read off the side length of the square, $\dfrac{\sqrt{32}}{\sqrt{2}} = \sqrt{16} = 4$. Line segment *EF* = 4, as does *ED*, *AF*, *AB*, *BC*, and *BE*. This makes the length of the rectangle 8 (4 + 4), while the width the rectangle is 4. Placing these values into the formula for the area of a rectangle gives you $4 \times 8 = 32$. Choice (C) is the correct answer.

The *parallelogram* and the *trapezoid* are two other 4-sided polygons to know. A parallelogram, like a rectangle, has opposite sides that are parallel and equal. Unlike a rectangle, the interior angles of parallelograms are not right angles. The opposite angles of a parallelogram are equal and they sum to 360, which makes sense if you remember that *n*-sided polygon formula.

Parallelogram   Trapezoid

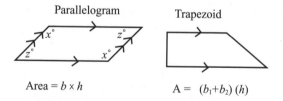

Area = $b \times h$ A = $(b_1 + b_2)(h)$

The area of a parallelogram is the base times the height. These values are determined similarly to the way you determine the base and height of a triangle. Pick the base, then draw a line perpendicular to it that intersects with the side across from it. That line is the height. The one difference is that the height of a parallelogram doesn't have to intersect with an angle.

As you can see, trapezoids do not have equal opposite sides or angles. In fact, to be a trapezoid, all you need is 4 sides, where 2 of those sides are parallel. In the trapezoid shown, the top and bottom sides are parallel.

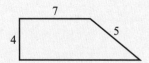

What is the area of the above figure?

A. 20
B. 28
C. 32
D. 34
E. 40

If you have no idea how to do this problem, you can at least eliminate choices (A) and (B), since you know that this trapezoid will be bigger than a rectangle with length 7 and width 4. That's because you can see how this trapezoid is like a rectangle with length 7 and width 4 with a triangle attached to it. Viewing it this way is the key to the problem. To find the area of a trapezoid, first draw a dotted line to turn the trapezoid into a rectangle and a triangle.

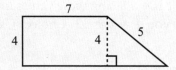

You can read off the third side of the triangle if you recognize that it is a 3-4-5 triangle. The area of the rectangle is 28, and the area of the triangle is $\frac{1}{2}(3)(4) = 6$. So the area of the trapezoid is 34, choice (D). You found the answer, and you also saw a way in which special triangles can be cropped and provide the key to a problem.

92

Circles

For many, circles evoke ideas like elegance and eternity. Sadly, elegance is not one of standards commonly tested on the GRE. Instead, the more mundane properties of the circle are focused on, so any musings about eternity must take a back seat to the definition of circumference.

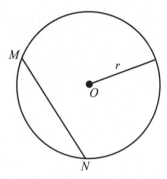

O is called the center of the circle, and all the points along the edge of the circle are the same distance from O. That distance, r, is called the *radius*. The radius is any line that goes from the center to the edge of the circle. If a line starts at the edge of the circle, runs through O, and continues on to the opposite edge, it is called the diameter. By definition, every diameter is made up of two radii, so *diameter* = 2(*radius*). Any line whose endpoints are on the edge of the circle is called a *chord,* like $\overline{MN}$. The diameter is one particular chord.

If you were to walk along the edge of a circle once, the distance you would have traveled is called the *circumference*. The circumference is like the perimeter of a polygon except that you have to be a little more sophisticated in calculating it because the circumference isn't composed of straight lines. This is the beauty of the concept of *pi*, often shown by the symbol π. Mathematicians way back when came up with this concept, and boy, does it help.

To dispel the mystery around it, π is simply defined as the circumference of a circle divided by its diameter:

$$\pi = \frac{circumference}{diameter}$$

The neat thing about π is that its value remains constant regardless of the size of the circle. The ancient mathematicians figured this value to be 3.14159 . . . and a bunch of other numbers, since *pi* goes on for a long, long time. For our purposes, just remember that it is a little bigger than 3, about 3.14.

From the definition of π, you can determine the formula for circumference:

$$\pi = \frac{circumference}{diameter} \rightarrow$$

$$\pi = \frac{c}{d} \rightarrow$$

$$\pi \times d = \frac{c}{d} \times d \rightarrow$$

$$\pi d = c$$

$$\pi \times diameter = circumference$$

or $c = \pi d$ for short. Remember that since the diameter is twice the radius, you can also state:

$$c = \pi d = 2\pi r$$

Let's go back to that mythical walk around the circle. If you only walked partway around the circle, the distance that you walked would be called an *arc* of the circle. Imagine you walked from *A* through *B* to *C* in the figure below:

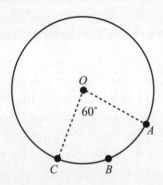

This arc would be referred to as arc *ABC*, since it starts at *A*, goes through *B*, and ends at *C*.

Note

The distance you walked is part of the circumference, but what part is it? To answer this, you must recall that there are 360 degrees in a circle. (If you think this is a foolish number, blame the Babylonians.) The angle of the arc is 60 degrees, and since there are 360 degrees in a circle, the arc angle is one sixth of the degrees in the circle $\left(\frac{60}{360}\right) = \frac{1}{6}$.

94

The arc length will have the same relationship with the circumference as the arc angle does with the total number of degrees in a circle. Therefore, $arcABC = \dfrac{1}{6}c$. All this can be encapsulated in a formula, the arc length = $\dfrac{n}{360} \times 2\pi r$, where n is the measure of the arc angle.

The area of a circle is πr^2. This means that if you know the radius (or the diameter) of a circle, you can find the area and the circumference of that circle. A common test question is to give enough information to find the radius of a circle and ask for the area or circumference of a circle.

Column A	**Column B**

The area of a circle is πy.

The diameter of the circle	$\dfrac{y^{\frac{3}{2}}}{y}$

If this question is a mystery to you, you can at least reason that Column A will have a y in it. This means that the two columns will probably have a definite relationship, so (D) is out. The trick is to make Column A look like something you can compare to Column B, which you can do if you figure out what the diameter of the circle is:

Area of a circle = πr^2

$$\pi y = \pi r^2 \rightarrow$$
$$\pi y \div \pi = \pi r^2 \div \pi \rightarrow$$
$$y = r^2 \rightarrow$$
$$\sqrt{y} = r$$

If that's the radius, then the diameter is twice that, or $d = 2\sqrt{y}$. Compare this with Column B after you sort it all out:

$$\frac{y^{\frac{3}{2}}}{y} = y^{\frac{3}{2} - \frac{2}{2}} = y^{\frac{1}{2}} = \sqrt{y}$$

(A) is greater.

If you didn't know that the *y* had to be positive since it is a distance, you would not know which column was greater.

A *tangent* to a circle is a line that has one point in common with a circle. The figure below is an illustration of a circle and one tangent line. Notice that the tangent line forms a right angle with the radius that shares a point with it. Tuck that fact away in your head because you might need it later.

Another word that might come up with circles or other shapes is *inscribed*. A polygon is inscribed (*in*-"scribed," drawn in) in a circle if each of its vertices lies on the circle. A circle can also be inscribed in a polygon if each of the polygon's sides is tangent to the circle. Circumscribed is related to inscribed in an antonym-like way.

Square inscribed in circle.
Circle circumscribing square.

Circle inscribed in square.
Square circumscribing circle.

Notice that when figures are inscribed and circumscribed, they share certain features. With the circle inscribed above in the square, the diameter of the circle is also the length of one side of the square. These sort of overlapping features are what the GRE focuses on when there are multiple figures involved in a problem. Be aware of what features figures share because that often is the clue to the answer.

Column A	Column B

l

w

The area of the above circle is 16π.

The area of the rectangle	6*l*

Look at the features the two figures share. Notice that the diameter of the circle is the width of the rectangle. If you can find the diameter, you can compare the two columns:

$$A = \pi r^2$$
$$16\pi = \pi r^2$$
$$16 = r^2$$
$$r = 4$$

If the radius is 4, then the diameter is twice that, so $d = 8$. The area of the rectangle is $8l$, which means that (A) is greater.

One last point: Concentric circles have the same center *but* do not have the same radius.

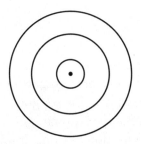

Coordinate Geometry

The above phrase refers to geometry done on a coordinate plane. When you see the following visual, you'll either remember coordinate geometry or playing the game *Battleship*! as a child. "B . . . 4 . . . Miss!"

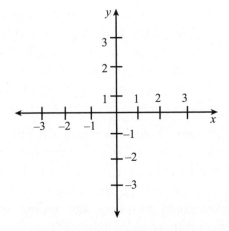

A coordinate plane is just two number lines perpendicular to each other. The one going up and down is called the *y*-axis, and the one going left and right is called the *x*-axis. Any point on the plane gets two coordinates, an *x* one and a *y* one, and they tell you where the point goes on the plane. The notation for this looks like this (*x,y*), with the *x*-coordinate always first.

The number in the *x* spot tells you where along the *x*-axis the point goes, and the number in the *y* spot tells you where along the *y*-axis the point goes. The points (−4,2) and (0,3) would be here:

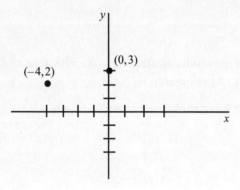

Say that a line was drawn between those two points. Would the slope be steep or flat? Looking at it, the slope would rise if you were going from left to right, and that is the direction that geometrists are always going on coordinate planes. Yet you can say more than "the slope is going up." You can give it a value since there is a mathematical definition of slope. It is the change in the *y* values over the change in the *x* values, also called the rise over the run.

In this case, the slope is

$$\frac{\Delta y}{\Delta x} = \frac{y_1 - y_2}{x_1 - x_2} = \frac{3 - 2}{0 - (-4)} = \frac{1}{4}$$

Always subtract the coordinate values of the point on the right from the coordinate values from the point on the left. The slope is positive one fourth, which means that the line goes up one in the *y*-direction for every four it goes over in the *x*-direction (again, if you are traveling left to right). A negative slope means that the line goes down from left to right instead of up.

The geometry part of coordinate geometry comes in when geometrical figures are put on the coordinate plane. In one way, this makes the geometry easier because you have the coordinate plane to help do the geometry. In another way, though, the test will up the complexity of a problem by expecting you to make inferences about the geometrical figures based on your knowledge of coordinate geometry.

Column A	Column B

A figure is defined by these points $(1,1)$, $(3,1)$, and $(1,-2)$ on a coordinate plane.

The area of the figure	The perimeter of the figure

If this question mystifies you, or you are short on time, realize that the perimeter of a figure and the area of a figure will have a definite relationship, and so the answer is probably not (D). That makes guessing a one in three chance. If you have the time to do the problem, you should suspect that this figure is a triangle since it is defined by three points. Regardless of what you suspect, though, the way to attack this problem is to quickly plot the points on a coordinate plane

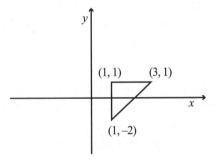

It is a right triangle, and you can use this fact to find both the area and the perimeter. Let's do the area first. The distance between $(1,1)$ and $(1,-2)$ is three units, so the height is three. The distance between $(1,1)$ and $(3,1)$ is two units, making it the base.

$$A = \frac{1}{2}bh$$

$$A = \frac{1}{2}(2)(3) = 3$$

The perimeter is the sum of the sides. You have

$$Perimeter = 2 + 3 + hypotenuse$$
$$Perimeter = 5 + \left(2^2 + 3^3\right)^{\frac{1}{2}}$$

The Pythagorean theorem was used for the hypotenuse. At this point, you don't have to finish the problem since this sum is clearly greater than 3. Therefore, choice (B) is the correct answer.

Data Analysis

If you read *USA Today* on a regular basis, you'll have experience with data analysis. The "data" that you are expected to analyze usually comes in the form of chart, graph, or table, three things that national newspapers love to print. It's visual information that needs to be understood and then used in some manner.

Before jumping into all the different graphs, there is one other topic often placed under the Data Analysis umbrella. What are the odds you can guess what it is?

Probability

If you flip a coin, what is the chance that it will land on heads? Pretty much everyone knows the answer is "one out of two" or "fifty-fifty." This is because there are two possible outcomes that are equally probable (landing heads, landing tails), so the chance the coin will land on heads is one out of two.

That's kid stuff, but you just covered the basics of probability theory. In any probability scenario, the probability of A occurring is the number of ways A can occur divided by the total number of possible outcomes. In our case, A is the coin landing on heads, and that can only happen one way.

There are two possible outcomes, heads or tails, so the probability is $\frac{1}{2}$.

$$\text{probability} = \frac{\text{number of desired outcomes}}{\text{total number of possible outcomes}}$$

Things get a little more interesting when you start talking about multiple event probability, but that's nothing you can't handle if you followed things thus far. Say you flip the coin again. What are the chances that it will land on heads this time? It's still $\frac{1}{2}$. If you thought otherwise, remember that each coin toss is independent and unaffected by previous coin tosses.

Moving up one more notch, what is the probability of tossing the coin twice and it landing on heads twice? It is the probability of the first event *times* the probability of the second event. Therefore, *probability* $= \left(\frac{1}{2}\right)\left(\frac{1}{2}\right) = \frac{1}{4}$. That's the basics of multiple-event probability. The probability of multiple events occurring is the product of the individual probabilities involved.

100

There are 5 boys and 7 girls in the fifth grade class at Saddleback Elementary. What is the probability that if 2 students are chosen at random from the class, that both students will be girls?

A. $\dfrac{7}{24}$

B. $\dfrac{7}{22}$

C. $\dfrac{1}{2}$

D. $\dfrac{7}{12}$

E. $\dfrac{11}{12}$

This probability problem involves two events, and you first need to determine the probability of each event. A girl getting picked first has a probability of $\dfrac{7}{12}$ since there are 7 girls and a total of 12 students in the class. The probability of a girl getting picked the second time is $\dfrac{6}{11}$. Why? Because one girl has been picked already, leaving only 6 girls left in the class of 11 students. Multiplying the two probabilities together gives you:

$$\frac{7}{12} \times \frac{6}{11} =$$

$$\frac{(7 \times 6)}{(12 \times 11)} =$$

$$= \frac{7}{22}$$

That's choice (B).

Workin' the Data

Data or information can come to you in lots of different forms. You are getting text information right now, for instance, as you read this sentence. Earlier you might have looked at the table of contents of this book to get some information about where to start reading. The GRE likes to test your ability to take in information and answer questions about that information. Specifically, the GRE math section will present information or data in the form of a line graph, a circle graph, a bar graph, a table, or some combination of all of these, and then expect you to answer questions about the information presented. You might think this sounds too easy, and in a sense it is. All the answers will be right in front of you in a graph or table. The hard part is that the GRE is pretty creative in coming up with complicated tables and charts and graphs, which makes understanding and using them a challenge.

> Usually you will see one or two sets of graphs and tables on the GRE math section. Each set will most likely have multiple parts, like a circle graph combined with a table or a diagram coupled with a bar graph. Each set will have 2–4 questions that refer to it.

Note

The first thing to do when you come upon a set of graphs and charts is read the title. It sounds simplistic, but do it. The simplest steps can make the great difference, so:

1. Read the title.

2. Read whatever key there is.

3. Read down any graph axis to see what information is being presented.

4. If there are two graphs or charts, look to see how they relate to each other.

Basically, spend 20 to 30 seconds getting familiar with the layout of everything, then proceed to the first question. This will not be a waste of time, as you will be able to answer each of the following questions more quickly. These kinds of questions try to trap you with an overload of information you have to wade through to get to the answer. If you don't have a good sense of what you are wading through, you will probably get bogged down and frustrated. That is why getting a sense of the information being presented is task one.

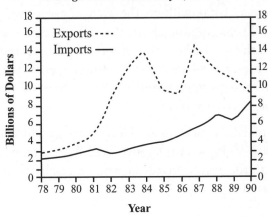

Foreign Trade of Country *Y*, 1978-1990

For which year was the ratio of exports to imports the greatest?

A. 1978
B. 1982
C. 1984
D. 1987
E. 1980

First, determine which line is for exports and which is for imports. Once you have that straight, you have to pull out the trusty concept of ratios. Remember that ratios can be expressed as fractions, and here the exports will be the numerator and the imports the denominator. To get a big ratio, you are looking for years when the exports were high and the imports were low. Eyeballing the graph, which years are candidates? In 1984 and 1987 the export-import lines are farthest apart, so these are the best candidates, and they are both answer choices. In 1984 the ratio was approximately $\frac{14}{4} > 3$, and in 1987 the ratio was approximately $\frac{15.5}{5.5} < 3$. Choice (C), 1984, is the correct answer.

This question shows how basic concepts like ratios are used in other areas to make questions more difficult.

What was the greatest consecutive two-year total of exports?

A. 14 billion
B. 18 billion
C. 24 billion
D. 26 billion
E. 28 billion

PETERSON'S
getting you there

You're looking for exports, so you're looking at the dotted line. The greatest consecutive two-year total will be the two consecutive years whose sum is the greatest. Eyeballing the chart, the sets of years that are the best candidates will be the ones where the export line spikes upward. You have two good candidates: 83–84 and 87–88. Summing each, you will find 83–84 is a little more than 26 billion, and 87–88 is about 76 billion. Therefore, choice (D) is the correct answer.

The previous example involved one line graph. Things can get a little more complicated when there are multiple graphs involved. Again, take a few seconds to get familiar with the graphs involved, and especially take note of how the graphs are related.

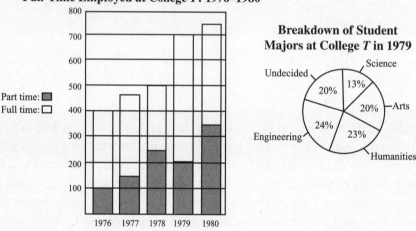

In what years did the percentage of part-time employed students at college *T* increase most dramatically?

A. 1976–1977
B. 1977–1978
C. 1978–1979
D. 1979–1980
E. 1977–1979

It might take a moment to determine whether the bar graph or the pie chart will provide the answer. Since part-time students are listed on the bar graph, that's where you should look. Specifically, you are looking for two years where the striped lines had the greatest *percentage* increase. The actual numbers won't be as important—indeed, they will be wrong answers—as the percentages you derive from them.

1978 to 1979 is out because it is a decrease. If time was running out, you could eliminate this choice and take a guess. Since the question concerns percentage change, take a close look at 1976 to 1977 because 1976 is small in comparison to the other years. 100 to 150 is a 50% increase. How about the other years? 1977 to 1978 have the raw numbers 150 to 250, which is a 66% increase (100 is 66% or two thirds of 150). 1979 to 1980 starts at 200 and goes to 350, which is a 75% increase (150 is 75% of 200). This is the biggest increase, so (D) is the correct answer.

Note

Percentage increases are greater when the starting numbers are very small, which is why a company like General Electric (GE) might improve its profits by 30 billion dollars and only have a 1% increase. The fact is that GE was already making so much cash, the additional amount is a small percentage increase. In contrast, if a kid sets up a lemonade stand and makes $1 on Saturday and $3 on Sunday, his/her profits increased by 300% from one day to the next.

Which of the following represents the greatest number of students?

A. Part-time employed in 1976
B. Full-time employed in 1976
C. Humanities majors in 1979
D. Engineering majors in 1979
E. Full-time employed in 1978

This question involves the bar graph and the pie chart. Look down the left side of the bar graph to get a sense of the numbers that the graph is displaying. Then, try to get the same sense with the pie chart.

Now attack the answer choices. You can eliminate (A) because all the full-time numbers are greater than all the part-time numbers. Reading (B) off the bar graph gets you 300. Looking at choices (C) and (D), you can see that the percentage of Humanities (23%) is less than the percentage of Engineering students, at 24%. (D) has to be greater than (C), so you don't even need to figure out the exact number for it. To calculate the number of Engineering majors in 1979, you'll need to establish the total number of students in that year. That number is the total height of the bars in the bar graph for 1979: 700 students. For Engineering majors, you must determine what is 24% of 700. It works out to a little less than 280. Reading (E) off the bar graph, it is 750. Choice (B) is the answer.

PETERSON'S
getting you there

Take It to
the Next Level

Math: The Multi-Step Complicated Stuff

The harder questions on the GRE do not require you to understand more sophisticated math. The math concepts required to answer a 500-level problem and a 750-level problem are, for the most part, the same. The difference is that the 750-level problem will challenge you to be more clever, creative, and inventive in your approach. Showing you how to "out-clever" the test will be a major focus of this chapter.

Before that starts, there are a few math concepts you are probably only going to see on harder questions. These harder concepts are really just extensions of what we've already covered in this chapter, so it's not as if the easier questions are algebra and the harder ones are calculus. Basically, the harder questions contain the basics revved up to make problems more interesting and difficult.

If a math concept comes up that you are not familiar with, or you can't remember exactly what it is, look back to the beginning of the chapter to see if it is covered there. If you've skipped the beginning of the chapter, it's not a bad idea to leaf through it anyway and make sure that all the math content is fresh in your mind. Once that's done, you can *Take It to the Next Level* and start honing your clever skills.

Advanced Arithmetic

Hard arithmetic problems will use jargon to make problems more complex. Problems will include multiple phrases like "the sum of the first three prime numbers" or "the product of two consecutive integers." The way to decode such math speak is to attack it piece by piece and phrase by phrase. Unless you are a math wunderkind, trying to conceptualize whole sentences of math speak at one time is impossible. At the least, it is foolhardy.

Let's decode these two phrases. The first three prime numbers are 2, 3, and 5, and their sum is 10. In the second phrase, since we don't know what the

106

first integer is, let's call it x. The product of x and the next integer is $(x)(x + 1)$. None of that was too difficult, but suppose a problem reads, "If the sum of the first three prime numbers plus 2 equals the product of two consecutive integers, what is the value of the first integer?"

Alert!

Using algebra in the form of the variable x to help describe an arithmetic expression is fairly common practice. Don't hesitate to draw information from any field of math if you believe it will help you solve a problem.

If you decode this jargon piece by piece, it is manageable. The sum of the first three prime numbers plus 2 is 12, and you already know what the product of two consecutive integers is. Therefore, you can set up the equation:

$$(x)(x + 1) = 12 \rightarrow$$
$$x^2 + x = 12 \rightarrow$$
$$x^2 + x - 12 = 12 - 12 \rightarrow$$
$$x^2 + x - 12 = 0 \rightarrow$$
$$(x + 4)(x - 3) = 0 \rightarrow$$
$$x = -4, 3$$

There's a bit of everything in the above problem, and that's not unusual for hard problems. You had to use arithmetic to decipher the problem and algebra to set up an equation. Then you had to do some factoring to split the equation $x^2 + x - 12 = 0$ in order to find the values for x. If you handle each step, though, the answer falls into your lap.

Column A	**Column B**

$$\frac{a}{b} + \frac{c}{d} + \frac{e}{f} \cdots$$

is a sum in which all the variables are
positive consecutive integers greater than 1
that increase in alphabetical order.

The third term in the sum	$\dfrac{a - 2}{a - 1}$

First, you must decode. Positive consecutive integers are things like 4, 5, and 6, and these increase in alphabetical order, which means that $b = a + 1$

Take It to the Next Level

107

PETERSON'S
getting you there

and $c = b + 1$. Notice that since $b = a + 1$, then $c = (a + 1) + 1 = a + 2$. This means that the sum can be rewritten

$$\frac{a}{a + 1} + \frac{a + 2}{a + 3} + \frac{a + 4}{a + 5} \cdots$$

This makes the third term $\frac{a + 4}{a + 5}$. That's Column A, so far.

Compare this to the fraction in Column B. The smallest value that a can have is 2, so it will be interesting to start with this number and see what you get. Column A becomes $\frac{6}{7}$, while Column B is

$$\frac{a - 2}{a - 1} = \frac{2 - 2}{2 - 1} = \frac{0}{1} = 0.$$

Column A is greater is this instance, but to play it safe, it helps to try another number. A small number was used the first time, so a large number can be plugged in this time for variety. Making $a = 10$, you get $\frac{14}{15}$ in Column A and $\frac{8}{9}$ in Column B. Column A is again greater, and placing an even larger number will probably not make a difference. The correct answer is (A).

Ratios are another arithmetic topic that can be made interesting. Suppose you are told the ratio of a to b is 4:7 and the ratio of b to c is 8:7. You are then asked, "What is the ratio of a to c?"

The easiest way to approach such a problem is to make the common element in both ratios, b, the same so that you can directly compare a and c. To do that, find a common multiple of 7 and 8, preferably the least common multiple. 56 works, since it's 7×8.

First ratio: a to $b = 4:7$. Multiplied by 8, this becomes

a to $b = 32:56$

Second ratio: b to $c = 8:7$. Multiplied by 7, this becomes

b to $c = 56:49$

For both ratios, b is now 56. This allows you write to both ratios as a single long ratio:

a to b to $c = 32:56:49$

You can now see that $a : c = 32 : 49$. If these numbers in the ratio had any common multiples, then the ratio should be simplified.

X-Ref

Finding a common element for these ratios is similar to the practice of finding a common denominator before adding and subtracting fractions. See page 54 of this chapter.

If m and n are integers and $(m + n)^2$ is even, then which of the following must be true?

I. Both integers are even.
II. Both integers are odd.
III. One integer is even and one integer is odd.

A. I only
B. II only
C. III only
D. I and II only
E. I and III only

To attack this one, you have to work through each option to see if it *must be true*. Using FOIL, you know that if $(m + n)^2$ is even, then $m^2 + mn + n^2$ is also even.

I. must be true because $m^2 + 2mn + n^2 \rightarrow even + even + even = even$. That eliminates choices (B) and (C). If you're pressed for time, you could guess now with one in three odds of guessing right.

II. can be written as: $m^2 + 2mn + n^2 \rightarrow odd + even + odd = even + even = even$. This does work, so (B) is out.

III. can be written as: $(m^2 + 2mn + n^2 \rightarrow even + even + odd = even + odd = odd$. This doesn't work, so (D) is the correct answer.

This approach uses basic facts about how even and odd numbers interact when multiplied and added together. If this approach is too abstract for you, just pick two numbers for m and n according to each scenario and work the problem through using those numbers. If you don't make a careless math error, you should get the same answer, (D).

Harder Algebra

There are three primary ways the GRE will increase the difficulty on algebra problems. The first relies on shock value. On this track, you are presented with one or more monstrous-looking algebraic expressions that are supposed to shock you into some form of problem-solving paralysis. If you overcome this initial shock, keep in mind that almost every ugly

Take It to the Next Level

PETERSON'S
getting you there

algebraic expression will have a way to simplify it quickly. These problems are designed to shock, but they almost always can be simplified quickly.

If you see an expression like $\dfrac{4x^2 + 14x + 6}{4x + 2}$, you should immediately think, "There must be a quick way to simplify it." With algebra in fractions, always be on the lookout for canceling terms that are in both the numerator and the denominator. Since the denominator is simpler, start there: $4x + 2 = 2(2x + 1)$. Now look for a $(2x + 1)$ in the numerator. Seek and ye shall find:

$$4x^2 + 14x + 6 = 2(2x^2 + 7x + 3)$$
$$= 2(2x + 1)(x + 3)$$

Therefore,

$$\frac{4x^2 + 14x + 6}{4x + 2} = \frac{2(2x + 1)(x + 3)}{2(2x + 1)} = x + 3$$

That whole mess boils down to a simple $x + 3$.

For an idea about where to start simplifying, think of these guidelines:

1. Look at the numerator and denominator and start with whichever one looks simpler.

2. Once you factor the simpler term, look for those factors in the harder term. They should be there in some form or another.

3. Cancel out any similar terms you can, and enjoy your new simplified equation.

Expecting cleverness is the second way that the GRE will try to make algebra difficult. A problem will expect you to make a clever algebra maneuver to finish the problem. You are especially liable to see this on QCs. The following problem illustrates this idea.

Column A	**Column B**

a and *b* are positive constants and $0 < x < y$.

$\dfrac{\frac{x}{a}}{\frac{b}{y}}$	$\dfrac{(x+y)^2}{ab}$

First simplify Column A. To do this, you have to divide each fraction before multiplying.

$$\frac{\dfrac{x}{a}}{\dfrac{b}{y}} \times \frac{\dfrac{y}{b}}{\dfrac{y}{b}} = \left(\frac{x}{a} \div \frac{b}{y}\right) \times \left(\frac{y}{b} \div \frac{y}{b}\right)$$

$$= \left(\frac{x}{a} \times \frac{y}{b}\right) \times \left(\frac{y}{b} \times \frac{b}{y}\right)$$

$$= \frac{xy}{ab}$$

As you can see, the second term cancels itself out, leaving only the single fraction $\dfrac{xy}{ab}$. Column B can be rewritten as:

$$\frac{(x + y)^2}{ab} = \frac{x^2 + 2xy + y^2}{ab}$$

You can disregard the denominators since they are the same in each column. Comparing the numerators, you can see a $2xy$ in Column B (among other values) compared to a single xy in Column A. Since the statement says that both integers are positive, it is clear that (B) is greater.

It didn't take earthshaking genius to solve the last problem. Instead, all you needed was confidence that the two columns could be readily compared and the ability to jump in and start performing mathematical operations to help compare the two.

Embedding algebra in a coordinate plane is the third way that the GRE will make algebra more challenging. You might encounter a polygon whose side lengths are given in terms of algebraic expressions, as opposed to simply numbers or constants. The key to solving such problems is to not be unnerved by the combination of geometry and algebra. Normally you will need to start with the geometry and see what you can infer from it, and then examine the algebra.

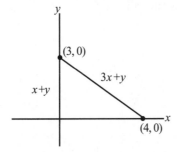

If you are given this figure and then asked to solve for x, start with the geometry. You have a right triangle, since the angle at the origin $(0, 0)$ is 90 degrees. The side along the y-axis is length 3, and the side along the x-axis is length 4. This means you have an old friend, the 3:4:5 right triangle, guest starring in a coordinate grid problem.

Now turn to the algebra. The diagram contains an expression, $3x + y$, for the hypotenuse, but you know that the length is 5 since it's a 3: 4: 5 right triangle. This gives you the equation $3x + y = 5$. From the side of length 3, you can get $x + y = 3$. Once you have two equations ($x + y = 3$ and $3x + y = 5$) and two variables, you can subtract the former equation from the latter and eliminate y. $2x = 2 \rightarrow x = 1$

No one single step in this problem was difficult, but the problem was involved since it was a messy pile of heaped-together geometry and algebra concepts. If you deal with them separately, and take each in its turn, the problem becomes quite manageable.

A symbol that might come up in an algebra problem is the "!". In English grammar, this is that excited bastion of punctuation, the exclamation point. In math, however, the "!" is the symbol for factorials. With a factorial, you take the initial number (say 5!) and multiply it by all integers between 5 and 1.

Sample factorials:

$$5! = 5 \times 4 \times 3 \times 2 \times 1 = 120$$
$$3! = 3 \times 2 \times 1 = 6$$

or

$$x! = x \times (x - 1) \times (x - 2) \times \ldots \text{(It goes on until the last term is 1.)}$$

Note

You can only take the factorial of an integer greater than 1.

If x is two greater than y, how can you simplify $\dfrac{x!}{y!}$?

A. $y^3 + 3y^2 + 2y$

B. $\dfrac{y^2}{x^2}$

C. $y^2 + 3xy^2 + 2xy$

D. $(y + 2)(y + 1)$

E. $(y - 2)(y - 1)$

Since $x = y + 2$, then

$$\frac{x!}{y!} = \frac{(y + 2)!}{y!} = \frac{(y + 2)(y + 1)(y!)}{y!} = (y + 2)(y + 1).$$

Factorials problems are pretty simple once you get over the freak-out element of seeing an exclamation point.

Word Problems

Word problems are common two-tier questions that prompt you to first translate English into algebra and then solve the algebra. The simplest way to make a word problem harder is to make the translation from English to algebra more difficult. The actual algebra that you will have to do on a 500-level word problem and 700-level word problem is going to be similar, but getting to the algebra becomes more of a challenge.

Here's a classic word problem set-up:

How many liters of a solution that is 15 percent water by volume have to be added to 3 liters of a solution that is 30 percent water by volume to create a solution that is 20 percent water by volume?

All that was a quite a tangle. To untangle it, there is a basic form to follow for mixture problems. It's called the *balance method* since you are balancing the left and right side of the equation. On the left side, put the original solution:

Number of original liters $(original\% - final\%) = 3(30 - 20)$

And on the right side put the new solution,

$n(final\% - added\%) = n(20 - 15)$

where n is the number of liters of the 15% solution. Now just solve for n:

$$3(30 - 20) = n(20 - 15) \rightarrow$$
$$90 - 60 = n(5) \rightarrow$$
$$30 = 5n$$
$$30 \div 5 = 5n \div 5 \rightarrow$$
$$6 = n$$

Take your time to muck through the English of a word problem and you will end up with a perfectly solvable algebraic equation.

Advanced Statistics

There are some interesting ways to manipulate statistical notions like *average* or *median*. Harder questions on the GRE math section will expect you to know the basic set of statistic notions—covered on pages 76–78 in this chapter—and how to use them creatively to problem solve.

For example, you commonly employ the concept of *mean* to find the average of a set of numbers, but suppose you were asked for the sum of the set of numbers instead? If 18 is the average of a set of numbers that has 10 members, then can you find the sum of the set of numbers? To do this, you have to multiply the mean average by the number of terms, $18 \times 10 = 180$.

That's simple enough, but it gets trickier. Suppose you are asked, "What is the sum of the integers 20 to 50 inclusive?" Actually adding all the terms up can't be the best way to solve this problem because that would take all day. You could do it, but there has to be a simpler way. The shortcut method here is that the sum of consecutive numbers is equal to the average of the numbers times the number of terms:

$sum = (average) \times (number\ of\ terms)$

In our problem, the average is 35 (halfway between 20 and 50), so

$sum = (35) \times (31) = 1,085$

The notion of weighted averages can make finding the average of a number set a little more interesting. A *weighted average* is when certain terms in a set are counted more (weighted more) than other terms in the set.

> In a certain class, the average boys' score is 50 and the average girls' score is 47. If there are twice as many girls in the class as boys, what is the class average?
>
> A. 49.5
> B. 49
> C. 48.5
> D. 48
> E. 47.5

There are not equal amounts of girls and boys, so you have to weight their averages to get to the overall average. Since there are twice as many girls as boys, there are twice as many terms that go into the 47 average. The simplest way is to assume a three-person class where there is one boy and two girls. The boy scored a 47 and the girls scored 50s, so

$$average = \frac{1 \times 50 + 2 \times 47}{3} = \frac{144}{3} = 48$$

The denominator is 3 because there are three terms in this number set (50, 47, and 47) to reflect the mythical three people in the classroom.

Another variation on the average is when you start with a number set, add or subtract a term, and then must find the new average.

Column A	Column B

The mean average of 4 numbers is −6.
One number is taken from the set,
and the new mean is −3.

The number taken from the set	The largest number left in the set

Start with Column A unless you see something that makes you feel Column B is simple. For Column A, the number taken must be the difference between the sums of the two sets:

(*original sum*) − (*new sum*)

$(-6 \times 4) - (-3 \times 3) = -15$

For Column A, you know that −15 was taken from the number set. Think about how this number is much lower than the average after it left and before it left. −15 was obviously one of the lower numbers in the set, and the higher numbers brought the average up to −6 and then up to −3. It makes sense that Column B definitely contains a number larger than −15, so choice (B) is the correct answer for this average problem.

Compound interest problems involve a loaded math concept. Simple interest is when the interest applies only to the principal over a given period. If a $10,000 account has a 5 percent simple interest rate compounded annually, then after six months the interest will be:

$$\begin{aligned} principal \times rate \times time &= 10,000 \times 0.05 \times 0.5 \\ &= 5,000 \times 0.05 \\ &= 250 \end{aligned}$$

The first number is the cash, the second value is the percent interest expressed in decimal form as 0.05, and the 0.5 at the end shows that you are halfway (six months) through the annual interest period.

Things get a little more complicated with compounding interest. Under this format, the interest rate is applied to the principal and to the

Take It to the Next Level

accumulated interest. There is a complicated formula for compound interest, but you can do without it. If you come across a compound interest problem, simply calculate the simple interest for the scenario, and the compound interest will be a little more than this. There is typically a small difference between the two because the interest accrued on the interest will be small.

> Supposedly, many savings accounts at banks work on the concept of compound interest, but like many Americans, the author has never experienced this fact firsthand. The author is, however, well aware of the interest formulas used by credit card companies.

Alert!

Geometry

To double the geometric fun (and the difficulty), harder geometry problems will include multiple geometric shapes. A square might be inscribed in a circle. A triangle might be located inside a trapezoid. Regardless of the particulars, the idea behind increasing the difficulty is the same. Things look cluttered when there are multiple figures, and that clutter can distract you from problem-solving tasks. You combat the clutter by:

1. First determining exactly what you are trying to find

2. Considering each of the figures separately

3. Trying to find the relationships between the figures that will help solve the problem

All three steps are important, but the third step is the one that holds the key to most of these questions. To try out this methodology, consider a square inscribed in a circle like the following:

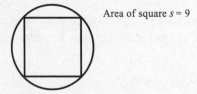
Area of square $s = 9$

Your goal is to find the radius of the circle, but all you have been given is the area of the square. First, locate the radius of the circle. If you think about it, you can see that the diagonal of the square is also the diameter of the circle, and the radius is always half a circle's diameter. So half of the diagonal of the square will equal the radius. Second, you can use the area formula of a square to figure out the length of the sides. If area is 9, then the sides are all length 3.

116

Now imagine the diagonal. If you draw it out, you would see yourself making two 45-45-90 right triangles out of the square. Finding the hypotenuse of one these triangles is equal to finding the square's diagonal, and that is equal to the circle's diameter. Follow all the steps (try it on your own), and you should end up with a radius of $\dfrac{3\sqrt{2}}{2}$.

To help you recognize the relationship that two or more figures share, ask yourself questions like, "Do they share a side, or an angle?" or "What is the relationship between their areas?" Once you have picked out the relationship that links the two figures together, the actual geometry is often no harder than what is covered in the first section.

Column A   **Column B**

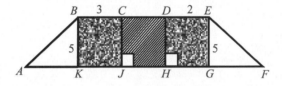

The difference of the areas of trapezoid *ABDH* and trapezoid *FECJ* is 15.

The area of the   The area of the
dotted region   striped region

Locate the two trapezoids. How are they geometrically related? Both share the striped region and they have the same height, 5. Now you can try to compare the striped region and the dotted region. Can you determine the area of the dotted region? Yes, since both are rectangles with length and width readily obvious. However, you cannot determine the area of the striped region, since there's no way to figure out its width. The difference in areas of the trapezoids does not help us, for when the areas of the trapezoid are subtracted, the area of the striped region in each just cancels out. Those triangles on both ends of the figure hold an unknown amount of area for both trapezoids, making any attempt to subtract one trapezoid's area from the other impossible. Therefore, (D) is the correct answer.

Take It to the Next Level

PETERSON'S
getting you there

Coordinate Geometry

Reach back into your past and dust off the equation $y = mx + b$. This formula can be used to describe a straight line in a coordinate plane. The y and the x variables stand the value of y and x, respectively, of any point on a particular line. m is the slope of the line and b is the y-intercept (where the line crosses the y-axis). The beauty of this equation is that if you are given some of the parts—such as the slope and one point on the line—there is a way to figure out all the other parts of the equation.

To be able to use this formula and just read off the slope or the y-intercept, the equation has to be in the $y = mx + b$ form, with y by itself on one side, and the x on the other side summed with b. If you are given a linear equation of a line in the form $2y + 5x = b$, you would have to do some manipulating:

$$2y + 5x = -3 \rightarrow$$
$$2y + 5x - 5x = -3 - 5x \rightarrow$$
$$2y = -5x - 3 \rightarrow$$
$$(2y) \div 2 = (-5x - 3) \div 2 \rightarrow$$
$$y = -\frac{5}{2}x - \frac{3}{2}$$

The slope is negative five halves, $\left(-\frac{5}{2}\right)$, and the y-intercept is negative three halves, $\left(-\frac{3}{2}\right)$.

The slope equation works for a line—but nothing else. You won't see many things graphed besides lines on the GRE, but you might see a quadratic equation (an equation that has a squared term like $y = x^2$). To make things more confusing, the y may be exchanged for an $f(x)$ so it looks like this: $f(x) = x^2$. Then the whole thing is renamed a *function*. It is simplest to just think of the $f(x)$ as a more complicated way to write y. As you might imagine, the graph of this quadratic is not as simple as the graph of a line, but it has a basic form that simplifies it.

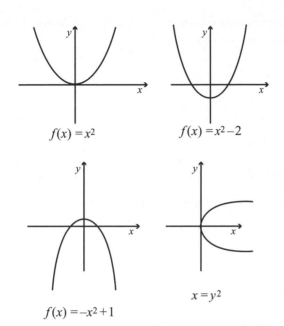

$f(x) = x^2$

$f(x) = x^2 - 2$

$f(x) = -x^2 + 1$

$x = y^2$

Each of these graphs shares a basic shape called a *parabola*. Examine the different graphs and you should see the logic of how they are graphed. For example, a negative squared term like $f(x) = -x^2 + 1$ creates an upside-down hump. If there is an integer after the squared value, then this number is the value of y where the crest of the hump occurs. You could see this with $f(x) = -x^2 + 1$ with a crest at 1 and $f(x) = x^2 - 2$ with a crest at $y = -2$.

The last coordinate geometry concept to cover is the *distance formula*. It allows you to find the distance between two points on the coordinate plane using the following formula:

$$d = \sqrt{(x_1 - x_2)^2 + (y_1 - y_2)^2}$$

If you know two points, just plug in the x values and the y values into the equation and then solve for the distance. It's that simple.

Note

If the distance formula reminds you of the Pythagorean theorem, you're quite observant, because the distance formula is based on it.

If $A(2, -4)$ and $B(3, 6)$ are two points on a rectangular coordinate system, what is the distance between A and B?

A. 1
B. 10
C. $\sqrt{101}$
D. 11
E. 15

Hauling out the distance formula:

$$d = \sqrt{(x_1 - x_2)^2 + (y_1 - y_2)^2} = \sqrt{(2 - 3)^2 + (-4 - 6)^2}$$
$$= \sqrt{1 + 100}$$
$$= \sqrt{101}$$

This is choice (C).

That might look like a big number, but it actually is just a little bit bigger than 10. If you visualize where the two points are, this answer makes sense.

3-D Figures

Another way to up the geometry ante is by upping the number of dimensions from two to three. The 3-D figures that you will come across on the GRE are all built upon the figures that were covered in the first section (rectangles, squares, circles, triangles). The 2-D figures are given height, so instead of dealing just with a square you now get a cube, a 3-D figure composed of six squares.

If you need a refresher on the 2-D geometry, buzz through the geometry section earlier in this chapter. If not, go ahead and dive into the 3-D geometry.

Rectangle Solid

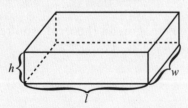

Volume = $h \times l \times w$

Surface Area = $2(lw + lh + wh)$

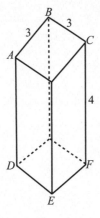

The above figure is a rectangular solid. What is the shortest distance from *A* to *F*?

A. $\sqrt{18}$

B. $\sqrt{20}$

C. $\sqrt{28}$

D. $\sqrt{34}$

E. 6

The shortest distance between two points is a line, so the question is asking you to find the distance of the line *AF*. If you want a hint about how to find it, think triangles.

Notice that *AF* is the hypotenuse of $\triangle ACF$, which is a right triangle. If you find *AC*, you can use it along with *CF* in the Pythagorean theorem to find *AF*.

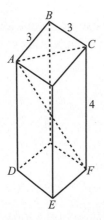

Look at the top surface of the figure. You should see a square with sides of length 3, and the diagonal is the hypotenuse of a 45-45-90 right triangle, just like it was earlier in this chapter. This makes $AC = 3\sqrt{2}$, since it is the hypotenuse of a 45-45-90 triangle with smaller sides of length 3.

Put that value into the next Pythagorean theorem as follows:

$$(AF)^2 = (AC)^2 + (CF)^2$$
$$(AF)^2 = \left(3\sqrt{2}\right)^2 + 16 = 18 + 16$$
$$(AF)^2 = 34$$
$$AF = \sqrt{34}$$

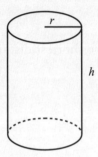

Volume = $\pi r^2 h$

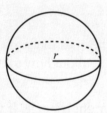

Volume = $\dfrac{4}{3}\pi r^3$

If a sphere has a radius of r, what is the greatest distance along the surface of the sphere that two points could be from each other?

- **A.** $2r$
- **B.** πr
- **C.** $2\pi r$
- **D.** $\dfrac{4}{3}\pi r$
- **E.** $\dfrac{4}{3}\pi r^2$

Sometimes coming up with a real-life situation will help you understand an abstract geometrical one. For our purposes, think of the earth as a sphere. In real terms, the questions is asking, "If you are at the North Pole, what point on the earth is farthest from you if you had to travel along the earth's surface?"

Alert!

Technically, the earth is an oblate spheroid, not a sphere. Thankfully, oblate spheroids are NOT on the GRE.

Viewed in this way, the answer, "the South Pole," should be obvious. The same is true for the abstract sphere question. To determine that distance, imagine drawing a circle on the surface of the sphere that runs through its North and South Pole. You can see then that those two points are a half circumference of that circle from each other. The radius of that circle is r, the same as the radius of the sphere. This makes the circumference $2\pi r$, and half of that is πr. That's choice (B).

Data Analysis

Measures of Central Location and Dispersion (or How Close and Far Apart Stuff Is)

Mean, *median*, and *mode* were covered earlier in this chapter. These are notions from statistics that give different ways to measure the central location of a number set. Basically, they are different ways to say where the middle of a bunch of numbers is.

The *dispersion* of a number set is the opposite of the "middleness" or "clusteredness" of a number set. The range is one measure of the dispersion since it tells you how far apart the extremes are. *Standard deviation* is another measure of dispersion. It measures on average how much numbers of a set differ from the middle of that set (basically how spread out the numbers are). There is an involved way to calculate the standard deviation, but you don't need to bother with that. Standard deviation, though, might appear on a question, and so you will need to grasp the concept. To that end, consider the following problem.

Column A	Column B
Standard Deviation of this number set [5, 10, 2, 4]	Standard Deviation of this number set [1, 14, 3, 22]

You don't need to actually calculate the two standard deviations to answer this question. Estimate the mean of the number set in Column A. It's

Take It to the Next Level

123

probably around 4 or 5, and the numbers in the set deviate from this by, at most, 6. So, the standard deviation will be something less than 6. Now estimate the mean for Column B. It's probably around 11, and the number set deviates from this by 10 or more. The standard deviation is going to be greater in Column B. The answer will be Column B, in part because the numbers in Column B are more spread out than the numbers in Column A.

Standard deviation is not the only way to make these statistics concepts interesting. The test-writers can craft difficult problems with median, mode, range, and average.

Column A	Column B

A number set is composed of five non-negative integers, and its average is 20.

The greatest possible range of the number set	The sum of the number set

Start with Column B. The sum of the number set is the average times the number of elements:

$$\frac{sum}{5} = average \rightarrow sum = 5 \times 20 = 100$$

Column B is 100.

As for Column A, the greatest possible range will maximize the highest element and minimize the lowest element. The set is composed of non-negative integers, so the smallest element possible is 0. There is no mention that the elements are distinct, so four of the elements could be zero. In that case, the fifth element would have to be 100 for the sum to be 100. 100 is actually the greatest that a number in the set could be, since the sum cannot exceed 100 and there are no negative numbers to add. So the greatest possible range is $100 - 0 = 100$. Column A and B are equal, making (C) the correct answer.

Counting Stuff

There are a few different kinds of word problems on the GRE that involve counting possible outcomes or permutations of a set of items. Each has a different kind of way to solve them, so we'll review them one by one.

Different Ways to Count Stuff

1. If one task has n possible outcomes and a second one has m possible outcomes, then the joint occurrence of the two tasks has $n \times m$ possible

124

outcomes. That postulate was a bit vague, so consider an example. If between Town *A* and Town *B* there are four roads, and between Town *B* and Town *C* there are five roads, how many different routes are there from Town *A* to Town *C* that travel through Town *B*? One way to attack this problem is to sketch out the scenario and start counting up the possibilities. The other way is to use our nifty little formula, $n \times m = 4 \times 5 = 20$.

2. Permutation problems prompt you to determine how many different *permutations*, or outcomes, are possible. A permutation word problem might ask, "If there are six car spots at the Destin Apartments and six different cars owned by the renters, how many different arrangements of cars are possible in the parking lot?" You solve this problem by multiplying the number of possibilities for the first spot (6 cars can park there) times the number of remaining possibilities for the second spot (5 cars can if the first spot is filled) times the number of remaining possibilities for the third spot (4) and so on. In other words, $6 \times 5 \times 4 \times 3 \times 2 \times 1$. This is the same thing as 6!, our good friend the factorial. In general, when you come across a permutation problem like this one, you can use this factorial shortcut rather than going through all the logic. The basic formula is $n!$; the number of ways that n different objects can be ordered is $n!$.

3. The last kind of counting problem involves determining the number of different ways that sets of items can be selected from a larger set of items. A good example of this is selecting committees of three people from a group of five people. How many different ways can this be done? You could try to work out the possibilities with a systematic use of logic, or you could use the handy-dandy formula that has all the logic packed into it. The formula is $\frac{n!}{(n-r)!r!}$, where n is the size of the larger set, and r is the size of the groups being selected. In our example, the formula would be applied like this:

$$\frac{5!}{(5-3)!3!} = \frac{5 \times 4 \times 3!}{2!3!} = \frac{20}{2!} = 10$$

Probability

The basics of single and multi-event probability were covered in the first section. Yet there are some multi-event probability scenarios that go beyond the basic. If two events are independent, then the probability of both events occurring is the product of the two individual probabilities. Now suppose you know the probabilities of event *A* and event *B*

Take It to the Next Level

PETERSON'S

getting you there

individually and want to find the probabilities of either *A or B* occurring (as opposed to the probability of *A and B* occurring).

A fundamental rule of probability is:

$$P(A \text{ or } B) = P(A) + P(B) - P(A)P(B)$$

Suppose there is a one-in-two chance of event *A* occurring and a two-in-five chance for event *B*. Expressed in decimal terms, this makes the probability of $A = 0.5 \left(\frac{1}{2}\right)$ and probability of $B = 0.4 \left(\frac{2}{5}\right)$. Putting these values into the formula gets you:

$$P\left(A \text{ or } B\right) = P\left(A\right) + P\left(B\right) - P(A)P(B)$$
$$P\left(A \text{ or } B\right) = 0.5 + 0.4 - \left(0.5\right)\left(0.4\right)$$
$$P\left(A \text{ or } B\right) = 0.9 - 0.2 = 0.7$$

0.7 translates to a seven-in-ten chance, showing that the probability of *A* or *B* occurring is larger than the probability of either single event occurring.

A bag of marbles contains 12 red marbles, 8 blue marbles, and 5 green marbles. What is the probability that a green and then a blue marble will be chosen in two attempts?

A. $\dfrac{1}{15}$

B. $\dfrac{1}{10}$

C. $\dfrac{1}{5}$

D. $\dfrac{12}{25}$

E. $\dfrac{13}{25}$

Determine the probability of each event individually. The probability of the first event is:

$$\frac{5}{12 + 8 + 5} = \frac{5}{25} = \frac{1}{5}$$

The numerator, 5, is the number of green marbles divided by the total number of marbles. For the second probability, you must remember to take the first transaction into account. This means there are only 24 total marbles and 4 green marbles.

This makes the blue marble equation:

$$\frac{8}{12 + 8 + 4} = \frac{8}{24} = \frac{1}{3}$$

The probability of both occurring is the product of the individual probabilities:

$$\frac{1}{3} \times \frac{1}{5} = \frac{1}{15}$$

The correct answer is (A).

Note

Given the same scenario, what would the probability of picking a green marble first or a blue marble second?

$$P\,(A \text{ or } B) = P(A) + P(B) - P(A)P(B)$$
$$= \frac{1}{5} + \frac{1}{3} - \frac{1}{15}$$
$$= \frac{8}{15} - \frac{1}{15}$$
$$= \frac{7}{15}$$

Column A	Column B

There are 24 students in a class. Half are male and half are female. At random, 3 students are chosen successively from the class.

Column A	Column B
The probability of a boy, then a girl, then a girl, being chosen	The probability of a girl, then a boy, then a girl being chosen

These are both *and* situations, not *or* situations. The probability of either first event is 0.5 since the class is evenly split. The second event in both columns then switches genders, so again the probability would be the same, $\frac{12}{23}$. For the third event, in both columns a girl and a boy have already been chosen, so the probability of picking a male or female is again the same. So the third events also have the same probability. The products of equal factors are equal, so (C) is the correct answer.

Get Graphical with the Data

You will see one or two sets of graphs and charts on the GRE math section. Each set will have 2 to 4 questions, so understanding and interpreting the graph sets are important. As was said in the first section, there is good news and bad news for this. The good news is that the answers for the graph set questions are always right in front of you. The bad news is that the GRE can come up with some pretty complex graph sets that make finding the answers a challenge. The way to combat this "complexifying" is to spend 10 to 20 seconds familiarizing yourself with a graph set when it comes up. Scroll all the way down so that you see all the pertinent information. Look at any key. Read the titles of everything. Inspect graph axes so that you know with what units the information is being presented. Basically, get comfortable with the graph sets. This way, when you start on the questions you will be ready to hone in on whatever information a question asks for.

There are two ways that the GRE increases the difficulty of these kinds of problems. The first is to give you wackier or more unconventional graph sets. Instead of getting just a line graph and a bar graph, you might get a line graph that has a right and left axis with different figures graphed, and also a vertical pie chart. The second way the test-makers increase the difficulty is by increasing the number of steps needed to find the answer. Instead of just having to read the answer off a bar graph, you might have to take information from both graphs and then do a little math. Although these multi-stage problems take time, graph set questions will not involve more than two or three steps. The GRE tests your ability to quickly and correctly interpret graph sets, not your ability to do sophisticated analysis of the information presented.

Survey of 250 European Travelers

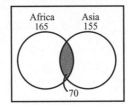

Breakdown of European Travelers Surveyed Who Traveled to Asia

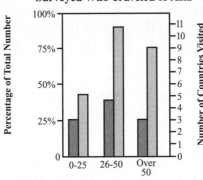

■ – Percentage of Total Group
■ – Average Number of Countries Visited in Asia

What percentage of the European Travelers surveyed did NOT travel to Africa?

A. 34%
B. 43%
C. 57%
D. 63%
E. 70%

This question only involves the Venn diagram, so focus on it. You will find that the total number of European travelers is 250 (165 African travelers + 155 Asian travelers). You will note that by looking closely at the Venn diagram that there is a shaded region shared by both Africa and Asia (represented by 70).

You'll calculate the travelers represented in the non-shaded portion of the Venn diagram by subtracting 70 from both sides. So, for Africa 165 − 70 = 95 travelers. And Asia, 155 − 70 = 85 travelers.

Remember our total amount of European travelers is 250. Therefore, for Africa $\frac{95}{250}$ (or approximately 38 percent) and for Asia $\frac{85}{250}$ (or approximately 34 percent). The question only asks for the percentage that did NOT travel to Africa, so the correct answer is (A), 34 percent.

How many of the European travelers surveyed are over 50 and have traveled to Asia?

A. 28
B. 38
C. 42
D. 50
E. 54

This question involves both figures. The Venn diagram indicates there are 155 travelers to Asia, so the percentages in the bar graph are percentages of 155. Find the 51–100 category and read the value of the lightly-shaded column. It is about midway between 25% and 30%, so estimate it at 27.5%.

Ten percent of 155 is 15.5, and so 20% is 31. Five percent of 155 is 7.75. If we add the 20% number to the 5% number, we should get (31 + 7.75 = 38.75). If 25% of 155 is 38.75, then 27.5% must be a little higher than this. Choice (C) is in the right neighborhood.

You might also see a less conventional graph set than the previous one. The test likes to see if you can think on your feet by presenting information in a format that you might not be expecting. Don't be surprised if you see something wacky like the following on test day.

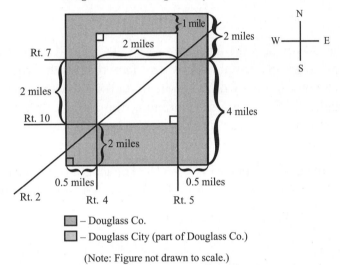

Douglass Co. and Douglass City

▢ – Douglass Co.

▢ – Douglass City (part of Douglass Co.)

(Note: Figure not drawn to scale.)

Since the city was laid out on a grid, all lines and roads that appear parallel are parallel, and all roads that appear perpendicular are perpendicular.

How many miles is the section of Rt. 2 that runs through the city limits of Douglass?

A. 2
B. $\sqrt{6}$
C. $\sqrt{8}$
D. 3
E. $\sqrt{12}$

Rt. 2 in the city limits works out to be the hypotenuse of two different right triangles. You can determine the length of the section of Rt. 2 with either triangle, so pick one and go with it. Both of the other sides of the triangles are 2 miles, so both triangles are 45-45-90 triangles. The length of the hypotenuse can simply be read off, $2\sqrt{2}$, which is equal to choice (C).

What approximate percentage of Douglass County is within the city limits of Douglass?

A. 20%
B. 33%
C. 42%
D. 50%
E. 66%

The areas of the county and the city have to be determined to find this percentage. This is greatly simplified by the fact that both areas are rectangles, which you can infer from the note that all the lines are parallel and at right angles in the diagram. Examining the right length of the diagram, the length of the diagram is 6 (4 miles +2 miles). The width is 3 (read off from the bottom width as 0.5 +2 + 0.5).

This makes the area of the county $3 \times 6 = 18$. The length of the city is 3 and the width is 2, so the city's area is 6. The ratio of city area to county area then is $\frac{6}{18} = \frac{1}{3} \approx 0.33$. The correct answer is (B).

You can drop the units since all the units are the same and will cancel each other out.

Tip

If you are 2 miles due southeast of the intersection of Rt. 7 and Rt. 4, where are you?

A. In the city
B. Outside the city but in the county
C. Outside the county
D. Along Rt. 10
E. Along Rt. 2

First find the intersection of Rt. 7 and Rt. 4. It is on the left side. According to the compass rose, Rt. 4 runs north-south and Rt. 7 runs east-west. Southeast then would be halfway between heading east on Rt. 7 and south on Rt. 4. If there were a line defining this direction, it would form a 45-degree angle with Rt. 7 and with Rt. 4. If that line is long enough, it will form two 45-45-90 triangles like you saw that Rt. 2 did two questions back. However, in that instance you found that the length of Rt. 2 in the city was $2\sqrt{2}$ miles, which is greater than 2 miles. So 2 miles southeast of the intersection is not outside of the box defined by the city limits south of Rt. 7. So you would be inside the city, choice (A).

A Final Word

The *Next Level* section of this chapter covers many of the favorite ways to make a GRE problem hard, but not all of them. Invariably, if you are doing really well on the GRE Math section, you will encounter something that at first glance looks impossibly complex. Ask yourself, "How did the test-makers make this problem hard?" Is it a multi-step problem involving a host of equations? If so, the goal is often to find terms that cancel each other out. Does the question have a bunch of interconnected figures? If so, the key is usually to figure out facts about individual figures and then use this knowledge to gain information about other figures. With an aggressive attitude and a willingness to get creative and keep working, many of the hardest GRE problems will be yours for the taking.

Chapter 5

Verbal Review

The Perfect Charm for Those Shooting to Score above a 500

When people talk about standardized tests, they often fall into one of two camps. The first group believes that the tests are a reasonably accurate indication of a person's "intelligence." It stands to reason, then, that someone who scores well on a standardized test must be "smart." The second camp does not hold standardized tests in such a high esteem light. To people in the second camp, the only thing a standardized test measures is how well someone does on that particular standardized test. To them, standardized tests are too arbitrary and narrowly focused to be any kind of accurate indicator of intelligence.

By the time you are finished reading through this section (and this book), many of you in the first camp will have migrated to the second camp. This is because many of you will no longer think of the GRE Verbal section as a comprehensive, multiple-choice exam that uses a variety of question formats to accurately gauge a person's level of English mastery. In place of this idea, many of you will view the test in a much different way.

The GRE Verbal Section Is a Vocabulary Quiz Gone Wild

For the Verbal section, you get 30 minutes to answer 30 questions that come in four different types:

1. Antonyms

2. Analogies

3. Sentence Completions (just SC if you're in a hurry)

4. Reading Comprehension (RC for those on the go)

A chart describing these four question types—as well as a discussion about the basic approach to the GRE Verbal test—can be found starting on page 25. Be sure to read this section if you haven't already done so. The bulk of this chapter will discuss each question type in detail, but you need to fit these individual ideas into the overall Verbal strategy covered in the earlier section.

Like the Quantitative section, the GRE Verbal section is scored on a scale from 200 to 800, with 800 a perfect score. Theoretically, a 500 would be an average score, and this chapter is going to emphasize strategies to help you score above a 500 on the GRE Verbal section. A Verbal score in the high 500s to mid 600s can be considered a solid score, although if you are applying for an English program you will most likely want to stay above 600. The fact that the scores are scaled makes for some strange discrepancies between the percentile scores and scaled scores. For example, a 700 Verbal might translate to the 96th percentile, meaning that this score was better than 95 out of 100 test-takers. However, a higher Quantitative scaled score might translate to a lower percentile score because of the results of all the other people taking the GRE CAT. On the same test where a 700 Verbal equals the 96th percentile, a 760 Quantitative scaled score might only rank in the 83rd percentile. Even though the scaled score is higher, the percentile ranking is lower. If this seems a little odd, that's because it is. The end result is that it is usually tougher to get a high Verbal scaled score than it is to get a high Quantitative scaled score because the pool of GRE test-takers is skewed with people who score better in Verbal than Math.

Alert!

You receive your scaled scores immediately after completing the entire test. There are also percentile scores (0–99%) for both the Verbal and Quantitative sections. These percentile scores can be found in the same letter that gives you your Analytical score. The percentile score can be a little strange, since it varies over time depending on all the people taking the test. Most graduate programs are more interested in the scaled scores, so don't lose too much sleep trying to figure out the vagaries of percentile scores.

Although there are four different question types, the first three all have a heavy vocabulary component. The first question type, Antonyms, is almost exclusively a vocabulary quiz, since you often need to know the definition of a word in order to pick its opposite. There are some guessing techniques that enable you to work on an antonym problem even if you don't know the definition of the word, but for the most part many antonym problems boil down to, "Do you know the word or not?"

PETERSON'S
getting you there

Both analogies and sentence completions have formats that are more complicated than antonyms, and both formats can be approached with a host of methods. However, the presence of difficult vocabulary words in the answer choices can make things difficult. For instance, you might read a SC problem and realize the word in the blank needs to mean something akin to "small," but then look down and see that your answer choices are:

A. weighty
B. pulchritudinous
C. pusillanimous
D. voluminous
E. angry

Choices (A) and (E) are well-known words, but (B), (C), and (D) are not as common. For this question, you could eliminate (A) and (E) since you know that neither of these words means "small," but you would then be left with a choice of (B), (C), and (D). Many of you might be able to look at *voluminous* and recognize the root *volume* in the word, making this choice unlikely to be the answer. This would leave you with two choices to guess from, illustrating how good test strategies can take you a long way, but sometimes not all the way to finding the answer outright. For the last push, you would have to know that *pulchritudinous* is an ugly-sounding word that surprisingly means "beautiful," while *pusillanimous* is a very large word that means "small." How's that for opposites?

Three fourths of the GRE Verbal question types have a vocabulary component to them. Combine this with the fact that the first 3–6 questions you face will be both antonyms and analogies, and that the first questions on a computer adaptive test section count more than the questions at the end. The end result is a GRE Verbal exam that is a lot like a "souped-up" vocabulary test, or a vocabulary quiz gone wild.

If you wanted to practice your Analytical skills, you can write an essay showing why the GRE Verbal section is *not* like a vocabulary quiz on steroids. You could go through and find the flaws in the author's argument, which admittedly is not airtight. This might help you improve your Analytical score, but it won't do much for the GRE Verbal score. For help in this area, the first thing you should do is improve your vocabulary, because it plays a huge part on the GRE Verbal.

Upgrading Your Personal Lexicon

In the ideal scenario, you are reading this book when you are 5 years old. It might be the first book you ever read. If this is the case, then the GRE CAT is almost two decades away, and you have an ample amount of time to learn a ton of tough vocabulary words. Put the lollipop down and crack open that dictionary, youngster!

Sadly, most of you reading this book do not have as much time as the wee child described above. That's okay, too! It means you have an actual life. The simple fact is that the more time you have before the test, the more vocabulary words you can learn.

Tips on Learning New Vocabulary

1. Strive for Quality over Quantity. Sort of learning the definition of 1,000 words is not as good as actually learning 100 words. Building vocabulary for a single test is a bit problematic to begin with, since there's no way you can cover all the possible words that might appear. Therefore, don't blow a gasket trying to guarantee you'll recognize every word you see, since it just isn't going to happen. Instead, make sure the new words you do learn are remembered. That way, if one of these words shows up as an antonym, you have a great chance to answer that question correctly.

People learn at different rates. Learning about 30 new words a week is a nice goal. If you start six weeks before the test, that gives you almost 200 new words. Feel free to adjust the 30 words/week figure up or down depending on your own ability and available time. Just make sure that you actually learn—and remember—the definitions of the words you are studying.

2. Don't Let an Unknown Word Cross Your Path Again. The best way to learn new words is when a word appears in the context of other words. Suppose you happen to be reading a magazine, book, or newspaper when you come across the word *charivari*. Looking at the context of the word (how the word is used in the sentence), you can sort of figure out its meaning. This allows you to keep on reading, even if you don't know exactly what *charivari* means.

Instead of settling for this quasi-comprehension, write the unknown word down and then look it up later. Or look it up right then, if you have a dictionary nearby. The goal is to add that word to your mental stable of words, and it's much easier to do this with words that you actually encounter in the course of a day. Encountering the word in context helps anchor the word in your mind.

Note

You can keep a small notebook with you to write unknown words down, or if you're techno-savvy you can store the words in a PDA or some similar device. For optimal benefit, write down the unknown word and the sentence in which it appears. When you look up the definition, you can then add the definition to the word and the sample sentence you already have. It almost goes without saying that creating a list this way gives you a vocabulary review sheet at the same time.

Writing down and learning the meaning of unknown words will help improve your vocabulary, and it will have benefits beyond the GRE CAT Verbal. You might be able to use some of these tough words on the Analytical essay, and in general you'll just have more words at your disposal on a day-by-day basis. You will find that a large vocabulary can be very helpful in social, educational, and business settings.

3. Do Some Test-Specific Vocabulary Reading. If context learning is the best way to pump up your GRE vocabulary, the second-best way is to buy a "Boost Your GRE Vocabulary" book. There are also a slew of Web sites covering GRE vocabulary.

Regardless of what source you use, a GRE-specific vocabulary list can help focus your studies to cover words that have a good likelihood of appearing on the GRE. However, this advantage is offset by two opposing factors. The first factor is that learning words from a book does not guarantee that you'll remember the word in the future. Typically, the high density of new words you encounter and the artificial method in which you experience them translates to a lower retention level. Instead of anchoring the word in your mind, you might see it on the test and say, "Oh yeah, I remember that was one of the words I studied." This recollection might lead you to recall the word's definition, but often all you have is a vague idea of what the word means. Still, this is better than nothing.

The second problem is that even if you do memorize 200 GRE-specific words, the chances you will encounter a bunch of them on the actual test is still rather small. Picture the Gulf of Mexico in your mind. Even if you know every fish off the coast of Florida, does this mean you know every fish in the entire gulf? The answer is no, because the volume of water in the gulf is simply too big. The same holds true for the amount of vocabulary that might appear on the GRE. The number of possible words is too large for any single book, or volume of books, to contain.

This doesn't mean you must gnash your teeth and scream to the stars about the injustice of the GRE, although if that makes you feel better, go right ahead. Instead, simply realize that you will not know the exact

138

definition of every word you encounter. That's fine. Everybody else taking the GRE is in the same boat as you, to one extent or another. Studying from a GRE-specific list might place 1–3 problems right in your lap. Since the test is only 30 questions long, every question helps. If some recently learned vocabulary helps you on the first 5 questions, then it will have been worth it.

The rest of the chapter will cover various question-specific techniques you can employ. Vocabulary was covered first since some of these techniques hinge upon whether or not you know the definition of the words used. Compiling new vocabulary words and learning questions strategies go hand in hand, so let's get started.

Antonyms

In test-taking lingo, a GRE antonym question consists of a "stem word" followed by 5 answer choices. For example:

CIRCUITOUS :

A. direct
B. electrical
C. wooden
D. oblique
E. long-winded

The stem word is *circuitous*, and one of the five answer choices below this stem word has a meaning that is "most nearly opposite" in meaning to circuitous. Don't look yet at the answer choices, though. The best way to approach every antonym problem is to focus on the stem word first and answer this question as honestly as possible: "Do I know the meaning of this word?"

> **Tip**
>
> Although these questions are commonly referred to as antonyms, not every stem word/correct answer is an antonym pair in the purest sense. This is why the phrase "most nearly opposite" (or something similar) will be used to describe these questions. The phrase is vague enough to give the test-writers wiggle room if they want to use two words that aren't exactly antonyms, but do have meanings that are fairly opposite.

This question triggers your approach to every antonym problem. Looking at the answer choices before answering it might influence your thinking, as you make an incorrect connection with the stem word and an answer choice that is incorrect. The reason for this common mistake has to do with the way wrong answer choices are created. In general, wrong answer choices often take the form of words that can commonly be associated with the stem word. Call this the "Salt-and-Pepper Trap." The stem word is *salt*, and directly below it is the answer choice *pepper*. Your mind commonly associates these two items together, in kind of an opposite way. So like the old tongue-twister you pick *pepper*, even though the two words are not antonyms. They aren't really related in any way except for the fact that they are both common spices. Focusing on the stem word definition first prevents you from falling into the Salt-and-Pepper Trap. Achoo!

Answering the question, "Do I know the meaning of the stem word?" produces three outcomes, "Yes," "No," and "Maybe." Each of these answers leads to a different technique.

Outcome #1: Yes, I Know the Meaning of the Word

As you might expect, this is the answer you want the most. If you do know the meaning of *circuitous*, define it mentally in a sentence like, "Circuitous means a long, round-about course or path." Now, **anticipate** what the antonym of *circuitous* will be. By anticipating the antonym, you approach the answer choices with a focus that will help you separate the wrong answers from the better choices. People who don't approach the answer choices with such a clear focus often "shop" the answer choices, looking at each one and trying them on to see if they fit as the stem word's antonyms. Since these wrong answers are designed to be tempting, this approach can easily lead to a poor choice.

By anticipating the antonym, you give yourself a clear idea of what you are looking for. You don't have to spend minutes crafting a perfect response, just compose a mental sentence along the lines of, "the antonym of *circuitous* will be a word like *straight* or *blunt*."

   A. direct
   B. electrical
   C. wooden
   D. oblique
   E. long-winded

Using this mental sentence as a guide, choice (A) stands out as the correct answer. You might not know exactly what *oblique* means, so you don't have to cross out that answer if you don't want to. All other choices are clearly wrong, although if you went shopping in the answer choices, you might have liked *electrical* since the word *circuitous* has the word *circuit* in it.

If you know the meaning of the stem word, chances are good you would get the answer correct even without anticipating the correct choice. Even so, anticipating the correct answer virtually eliminates the chance of a wrong answer. It's a sound test-taking strategy, and one you should always employ.

Outcome #2: I Sort of Know the Meaning of That Word . . . Maybe

There are many words that fall into this category. They are like the neighbors you occasionally see down the street or the people who work at your local grocery store. You recognize them when you see them, but if pressed, you have to admit that you don't know that much about them.

People encounter these "passing acquaintance" words every day. If you are following the suggestions listed earlier in this chapter, you are writing down these words and then looking up their definitions later. This allows you to change your answer from "Maybe I know this word" to "Yes, I know this word," something that greatly helps your GRE Verbal chances. Still, there will always be some words that you recognize but can never quite define.

BRAVADO :

A. callowness
B. greed
C. swagger
D. timorousness
E. hapless

Assume that you don't quite know the definition of the stem word *bravado*. However, you have seen the word in some novels, and you think that *brav-* in *bravado* is the same as the *brav-* in *brave* or *bravery*. This would mean that *bravado* means something similar to *brave* or courageous . . . if the *brav-* is the same for both words.

The above train of thought is commendable, and it shows someone working to decipher the meaning of a word with an educated guess. This is a good strategy. To determine whether or not the guess is correct, you need to develop your awareness of how the computer adaptive GRE works. For example, if *bravado* is the first question in the GRE Verbal section, which would imply that it is a question of medium difficulty. This question won't be simple, but a little work—like figuring out the definition by comparing the root *brav*—should place you on the right course. In this scenario, *bravado* probably does share some similarity with the more common word *brave*.

However, if *bravado* is the fifth question, and you're very confident you've answered the previous four questions correctly, then the scenario is different. You should realize that your correct answers have caused the test to adapt and start feeding you harder problems, so the root *brav-* in *bravado* is a decoy put there to catch unwary students. There's no way a hard GRE Verbal question would be so easy to decipher.

If the previous paragraph makes sense to you, then you are well on your way to becoming a great test-taker.

For this example, suppose *bravado* is the first question you encounter on the GRE Verbal, which means the *brav-* root theory is valid. Since you sort of know the definition, you can sort of anticipate an answer. The opposite of *bravery* would be *cowardice* or something similar, so the opposite of *bravado* should be something like *cowardice* as well. Glancing at the answer choices, you have:

A. callowness
B. greed
C. swagger
D. timorousness
E. hapless

Note

Some people like to think in terms of positive/negative words. Painting with broad strokes, positive words mean things like larger/happier/better/ good, while negative words mean the opposite. *Bravado* has the root *brav-* in it, and *bravery* would be considered positive. You can could then go into the answer choices and look for negative words. This technique does not always work, though, as many answer choices are negative words but with different meanings. Nevertheless, thinking in terms of positive/negative can help for some words in which the only thing you can recall about them is whether or not they mean something good or bad.

These choices illustrate the influence that vocabulary has on the GRE Verbal, since some of the answer choice words are as hard as or harder than the stem word itself. Still, choices (B), (C), and (E) have nothing to do with cowardice, so you can cross them out. This leaves you with a 50/50 chance, not bad considering you aren't certain of the stem word definition. Therefore, the correct answer is (D).

Outcome #3: No, I Have No Idea What That Word Means

For most people, the question is not *if* you will encounter a word you don't know, but *when* you will run across that word. Don't beat yourself up about this, as the words used on the GRE Verbal section reflect a pretty advanced vocabulary pool. For example:

WINSOME :

- A. unpleasant
- B. defeated
- C. garrulous
- D. whiny
- E. spurious

If you don't know what the word *winsome* means, and if your mind can not even summon up a passing memory of seeing the word in print, then there's no way to anticipate the answer. Instead, you need to attack the answer choices, scrutinize them and try to eliminate unlikely answers, and then take a guess.

There are two primary ways to attack answer choices. The first one has been touched on in the previous section, where you took your knowledge of the adaptive test format and used it to your advantage. Suppose the word *winsome* appears after you have answered several questions correctly. Personally, you think it's a tough word (which is true), and that you are in a hard portion of the GRE Verbal (a good assumption if you've been answering questions correctly). This means there's no easy shortcut on this problem. In fact, anything that looks like a shortcut is probably too good to be true, and can be eliminated.

The root *win-* appears in the word *winsome*, which might lead some to think the word has something to do with victory or winning. Choice (B) then practically screams, "I must be the answer!" Knowing where you are on the test, and how tough a word *winsome* is, you can therefore eliminate choice (B). You know it's there to catch unwary test-takers looking for an easy out when there isn't one.

One answer choice is out, but four remain. The second elimination technique can now be employed. Call it the "Sandwich Technique." Try to answer the question, "What is the opposite of sandwich?" Is it a pizza? Soup? A salad? The point is there is no opposite word for *sandwich*. Many words have no opposite, or you have to get very creative to come up with an opposite. Words without true opposites are very poor candidates to be the correct answer on an Antonym problem, so you can cross them out on hard problems.

PETERSON'S

getting you there

Looking over the four remaining choices, choice (A) has a very clear opposite. You might not know what *garrulous* or *spurious* means, so you can't eliminate them if you don't know what they mean. It turns out both have valid opposites. Look at (D), though, *whiny*. What is the opposite of *whiny*? Unwhiny? Polite? Not annoying? You can make a case that there is a word that means the opposite of *whiny* . . . but you have to make a case in order to do so. This makes it unlikely to be the right answer, so you can eliminate choice (D).

You are left with three choices. Take a guess, and keep in mind that one-in-three odds are not too bad when you are dealing with a completely unfamiliar word. The correct answer choice happens to be the one that could easily be an antonym. A *winsome* person is charming and pleasant, the opposite of *unpleasant*, choice (A).

There are several methods for dealing with antonym problems, but vocabulary plays a large part in the overall strategy. The same can also be said of another vocabulary-centric question type, the analogy questions.

ANALOGY is to GRE as FEATHER is to OSTRICH

Analogies are similar in form to antonyms, and they also have a heavy vocabulary component. However, where there is only one stem word for an antonym, an analogy question starts off with two stem words that bear some type of relationship to one another. As you will see, understanding the relationship between the two stem words is the critical skill to master when handling analogy problems.

FEATHER : OSTRICH ::

A. beak : raven
B. scale : lizard
C. foot : chicken
D. desert : cactus
E. tail : mammal

There's a colon between the two stem words, but there is also some kind of link between the two words. One of the answer choices—the correct one—will share this same link, or analogous relationship. Hence the term, *analogies*.

To get a clearer picture of what is needed on an analogy problem, it helps to get rid of the colon and format the question in the following manner:

FEATHER _____ OSTRICH ::

A. beak _____ raven
B. scale _____ lizard
C. foot _____ chicken
D. desert _____ cactus
E. tail _____ mammal

If the question were set up this way, it would be easy to see that what you need to do is write some text that shows the link between the two stem words. You can have something like

a FEATHER is part of an OSTRICH ::

Creating a link between the two stem words is the first step of every analogy problem. If you can create a good link, then you can take that link down into the answer choices and see which answer choices share that link.

Tip

Granted, you can't create a link between the stem words if you don't know what one or both of the words means. Strategies to deal with these circumstances are covered later in the chapter.

A. beak is part of a raven
B. scale is part of a lizard
C. foot is part of a chicken
D. desert is part of a cactus
E. tail is part of a mammal

A *desert* is NOT part of a *cactus*, so choice (D) is not going to be the right answer on this problem since it does not contain the same link as the two stem words (*desert* : *cactus* do share a link, it's just not the right one for this problem). Choices (A), (B), (C), and (E) all seem to share the same link. This does not mean that all four choices are correct. Instead, we must refine our initial link and be a little more precise in describing how the words *feather* and *ostrich* are connected. A little bit of thinking here will make the problem easy to solve.

Some people might say that feathers are used by birds to fly. This is somewhat true, although it could be argued that the wings are what enable a bird to fly. In any case, the ostrich is a flightless bird, so creating a link that states, "A feather is part of an ostrich that is used to fly" would be incorrect.

What do the feathers do for an ostrich? Without over-thinking it, feathers cover the outside of the bird and protect it in the same way that skin protects us. You can then modify our initial linking sentence to read something like:

> a FEATHER is part of the outer covering of an OSTRICH

> a FEATHER is the part of an OSTRICH found along the outside of its body

> a FEATHER is the part of an OSTRICH that covers it like skin

All three of these sentences give a more precise definition of the connection between *feather* and *ostrich*. Use any of them above and see how they fit in with the remaining answer choices.

A. beak is part of the outer covering of a raven
B. scale is part of the outer covering of a lizard
C. foot is part of the outer covering of a chicken
E. tail is part of the outer covering of a mammal

You could try to make the case that choices (A), (C), and (E) are still valid, but it should be clear that choice (B) is the best answer for this analogy problem. Scales cover the outside of lizards, and feathers cover the exterior of ostriches.

If you know both the stem words for an analogy question, then you should focus on creating a link that describes the connection between the two words. Once this is done, you simply take that link and check it against all the answer choices to find the one that shares the same relationship. That is your correct answer.

Creating good links can take some practice. Quite often, you might start out with a general link and then have to modify it to be more specific. The chart below discusses some of the more common types of Analogy links that will be encountered on the GRE.

Common Types of Analogies

1. **Synonyms:** Synonyms are fairly simple analogies, since the two words mean the same thing. An example would be PREVARICATE : LIE, since prevaricate is just a fancy word meaning "to lie." Synonym analogies like to combine one tough word with a simple one, leaving you to wonder what the relationship between the words are. The words could be synonyms, or . . .

2. **Antonyms:** These analogies are exactly what you would expect them to be. PREVARICATION: TRUTH is an example of an antonym analogy. Many synonym and antonym analogies use adjectives as the stem words.

146

3. **Degree:** Degree analogies combine two things that are similar in nature but different in scale. BREEZE : GALE is a good example since they are both winds, although a gale is much stronger.

4. **Set/Subset:** Fans of categories will like these analogies. Subset analogies often employ linking phrases such as "kind of" or "part of." ELM : TREE is a simple example, since an elm is a kind of tree. FEATHER : OSTRICH could also be considered one of these analogies, but if you disagree, that's fine, too. These categories should be used if they help you come up with good links, but it doesn't really matter whether or not each category is distinct from all the others.

5. **Function:** Certain things have been made with a specific purpose or function. For instance, what do gloves do? GLOVES : HANDS is a good example of a function relationship, since gloves are meant to be worn on the hands.

Note

You might also think that GLOVES : WARM is a good link, but this is not as strong. Gloves can be used to keep your hands warm, but gloves can also be worn for other purposes. A person wearing gloves while washing dishes is wearing gloves for protection, not warmth. The two stem words will always have a strong link, but the words in the answer choices do not always contain strong links. If you saw GLOVES : WARM as an answer choice, you could eliminate it as a likely answer choice because the link between the two words is not very strong.

6. **Definitional:** This is a big catch-all category. One stem word often plays a big part in defining the other stem word. CANDLE : WAX is an example, since it is hard to describe a candle without using the term *wax*. While there are some candles that might not be made out of wax, the overwhelming majority are, so a link like "a candle is made out of wax" might be all you need to answer a problem correctly. There is the possibility you would have to get more specific, so you could modify this first definition and change it to something more precise such as, "A candle is made out of wax, which is then burned away."

This list could be given more categories, but the overall goal is to show you some common routes you can take to create a link between the stem words. Look at the two analogies questions below, and come up with strong links that describe a connection between the two words. See if your links are good enough to enable you to answer both questions correctly.

SHEPHERD : FLOCK ::

A. apothecary : drugs
B. butcher : carcass
C. physician : patients
D. farmer : corn
E. businessperson : employer

BANEFUL : BENEFIT ::

A. helpful : cure
B. tragic : end
C. toxic : poison
D. flawless : aberration
E. disguised : concealment

You can describe the first two stem words in either functional or definitional terms:

Functional route:

he function of a SHEPHERD is to take care of his/her FLOCK.

Definitional route:

A SHEPHERD is someone who takes care of a FLOCK.

Both links do a good job of describing the connection between a shepherd and a flock. Taking either link and heading into the answer choices, you should see that choice (C) works better than any other. A PHYSICIAN is someone who takes care of his/her PATIENTS. Some people will balk at this choice, mainly because they do not want to be compared with sheep. Yet the whole point of analogous relationships is to show a shared similarity between two seemingly dissimilar groups.

For the second analogy problem, the words *baneful* and *benefit* have opposite connotations. Something that is BANEFUL has no BENEFIT, so you can use the link "has no" to check all the answer choices. Choices (C) and (E) are mostly synonyms, so while there is a strong link between the words in these answer choices, they do not have the link you are looking for. Something FLAWLESS has no ABERRATION, making (D) the correct answer.

The words used in the second problem were deliberately a lot tougher than the words in the first problem. If you didn't know what *baneful* meant, it would be hard to make a link between the two stem words. There will be some tough stem words on the GRE, so there are some strategies you can use to approach these problems.

What to Do When the Stem Words Are Just Too Freaky

There will always be a strong link between the two stem words. This is not the case with the answer choices. Some of these will have weak links, or even no links at all. Since the correct answer must have the same, strong link as the two stem words, any answer choices with weak links can be eliminated. There's no way they could be the right answer, because the right answer must have a strong link.

This is the best elimination technique you have, so be prepared to use it on lots of problems. Let's look back at the very first analogy problem in this section.

FEATHER : OSTRICH ::

A.   beak : raven
B.   scale : lizard
C.   foot : chicken
D.   desert : cactus
E.   tail : mammal

Assume you have no idea what the word *feather* means. Go down to your answer choices and try to make links between the two words.

A.   beak : raven—a BEAK is like the mouth of a RAVEN
B.   scale : lizard—a LIZARD is covered in SCALES (It's OK to reverse direction if you need to, and you can add a plural if you like)
C.   foot : chicken—a CHICKEN kinda has a FOOT
D.   desert : cactus—a DESERT is where you commonly find CACTUS
E.   tail : mammal—a TAIL can often be found on a MAMMAL, but not always

Choice (C) is not really a strong link, and (E) is pretty shaky, too. Mammals can have tails, but not every one does. Both (C) and (E) are weak choices that can be crossed out as possible answers. Choices (A) and (D) have fine links. But if (D) is the right answer, then the stem words would have to share the same link, meaning that a FEATHER "is where you commonly find" an OSTRICH. You would pick this if you thought there was a specific word out there meaning, "the place where ostriches are commonly found." The existence of such a word is unlikely, so this takes (D) out of the picture. You are left with (A) or (C), two solid choices.

Let's revisit choice (C) once more before bidding a fond farewell to this problem. Since *foot* and *chicken* do not share any real connection, why is this choice even here? The reason lies in the fact that most people like to play the "Connect the Words" game when tackling tough analogies problems. This means they might connect the second stem word with the second word in an answer choice, or maybe they'll take the first stem word and make a connection with the second word of a different answer choice. They'll make links however they can, with no regard for the strict rules regarding analogous relationships. In terms of this question, this means people will link *ostrich*, a bird, with *chicken* or *raven*, two other birds. Who cares what the first words are? Chickens and ostriches are both birds, aren't they?

None of these "Connect the Words" links are valid. They are traps designed to lead you astray. It doesn't matter that *chicken* and *ostriches* are both birds. You can only make links between the two paired words, and then compare links to one another.

The temptation to play "Connect the Words" gets stronger when you have some tough words that you might not know.

> Looking back at the *shepherd* and *flock* problem, you can see two answer choices designed to catch people making incorrect connections. The words *farmer* and *corn* do not really have a strong link, since farmers can grow many other things besides corn. It's there to catch people combining *shepherd* and *farmer*, two pastoral occupations. Some people might equate shepherds with tending herd animals of some sort, and these animals often end up with a *butcher*, the first word in choice (B).

Note

BANEFUL : BENEFIT ::

A. helpful : cure
B. tragic : end
C. toxic : poison
D. flawless : aberration
E. camouflaged : concealment

If you don't know what *baneful* means, attack this question by heading into the answer choices to test the links there. Choice (C) contains two synonyms, so it remains a likely pick if you think *baneful* and *benefit* are synonymous. When you try to make a link for choices (A) and (B), you will find that the words are not really related. Choice (A) is probably there for people connecting *cure* and *benefit*, two positive words. You should realize by now that choice (A) is wrong for two reasons: It has a weak link, and it's a trap for folks playing "Connect the Words."

150

Choices (C), (D), and (E) all contain good links, so they should all remain. A one-in-three chance may not be ideal, but it shows once again that you can use techniques to give yourself a fighting chance even on problems where you don't know the meaning of some of the words.

This _____ of the Book Deals with Sentence _____

If you could figure out that heading, you are well on your way to succeeding on Sentence Completions (SC) problems. Like the heading, SC problems feature a sentence—often a convoluted one filled with multiple types of punctuation (commas, semicolons, and so forth), kind of like the sentence you are currently reading—that has one or more words missing from it. A sample SC problem would look like:

> SC problems feature a sentence—often a convoluted one filled with multiple types of _____ (commas, semicolons, and so forth), kind of like the sentence you are currently reading—that has one or more words missing from it.
>
> A. pauses
> B. punctuation
> C. grammar
> D. issues
> E. subjects

Using context is the critical element with SC problems. You are not required to conjecture randomly to figure out what the missing word should be. Instead, every sentence will contain hints and clues in the context that should steer you toward the right word to place in the missing blank. In the sample sentence above, two words immediately following the blank are *commas* and *semicolons*, both forms of punctuation. These are the main clues that should lead you to the correct answer of choice (B), *punctuation*. Of course, having the entire sentence directly above the problem also helps.

PETERSON'S
getting you there

X-Ref

The idea of context should be familiar to everyone enhancing their vocabulary by grabbing unfamiliar words in the context of everyday reading. (This topic was discussed on page 137 in this section.) When you encounter an unfamiliar word in context, you can often determine its meaning from the way it is used in the sentence it is in. You figure out the meaning of the word through its context, and this practice is very similar to the strategy used to determine what word should appear in the blank space of the Sentence Completion problem.

Just like antonym problems, anticipating the answer will help you on SC problems. People who read the original sentence and then go shopping in the answer choices increase their possibility of picking a wrong answer. The incorrect answers are created to catch shoppers, so don't follow this pattern of behavior. Instead, read the original sentence slowly, and try to decide what word would fit best in each blank.

Figuring out a word can be difficult, but remember that every sentence will contain context clues to help you determine the right answer. If the missing word doesn't come to you right away, scan the sentence and look for words or phrases that provide a clue. There will always be some. If you come up with a word but are a bit uncertain it is the correct one, finding the context clues can help you decide whether or not you made the right choice.

> Determined to bring back an egg of the Emperor penguin, Apsley and his companions struggled through ferocious blizzards, _____ low temperatures, and across dangerously unknown Antarctic _____ in order to complete their mission.
>
> A. appallingly..terrain
> B. terrifyingly..errors
> C. cryptically..ice
> D. bitingly..forces
> E. stingingly..circumstances

Tip

The sample sentence also contains *directional words*. These are words that change or continue the flow of a sentence. A conjunction like *and* continues the flow of a sentence, while words like *but, although*, or *however* change the flow of sentence. Since changing the flow makes the meaning of a sentence harder to determine, you can expect to see at least some changing directional words on your SC problems.

This two-blank SC problem has a host of context clues. We can break down this entire sentence and discuss the relevance of all the words.

Word or Phrase	Significance
"Determined to bring back an egg of the Emperor penguin"	On many SC problems, the introductory phrase is employed to set up a change in the flow of the sentence. These introductory phrases start with words like *although*, *while*, and something related. However, this phrase does not do this. The key words in this phrase might be *Determined*—showing resolution—and *Emperor penguin*, which would lead to start thinking about cold weather, since penguins are associated with cold weather.
"Apsley and his companions"	Not much here except for the fact that Apsley's a decidely British name? In terms of answering a SC question, the phrase *and his companions* is completely worthless. Whether or not Apsley acted alone or with an entire troupe of clowns does not help you figure out the missing words. Think of these worthless phrases as sentence completion chaff.
"struggled through ferocious blizzards"	Here's a big clue that ties in well with the penguin clue from earlier. The words *penguin* and *blizzards* should evoke images of very cold weather. The words *struggled* and *ferocious* reinforce the idea that the place Apsley is at is very harsh and cold.
"_____ low temperatures"	Given the way this sentence is going, you should conjecture that the missing word should be something like "extremely" or "terribly." The phrase "pleasantly low temperatures" simply would not jive with everything you've read up to now.
"and across dangerously unknown Antarctic _____"	Apsley hasn't gone to poach penguin eggs from a zoo. He's obviously fighting to get eggs in the Antarctic. Picturing Antarctica in your mind, you might think the *ice* would fit well into the sentence. It would, but so would *land* or *ground*. Keep both options in mind.
"in order to complete their mission"	SC filler, but three cheers for completing the mission.

Now that you have potential words for each blank, look at the answer choices. Start with only one word, and eliminate any answer choices that do not fit the words you came up with. Start with the first blank and cross out any words that do not mean "terribly" or "extremely."

A. appallingly..terrain
B. terrifyingly..errors
C. ~~cryptically~~..ice
D. bitingly..forces
E. stingingly..circumstances

Choice (C) can be eliminated, since "cryptically low temperatures" does not make sense, and it does not mean the same thing as what you are looking for. Note that the second word in choice (C), *ice*, is a very good word to use for that blank. People shopping might pick choice (C) because the second word fits so well, even though the first word is a poor choice. If you work one blank at a time and eliminate improbable answer choices, you spare yourself this mistake.

For the second blank, *ice* works nicely but it's already gone. The word *errors* does not work very well, so (B) can be crossed out. This leaves (A), (D), and (E). The word *terrain* is synonymous with *ground*, making it the best choice from the ones left. (A) is your answer, then. You didn't start out thinking of the words *appallingly* and *terrain*, but you understood the context clues well enough to choose words that led you to these correct answers.

The approach outlined above should be used on all SC questions, one blank or two. As always, vocabulary plays a factor, since it is difficult to eliminate a word like *cryptically* if you are uncertain of what it means. Even though vocabulary works as a limiting factor on SC problems, the fact remains that sentence completion questions are very "techniquable." If you can understand the sentence, you have a shot at getting the answer right.

This is the best thing about SC problems. The worst thing is that there are usually fewer SC problems than any other question type. You might see as few as five, and these arrive near the back end of the test where their impact on scoring is lessened. Isn't it strange how the question type that's most solvable appears the least, while the question type that's little more than a "do-you-know-the-word-or-not?" appears the most? Hmm. . . .

Reading Comprehension, the Kevin Bacon of Standardized Tests (It's in *Every* Test)

Odds are high that you have already taken scads of tests containing Reading Comprehension (RC) problems. The format, then, should hold no surprise: You get a pile of words to read and must answer questions about these words to show that you understood said pile. RC on the GRE Verbal section is no different, although the twenty-first century techno-version of RC means that you must do your reading on a computer screen, scrolling up and down to read the words that appear in an annoyingly small text box.

Since the format is so familiar, there won't be any surprises when your first RC questions pop up on the screen. These questions do not focus on vocabulary as much as the other three question types, providing a bit of relief in that arena. These two aspects work to your advantage, but not everything about RC is rosy. The main drawback is that you have to spend an inordinate amount of time—compared to the other GRE problem types—to answer a small amount of questions. This can lead to problems if you are a very slow reader, as you might find yourself taking 4–6 minutes of a 30-minute test just to answer two measly questions. The ratio of what you put in to answer RC questions to what you get out of it is really lousy.

You should always take whatever time is needed to get a question right, even if this means having to guess on some questions at the very end. Many people tend to rush when taking a standardized test, and this is something you never want to do as it leads to careless errors. Careless errors are compounded by the adaptive nature of the GRE, so people flying through RC problems find themselves at an even greater disadvantage. To overcome any pacing problems before they appear, simply understand that you will have to take more time on RC problems, which means you should take less time on some other problems. For example, if you definitely know the answer to an antonym problem, it should only take you about 15 seconds to mark the correct answer.

Tip

A typical RC passage runs about 200 words in length and has 2–3 questions associated with it. Longer passages—those over and around 300 words—might have as many as 4 questions attached. On a normal GRE, RC questions are shy, appearing for the first time only after you have answered about 8–10 other questions.

Along with their different format, RC problems require a different approach. The overall goal is to make sure you answer the questions correctly in the shortest amount of time possible. To help you do this, read the question before you start reading the passage. Keep the question in the back of your mind when tackling the passage. If you can answer the question accurately before reading the entire passage, by all means do so. The whole goal is to answer questions, not while away time reading a bland passage.

The content of the passages is not going to electrify you. The passages are non-fiction and tackle a diverse range of scientific and non-scientific topics. It should be noted that all the information presented has to be accurate, and that the answers to the questions must also be factually accurate. Therefore, if you get a passage about the War of the Austrian Succession and you just happen to be a big fan of the Hapsburg dynasty, then you're in luck! On a more general note, you can use common sense to eliminate some answer choices that are unlikely to be real or true.

When you start reading the passages, try to understand the main point of the passage first. This is often found hiding out in the first paragraph. Your overall goal is to understand the main points of the passage and each of its paragraphs, but you don't need to waste time absorbing all the information into your long-term memory. Have an idea of where all the facts are, since you want to be able to go to the right part of the passage to answer any questions posed. At the same time, you don't want to waste any time reading information that's not essential to answering the questions, since answering questions is the only reason you're here. Finding the right balance between passage reading and question answering takes some practice, but that's why there are three pencil-and-paper tests in this book as well as others on the CD.

Here's a short sample paragraph:

Passage 1

Line   Viewing the underwater world through a land-based perspective, it is easy to consider a colony of coral—a broad term used to describe the marine organisms, like those of the genus *Corallium*, which inhabit many tropical waters—as something
(5)   similar to a bed of flowers. Both corals and flowers have many species that display brilliant markings and have intricate shapes pleasing to the human eye. Yet the relationship between flowers and corals is predominantly an aesthetic one, as the basic composition of a coral *polyp*, an animal, differs mark-
(10)   edly from that of a self-photosynthesizing plant like a rose or zinnia.

       It could even be argued that *lichen*, a fungus, bears more in common with corals than flowers, since both lichen and corals

(15) are typified by beneficial relationships with photosynthesizing algae. While there are some species of coral that can exist solely by capturing food, most corals receive energy by hosting millions of single-celled organisms commonly referred to as *zooxanthellae*. The *zooxanthellae* are provided safety from predation as well as certain by-products of the coral's

(20) metabolism, like ammonia, which *zooxanthellae* require to grow and reproduce. In return, a portion of the energy produced by the *zooxanthellae* through photosynthesis is used by the coral to further its own needs for sustenance, growth, and reproduction.

The text is wordy, the sentences are long, the style is bookish, and the topic somewhat dull. In short, it's your typical RC passage on a standardized test. Instead of trying to gain some deep insight from the text, just get an idea of what each paragraph is about and then dive into the questions.

The author of the passage uses the visual comparison of coral to a bed of flowers in order to illustrate

- A. how human perceptions of other habitats are influenced by their own environment.
- B. the zoological similarities that exist between corals and flowers.
- C. why a better understanding of corals is needed in order to preserve endangered forms.
- D. the multiple ways that the perspective organisms are regarded.
- E. the ability of underwater life to mimic that of the land-based world.

Note

If you were really cagy, you would have zipped down and read this question before tackling the text of the passage. It doesn't matter if you didn't do this for this question, but make sure to get in the habit of reviewing the questions before tackling the text.

This question covers a bit of text in the first paragraph, so don't try to answer the question without looking back at the first paragraph. There's a tendency for students who feel rushed to try to answer a problem "from memory," as if great amounts of time are saved by not referring back to the passage. Some seconds might be shaved off, it's true, but these seconds won't help much if you get the problem wrong. Go back and look over the first paragraph to give yourself the best shot possible to find the correct answer.

PETERSON'S
getting you there

Instead of jumping right to the correct answer, let's review why some of the other choices are not the right one. Choice (C) sounds good, and people who are very passionate about the environment might agree with the statement whole-heartedly. Yet the author of the passage never once mentions the environmental angle, so the answer choice is just there to trip up GRE-taking members of Greenpeace. Think of this as the "True, but So What?" wrong answer choice. There will be answer choices that sound really good but have nothing to do with the actual text you are working with. Cross these out.

Choices (B) and (E) both use words and phrases that can be found in the passage itself. Choice (B) has the words *corals*, *flower*, *similarities*, and the prefix *zoo-*, all of which appear in the passage. Choice (E) has *underwater* and *land-based* set up in a nice, contrasting way. Both of these choices offer looks over substance, since the actual meaning of each sentence makes them incorrect answer choices. They are like a bracelet made out of pearls and whipped cream. Even though the pearls look nice, the bracelet itself cannot be worn. Choice (B) actually states that there are deeper similarities between flowers and corals, when the whole paragraph is about how these similarities are superficial. The verb *mimic* in choice (E) makes this statement totally incorrect, since there is nothing in the passage to back up this claim.

This leaves only two choices, (A) and (D). Quite often, the correct answer for an RC question merely paraphrases, or restates, text from the passage using different words. The passage starts by showing how a land-based perspective can lead to the wrong conclusion about corals. In other words, people's perceptions of other habitats (the ocean) are influenced by their own environment, the land. That's choice (A), and that's your paraphrased correct answer.

From the second paragraph, it can be inferred that

A. lichen use *zooxanthellae* algae for use in photosynthesis.
B. lichen provides some form of photosynthesizing algae with the same basic nutrients that corals provide *zooxanthellae*.
C. *zooxanthellae* serve a function with corals that is served by some photosynthesizing organism in lichen.
D. corals are not as dependent on their photosynthesizing partners as lichen is.
E. corals and lichen are both able to capture food for themselves if necessary.

Tip

Most RC problems are not going to ask you to find information specifically stated in the passage. Instead, you will be asked to *infer* or *conclude* an answer, based on what was written. This means that while the correct answer is not stated directly, the clues needed to find the right answer are there. So, think like you did on the SC problems and search the passage text for the clues that lead you to the right answer. The clues will always be there; you need only find them and they will lead you to the correct answer.

If this question seems confusing, it's because it is. Many RC problems and answer choices appear to have been penned by Theodore Dreiser. (For those non-English majors, this joke means that they are very laboriously written.) The whole point of these choices is to get you unnerved to the extent that you hurry and make a poor decision. If you understand that this is the trap, you can avoid it.

First, you know where to look for the right answer, since the question states, "in the second passage." Accept any free information that's given. The answer choices continue to make various claims about the analogous—remember this word?—relationship between corals and *zooxanthellae* and lichen with some photosynthesizing organism. In other words,

CORAL : *ZOOXANTHELLAE* :: LICHEN : Some unnamed photosynthesizing organism

You can speak GRE, too!

Choices (B), (D), and (E) don't work because you don't know enough about lichen. There's nothing in the passage that says how dependent lichen is, choice (D), or whether lichen can capture its own food, choice (E). These answers wouldn't be inferences, they would be unfounded guesses. Furthermore, you don't know if lichen uses *zooxanthellae algae*—an unlikely choice (A) since lichen is not found underwater—or if lichen provides its guest algae with basic nutrients, choice (B). All you know is that there is an analogy between lichen and its photosynthesizing organism and corals with *zooxanthellae*. The correct answer is (C).

One last note: People with saltwater aquariums might have known about corals and their little sun-loving buddies, showing how outside knowledge can come in handy depending on the subject you get.

One Last Note about Vocabulary

And that note is, **study more vocabulary!** All the techniques discussed above are useful, but if you don't know the words, their effectiveness will be greatly reduced. The other advantage to studying vocabulary is that you can use these advanced words to make your Analytical essays sound more urbane and educated. For more advice on how to improve your essays, turn to Chapter 6 and start reading.

Take It
to the Next Level

Here There Be Wyverns
(and other Difficult Words)

Graduate programs use GRE scores in a bewildering variety of ways, but in the end it all basically comes down to making piles. Graduate programs start out with a huge pile of applicants, and they need to do things to make this big pile smaller. The big pile gets whittled down one way or another, and when it gets down to a manageable size, then people start to get seriously considered.

Your GRE score is one easy, easy way to whittle down a pile. Viewed this way, you can see that your goal is to have a GRE score good enough to keep from getting placed on the wrong pile. Some programs employ the combined Quantitative and Verbal scores, which is good for you because it is easier to gain points on the math side than it is on the verbal side. If you wanted to boost your score by about 100 points, you could shoot for a 70-point improvement in math and a 30-point increase in verbal.

Alert!

A higher number of humanities programs require the GRE, so the major proportion of people taking the test are better at the verbal portion than the math portion. This verbal-centric skew makes it harder to get a high verbal score, since relatively speaking most people are doing better on that section than on the math section.

Other graduate programs—like those with the word "English" in them—are often not concerned about your Quantitative score. These programs are going to whittle down their piles based on Verbal and perhaps Analytical scores. If this is the case for you, then gunning for a high Verbal score is the right plan. However, if the program is more concerned with overall score, keep in mind that it will be easier to gain extra points in the math portion.

Getting a high score in the GRE Verbal section—high 600s to low 700s—is not very simple, since it often boils down to one word. To be more precise, it comes down to one word that means all words: *vocabulary*.

A Simple Formula to Make Medium Verbal Problems Harder: Use Tougher Words

There are no different question types to separate medium problems from hard ones. Antonyms, analogies, and sentence completions will all have the same format, but instead of the antonym BULKY you'll have the word CORPULENT. Both words mean the same thing, but *corpulent* is a more difficult word. Analogies will still be formed using the common relationships described on page 144, but once again the words used will be tougher and not as commonly known. Ditto for sentence completions, as answer choices will come from the same stockpile of advanced vocabulary. The emphasis on tougher words will be slightest for reading comprehension, but even there passages may feature a large amount of technical and scientific jargon within the text. It will be like the coral/*zooxanthellae* passage on pages 156–157, but with even more terms such as "photosynthesizing organism" bandied about.

The adaptive format, and the manner in which the GRE Verbal starts, only exacerbates the problem. The first 3–6 problems you'll face will be either antonyms or analogies, and if you're shooting for a high score it's going to be important to get most of these questions right. Since these questions are little more than vocabulary problems, knowing the words used on these problems is going to take a combination of knowledge and luck. The knowledge will come in the form of a good lexicon, and the luck will come since not everybody knows the definition of every word.

Notice the term *exacerbates* is used instead of *increases*. To help your score, it makes sense to jump on the GRE Tough Words bandwagon.

Note

Since vocabulary is the key to getting a high Verbal score, the bulk of this chapter will focus on expanding the list of tough words you know. Before this occurs, though, a brief note about the various question types will be covered.

162

Similar Strategies, Harder Problems

The question-specific verbal strategies—covered earlier in this chapter—are the same for antonyms, analogies, and sentence completions. You always want to make a link between the stem words on an analogy, regardless of when the question shows up and how difficult the words are. Similarly, the approach to antonyms is the same: Focus on the stem word, decide whether or not you know the meaning of this word, and then proceed accordingly.

Difficult SC problems will typically have two blanks instead of just one, making you search for clues for both missing words. When the test decides to get really clever, you get a situation where you can't figure out either blank because they are linked. The sample sentence below shows this in action:

The guests were _____ at the _____ state of the basement.

The problem here isn't that you can't place any words. Rather, many different combinations of words work in the two places, since the clue to the first blank (a missing verb) is the second blank (an adjective describing the basement).

The guests could be:

delighted at the magnificent state of the basement.

disgusted at the slovenly state of the basement.

bemused at the whimsical state of the basement.

It's uncertain how you get a basement to be whimsical, but if you could, then the last choice works just as well as the others.

If you come across one of these two-blank SC questions, congratulate yourself for doing well on the test so far, since you wouldn't get one of these puppies if you were answering questions poorly. After you are done patting your back, determine what the link between the two missing words is. This link is usually just "similar" (like in the example above) or "opposite." An opposite SC would resemble:

The guests were not _____ at the _____ state of the basement.

The "not" flips the connection between the two words from similar to opposite.

The guests were _____ at the _____ state of the basement.

A. appalled..tidy
B. appreciative..flooded
C. befuddled..paltry
D. enthralled..singular
E. ambivalent..mildewed

Once you figure out the link, it's time to hit the answer choices and start sifting through the vocabulary. Choice (A) has opposites, so that's a wrong link. Choices (B) and (E) don't work very well, as the second term does not do a very good job of justifying the first one. Also, *flooded* and *mildewed* are two things that happen to real basements, so these answer choices are probably there to distract you. Paring things down to two good choices, (C) and (D), there is no reason to think people would be confused (*befuddled*) by a spare (*paltry*) basement. Choice (D) is the best answer, as something *singular* (wondrous) would cause people to be *enthralled* (captivated).

After you survive the first eight or so questions on the GRE Verbal, you'll get your first shot at the Reading Comp passage. If you are scoring very well, this passage should be a tough RC passage, which means a densely worded passage on some arcane topic. One way to handle this type of dense passage is to jot down notes on a sheet of scratch paper. Note-taking can help you understand the passage better, although it will slow you down a bit. However, imagine that you are in a classroom and listening to a professor drone on about a boring subject that you know will be on the mid-term. Will you understand the topic better if you take notes, or if you don't? Again, this takes additional time, but if you are gunning for a high score, you should have the time if your wide knowledge of vocabulary helped you sail through the antonym problems.

Jotting down a quick note about each paragraph will help you understand the content of each one. This will come in handy when you tackle the RC problems. It is highly unlikely that any of these problems will be a question as straightforward as, "What would be a good title for this essay?" Instead, expect to see convoluted problems like:

"If Dr. Andersen changes her mind about the social behavior of *nudibranchs*, then which of the following statements would she be most likely to agree with?"

Faced with this twisted piece of writing, you would first have to go into the passage to the section where Dr. Andersen discusses *nudibranchs* and/or social behavior. Then you would have to infer what she thinks about it, figure out what the opposite of that is, and then look through the answer choices to find the paraphrased answer that matches this opposite inference.

Tip

> You would have to *infer* what Dr. Andersen thinks because it is very doubtful anything will be given to you on a tough RC question. Nothing will just be waiting in the passage; you will have to take the clues in the passage and use them to deduce the information you need.

The additional work required to answer a hard RC problem makes these questions more involved and time-consuming. Yet they are still very solvable if you take the time to look back into the passage and infer the answer that you need.

Free Words! Free Words!

To acquire a comprehensive list of all the words that might appear on the GRE, simply go down to your local bookstore and look for a dictionary of at least 1,500 pages. For a slightly smaller list of advanced words, try the set below. There's no way to tell which batch of words you will get on your particular GRE, but any increase in your stockpile of tough words increases your odds of succeeding on the test.

To really get the most out of this list, write out each word and then provide a definition and sample sentence. You can put this list of words in a notebook, handheld PDA, or plain old flash cards. Use whatever media you are most comfortable with, but make sure to compile the list in a way that makes it easy for you to review the contents.

If you are willing to take the time, get a thesaurus and include a list of possible antonyms for each applicable word. Some words won't have antonyms, but many of them will, and studying the antonyms of difficult words has obvious, obvious advantages. Some of those antonyms will be hard words themselves, giving you an easy way to increase your vocabulary even further.

Take It to the Next Level

PETERSON'S
getting you there

The Word List

Word Origin | Latin brevis = *short. Also found in English* brevity.

abbreviate (verb)   To make briefer, to shorten. *Because time was running out, the speaker was forced to abbreviate his remarks.* abbreviation (noun).

aberration (noun)   A deviation from what is normal or natural, an abnormality. *Jack's extravagant lunch at Lutece was an aberration from his usual meal, a peanut butter sandwich and a diet soda.* aberrant (adjective).

abeyance (noun)   A temporary lapse in activity; suspension. *In the aftermath of the bombing, all normal activities were held in abeyance.*

abjure (verb)   To renounce or reject; to officially disclaim. *While being tried by the inquisition in 1633, Galileo abjured all his writings holding that Earth and other planets revolved around the sun.*

Word Origin | Latin abradare = *to scrape. Also found in English* abrasive.

abrade (verb)   To irritate by rubbing; to wear down in spirit. *Olga's "conditioning facial" abraded Sabrina's skin so severely that she vowed never to let anyone's hands touch her face again.* abrasion (noun).

abridge (verb)   To shorten, to reduce. *The Bill of Rights is designed to prevent Congress from abridging the rights of Americans.* abridgment (noun).

abrogate (verb)   To nullify, to abolish. *During World War II, the United States abrogated the rights of Japanese Americans by detaining them in internment camps.* abrogation (noun).

abscond (verb)   To make a secret departure, to elope. *Theresa will never forgive her daughter, Elena, for absconding to Miami with Philip when they were only 17.*

accretion (noun)   A gradual build-up or enlargement. *My mother's house is a mess due to her steady accretion of bric-a-brac and her inability to throw anything away.*

adjunct (noun)   Something added to another thing, but not a part of it; an associate or assistant. *While Felix and Fritz were adjuncts to Professor Himmelman during his experiments in electrodynamics, they did not receive credit when the results were published.*

adroit (adjective)   Skillful, adept. *The writer Laurie Colwin was particularly adroit at concocting love stories involving admirable and quirky female heroines and men who deserve them.*

adulterate (verb)   To corrupt, to make impure. *Unlike the chickens from the large poultry companies, Murray's free-roaming chickens have not been adulterated with hormones and other additives.*

Word Origin   Latin vertere = *to turn. Also found in English* adversary, adverse, reverse, vertical, *and* vertigo.

adversary (noun)   An enemy or opponent. *When the former Soviet Union became an American ally, the United States lost its last major international adversary.* adverse (adjective).

aesthete (noun)   Someone devoted to beauty and to beautiful things. *A renowned aesthete, Oscar Wilde was the center of a group that glorified beauty and adopted the slogan "art for art's sake."* aesthetic (adjective).

affability (noun)   The quality of being easy to talk to and gracious. *Affability is a much-desired trait in any profession that involves dealing with many people on a daily basis.* affable (adjective).

affected (adjective)   False, artificial. *At one time, Japanese women were taught to speak in an affected high-pitched voice, which was thought girlishly attractive.* affect (verb), affectation (noun).

affinity (noun)   A feeling of shared attraction, kinship; a similarity. *When they first fell in love, Andrew and Tanya marveled over their affinity for bluegrass music, obscure French poetry, and beer taken with a squirt of lemon juice. People often say there is a striking affinity between dogs and their owners (but please don't tell Clara that she and her bassett hound are starting to resemble each other).*

Take It to the Next Level

167

aggrandize (verb) To make bigger or greater; to inflate. *When he was mayor of New York City, Ed Koch was renowned for aggrandizing his accomplishments and strolling through city events shouting, "How'm I doing?"* aggrandizement (noun).

agitation (noun) A disturbance; a disturbing feeling of upheaval and excitement. *After the CEO announced the coming layoffs, the employees' agitation was evident as they remained in the auditorium talking excitedly among themselves.* agitated (adjective), agitate (verb).

alias (noun) An assumed name. *Determined not to reveal his upper-class roots, Harold Steerforth Hetherington III went under the alias of "Hound Dog" when playing trumpet in his blues band.*

allegiance (noun) Loyalty or devotion shown to one's government or to a person, group, or cause. *At the moving naturalization ceremony, forty-three new Americans from twenty-five lands swore allegiance to the United States.*

allocate (verb) To apportion for a specific purpose; to distribute. *The president talked about the importance of education and health care in his State of the Union address, but, in the end, the administration did not allocate enough resources for these pressing concerns.* allocation (noun).

amalgamate (verb) To blend thoroughly. *The tendency of grains to sort when they should mix makes it difficult for manufacturers to create powders that are amalgamated.* amalgamation (noun).

ameliorate (verb) To make something better or more tolerable. *The living conditions of the tenants were certainly ameliorated when the landlord finally installed washing machines and dryers in the basement.* amelioration (noun).

amortize (verb) To pay off or reduce a debt gradually through periodic payments. *If you don't need to take a lump sum tax deduction, it's best to amortize large business expenditures by spreading the cost out over several years.*

amplify (verb)   To enlarge, expand, or increase. *Uncertain as to whether they understood, the students asked the teacher to amplify his explanation.* amplification (noun).

Word Origin   Greek chronos = *time. Also found in English* chronic, chronicle, chronograph, chronology, *and* synchronize.

anachronistic (adjective)   Out of the proper time. *The reference, in Shakespeare's* Julius Caesar, *to "the clock striking twelve" is anachronistic, since there were no striking timepieces in ancient Rome.* anachronism (noun).

anarchy (noun)   Absence of law or order. *For several months after the Nazi government was destroyed, there was no effective government in parts of Germany, and anarchy ruled.* anarchic (adjective).

animosity (noun)   Hostility, resentment. *During the last debate, the candidates could no longer disguise their animosity and began to trade accusations and insults.*

anomaly (noun)   Something different or irregular. *The tiny planet Pluto, orbiting next to the giants Jupiter, Saturn, and Neptune, has long appeared to be an anomaly.* anomalous (adjective).

antagonism (noun)   Hostility, conflict, opposition. *As more and more reporters investigated the Watergate scandal, antagonism between the Nixon administration and the press increased.* antagonistic (adjective), antagonize (verb).

Word Origin   Greek pathos = *suffering. Also found in English* apathy, empathy, pathetic, pathos, *and* sympathy.

antipathy (noun)   A long-held feeling of dislike or aversion. *When asked why he didn't call for help immediately after his wife fell into a coma, the defendant emphasized his wife's utter antipathy to doctors.*

apprehension (noun)   A feeling of fear or foreboding; an arrest. *The peculiar feeling of apprehension that Harold Pinter creates in his plays derives as much from the long silences between speeches as from the speeches themselves. The policewoman's dramatic apprehension of the gunman took place in full view of the midtown lunch crowd.* apprehend (verb).

Take It to the Next Level

PETERSON'S getting you there

arabesque (noun)   Intricate decorative patterns involving intertwining lines and sometimes incorporating flowers, animals, and fruits. *Borders of gold and fanciful arabesques surround the Arabic script on every page of this ancient edition of the* Koran.

Word Origin   Latin arbiter = *judge. Also found in English* arbiter, arbitrage, *and* arbitrate.

arbitrary (adjective)   Based on random or merely personal preference. *Both computers cost the same and had the same features, so in the end I made an arbitrary decision about which one to buy.*

archaic (adjective)   Old-fashioned, obsolete. *Those who believe in "open marriage" often declare that they will not be bound by archaic laws and religious rituals, but state instead that love alone should bring two people together.* archaism (noun).

ardor (noun)   A strong feeling of passion, energy, or zeal. *The young revolutionary proclaimed his convictions with an ardor that excited the crowd.* ardent (adjective).

arid (adjective)   Very dry; boring and meaningless. *The arid climate of Arizona makes farming difficult. Some find the law a fascinating topic, but for me it is an arid discipline.* aridity (noun).

Word Origin   Latin articulus I = joint, division. Also found in English arthritis, article, *and* inarticulate.

articulate (adjective)   To express oneself clearly and effectively. *Compared to George Bush, with his stammering and his frequently incomplete sentences, Bill Clinton was considered a highly articulate president.*

asperity (noun)   Harshness, severity. *Total silence at the dinner table, baths in icy water, prayers five times a day—these practices all contributed to the asperity of life in the monastery.*

assail (verb)   To attack with blows or words. *When the president's cabinet members rose to justify the case for military intervention in Iraq, they were assailed by many audience members who were critical of U.S. policy.* assailant (noun).

170

assay (verb)   To analyze for particular components; to determine weight, quality etc. *The jeweler assayed the stone pendant Gwyneth inherited from her mother and found it to contain a topaz of high quality.*

assimilate (verb)   To absorb into a system or culture. *New York City has assimilated one group of immigrants after another, from the Jewish, German, and Irish immigrants who arrived at the turn of the last century to the waves of Mexican and Latin American immigrants who arrived in the 1980s.* assimilated (adjective).

assuage (verb)   To ease, to pacify. *Knowing that the pilot's record was perfect did little to assuage Linnet's fear of flying in the two-seater airplane.*

audacious (adjective)   Bold, daring, adventurous. *Her plan to cross the Atlantic single-handed in a twelve-foot sailboat was an audacious, if not reckless, one.* audacity (noun).

authoritarian (adjective)   Favoring or demanding blind obedience to leaders. *Despite most Americans' strong belief in democracy, the American government has sometimes supported authoritarian regimes in other countries.* authoritarianism (noun).

authoritative (adjective)   Official, conclusive. *For over five decades, American parents regarded Doctor Benjamin Spock as the most authoritative voice on baby and child care.* authority (noun), authorize (verb).

avenge (verb)   To exact a punishment for or on behalf of someone. *In Shakespeare's tragedy* Hamlet, *the ghost of the dead king of Denmark visits his son, Prince Hamlet, and urges him to avenge his murder.*

aver (verb)   To claim to be true; to avouch. *The fact that the key witness averred the defendant's innocence is what ultimately swayed the jury to deliver a "not guilty" verdict.*

avow (verb)   To declare boldly. *Immediately after Cyrus avowed his atheism at our church fund-raiser, there was a long, uncomfortable silence.* avowal (noun), avowed (adjective).

Take It to the Next Level

barren (adjective)   Desolate; infertile. *The subarctic tundra is a barren wasteland inhabited only by lichens and mosses. Women who try to conceive in their 40s are often barren and must turn to artificial means of producing a child.*

belligerent (adjective)   Quarrelsome, combative. *Mrs. Juniper was so belligerent toward the clerks at the local stores that they cringed when they saw her coming.*

belligerent (noun)   An opposing army, a party waging war. *The Union and Confederate forces were the belligerents in the American Civil War.*

Word Origin	Latin bene = *well. Also found in English* benediction, benefactor, beneficent, beneficial, benefit, *and* benign.

benevolent (adjective)   Wishing or doing good. *In old age, Carnegie used his wealth for benevolent purposes, donating large sums to found libraries and schools around the country.* benevolence (noun).

berate (verb)   To scold or criticize harshly. *The judge angrily berated the two lawyers for their childish and unprofessional behavior.*

boggle (verb)   To overwhelm with amazement. *The ability of physicists to isolate the most infinitesimal particles of matter truly boggles the mind.*

bogus (adjective)   Phony, a sham. *Senior citizens are often the target of telemarketing scams pushing bogus investment opportunities.*

bombastic (adjective)   Inflated or pompous in style. *Old-fashioned bombastic political speeches don't work on television, which demands a more intimate, personal style of communication.* bombast (noun).

boor (noun)   Crude, insensitive and overbearing. *Harold was well-known to be a boor; at parties he horrified people with stories of his past sexual exploits and old, off-color jokes.* boorish (adjective).

brazenly (adverb)   Acting with disrespectful boldness. *Some say that the former White House intern brazenly threw herself at the president, but the American public will probably never know the full truth.* brazen (adjective).

broach (verb)   To bring up an issue for discussion, to propose. *Knowing my father's strictness about adhering to a budget, I just can't seem to broach the subject of my massive credit-card debt.*

burgeon (verb)   To bloom, literally or figuratively. *Due to the extremely mild winter, the forsythia burgeoned as early as March. The story of two prison inmates in Manuel Puig's play* The Kiss of The Spiderwoman *is testimony that tenderness can burgeon in the most unlikely places.*

burnish (verb)   To shine by polishing, literally or figuratively. *After stripping seven layers of old paint off the antique door, the carpenter stained the wood and burnished it to a rich hue. When Bill Gates, the wealthiest man in the country, decided to endorse the Big Bertha line of Golf Clubs, many suggested that he was trying to burnish his image as a "regular guy."*

buttress (noun)   Something that supports or strengthens. *The endorsement of the American Medical Association is a powerful buttress for the claims made on behalf of this new medicine.* buttress (verb).

cacophony (noun)   Discordant sounds; dissonance. *In the minutes before classes start, the high school's halls are filled with a cacophony of shrieks, shouts, banging locker doors, and pounding feet.* cacophonous (adjective).

cadge (verb)   To beg for, to sponge. *Few in our crowd want to go out on the town with Piper, since he routinely cadges cigarettes, subway tokens, and drinks.*

calibrate (verb)   To determine or mark graduations (of a measuring instrument); to adjust or finely tune. *We tried to calibrate the heating to Rufus's liking, but he still ended up shivering in our living room.* calibration (noun).

castigate (verb)   To chastise; to punish severely. *The editor castigated Bob for repeatedly failing to meet his deadlines.* castigation (noun).

catalytic (adjective)   Bringing about, causing, or producing some result. *The conditions for revolution existed in America by 1765; the disputes about taxation that arose during the following decade were the catalytic events that sparked the rebellion.* catalyze (verb).

Word Origin	Greek kaustikos = *burning. Also found in English* holocaust.

caustic (adjective)   Burning, corrosive. *No pretensions were safe when the famous satirist H. L. Mencken unleashed his caustic wit.*

chaos (noun)   Disorder, confusion, chance. *The first few moments after the explosion were pure chaos: No one was sure what had happened, and the area was filled with people running and yelling.* chaotic (adjective).

charisma (noun)   Dynamic charm or appeal. *Eva Peron was such a fiery orator and had so much charisma that she commanded an enormous political following.* charismatic (adjective).

chary (adjective)   Slow to accept, cautious. *Yuan was chary about going out with Xinhua, since she had been badly hurt in her previous relationship.*

chronology (noun)   An arrangement of events by order of occurrence, a list of dates; the science of time. *If you ask Susan about her 2-year-old son, she will give you a chronology of his accomplishments and childhood illnesses, from the day he was born to the present. The village of Copan was where Mayan astronomical learning, as applied to chronology, achieved its most accurate expression in the famous Mayan calendar.* chronological (adjective).

churlish (adjective)   Coarse and ill-mannered. *Few journalists were eager to interview the aging film star, since he was reputed to be a churlish, uncooperative subject.* churl (noun).

Word Origin
Latin circus = *circle. Also found in English* circumference, circumnavigate, circumscribe, *and* circumvent.

circumspect (adjective) Prudent, cautious. *After he had been acquitted of the sexual harassment charge, the sergeant realized he would have to be more circumspect in his dealings with the female cadets.* circumspection (noun).

cleave (verb) NOTE: A tricky verb that can mean either to stick closely together or to split apart. (Pay attention to context.) *The more abusive his father became, the more Timothy cleaved to his mother and refused to let her out of his sight. Sometimes a few words carelessly spoken are enough to cleave a married couple and leave the relationship in shambles.* cleavage (noun).

coagulant (noun) Any material that causes another to thicken or clot. *Hemophilia is characterized by excessive bleeding from even the slightest cut and is caused by a lack of one of the coagulants necessary for blood clotting.* coagulate (verb).

coalesce (verb) To fuse, to unite. *The music we know as jazz coalesced from diverse elements from many musical cultures, including those of West Africa, America, and Europe.* coalescence (noun).

coerce (verb) To force someone either to do something or to refrain from doing something. *The Miranda ruling prevents police from coercing a confession by forcing them to read criminals their rights.* coercion (noun).

cogent (adjective) Forceful and convincing. *The committee members were won over to the project by the cogent arguments of the chairman.* cogency (noun).

Word Origin
Latin mensura = *to measure. Also found in English* measure, immeasurable, immense, *and* mensuration.

commensurate (adjective) Aligned with, proportional. *Many Ph.D.s in the humanities do not feel their paltry salaries are commensurate with their abilities, their experience, or the heavy workload they are asked to bear.*

Take It to the Next Level

commingle (verb) To blend, to mix. *Just as he had when he was only five years old, Elmer did not allow any of the foods on his plate to commingle: The beans must not merge with the rice nor the chicken rub shoulders with the broccoli!*

complaisant (adjective) Tending to bow to others' wishes; amiable. *Of the two Dashwood sisters, Elinor was the more complaisant, often putting the strictures of society and family above her own desires.* complaisance (noun).

compound (verb) To intensify, to exacerbate. *When you make a faux pas, my father advised me, don't compound the problem by apologizing profusely; just say you're sorry and get on with life!*

conceivable (adjective) Possible, imaginable. *It's possible to find people with every conceivable interest by surfing the World Wide Web—from fans of minor film stars to those who study the mating habits of crustaceans.* conception (noun).

concur (verb) To agree, to approve. *We concur that a toddler functions best on a fairly reliable schedule; however, my husband tends to be a bit more rigid than I am.* concurrence (noun).

condensation (noun) A reduction to a denser form (from steam to water); an abridgment of a literary work. *The condensation of humidity on the car's windshield made it difficult for me to see the road. It seems as though every beach house I've ever rented features a shelf full of Reader's Digest condensations of b-grade novels.* condense (verb).

condescending (adjective) Having an attitude of superiority toward another; patronizing. *"What a cute little car!" she remarked in a condescending fashion. "I suppose it's the nicest one someone like you could afford!"* condescension (noun).

condone (verb) To overlook, to permit to happen. *Schools with Zero Tolerance policies do not condone alcohol, drugs, vandalism, or violence on school grounds.*

congruent (adjective) Coinciding; harmonious. *Fortunately, the two employees who had been asked to organize the department had congruent views on the budget.* congruence (noun).

Word Origin Latin jungere = *to join. Also found in English* injunction, junction, *and* juncture.

conjunction (noun) The occurrence of two or more events together in time or space; in astronomy, the point at which two celestial bodies have the least separation. *Low inflation, occurring in conjunction with low unemployment and relatively low interest rates, has enabled the United States to enjoy a long period of sustained economic growth. The moon is in conjunction with the sun when it is new; if the conjunction is perfect, an eclipse of the sun will occur.* conjoin (verb).

consolation (noun) Relief or comfort in sorrow or suffering. *Although we miss our dog very much, it is a consolation to know that she died quickly, without much suffering.* console (verb).

consternation (noun) Shock, amazement, dismay. *When a voice in the back of the church shouted out, "I know why they should not be married!" the entire gathering was thrown into consternation.*

convergence (noun) The act of coming together in unity or similarity. *A remarkable example of evolutionary convergence can be seen in the shark and the dolphin, two sea creatures that developed from different origins to become very similar in form and appearance.* converge (verb).

Word Origin Latin vivere = *to live. Also found in English* revive, vital, vivid, *and* vivisection.

conviviality (noun) Fond of good company and eating and drinking. *The conviviality of my fellow employees seemed to turn every staff meeting into a party, complete with snacks, drinks, and lots of hearty laughter.* convivial (adjective).

Word Origin Latin volvere = *to roll. Also found in English* devolve, involve, revolution, revolve, *and* voluble.

convoluted (adjective) Twisting, complicated, intricate. *Income tax law has become so convoluted that it's easy for people to violate it completely by accident.* convolute (verb), convolution (noun).

Take It to the Next Level

PETERSON'S
getting you there

cordon (verb)   To form a protective or restrictive barrier. *Well before the Academy Awards ceremony began, the police cordoned off the hordes of fans who were desperate to ogle the arriving stars.* cordon (noun).

corral (verb)   To enclose, to collect, to gather. *Tyrone couldn't enjoy the wedding at all, since he spent most of his time corralling his two children into the reception room and preventing them from running amok through the Potters' mansion.* corral (noun).

corroborating (adjective)   Supporting with evidence; confirming. *A passerby who had witnessed the crime gave corroborating testimony about the presence of the accused person.* corroborate (verb), corroboration (noun).

corrosive (adjective)   Eating away, gnawing, or destroying. *Years of poverty and hard work had a corrosive effect on her strength and beauty.* corrode (verb), corrosion (noun).

cosmopolitanism (noun)   International sophistication; worldliness. *Budapest is known for its cosmopolitanism, perhaps because it was the first Eastern European city to be more open to capitalism and influences from the West.* cosmopolitan (adjective).

covert (adjective)   Secret, clandestine. *The CIA has often been criticized for its covert operations in the domestic policies of foreign countries, such as the failed Bay of Pigs operation in Cuba.*

covetous (adjective)   Envious, particularly of another's possessions. *Benita would never admit to being covetous of my new sable jacket, but I found it odd that she couldn't refrain from trying it on each time we met.* covet (verb).

craven (adjective)   Cowardly. *Local Gay and Lesbian activists were outraged by the craven behavior of a policeman who refused to come to the aid of an HIV-positive accident victim.*

credulous (adjective)   Ready to believe; gullible. *Elaine was not very credulous of the explanation Serge gave for his acquisition of the Matisse lithograph.* credulity (noun).

cryptic (adjective)   Puzzling, ambiguous. *I was puzzled by the cryptic message left on my answering machine about "a shipment of pomegranates from an anonymous donor."*

culmination (noun)   The climax. *The Los Angeles riots, in the aftermath of the Rodney King verdict, were the culmination of long-standing racial tensions between the residents of South Central LA and the police.* culminate (verb).

culpable (adjective)   Deserving blame, guilty. *Although he committed the crime, because he was mentally ill he should not be considered culpable for his actions.* culpability (noun).

curmudgeon (noun)   A crusty, ill-tempered person. *Todd hated to drive with his Uncle Jasper, a notorious curmudgeon, who complained non-stop about the air-conditioning and Todd's driving.* curmudgeonly (adjective).

cursory (adjective)   Hasty and superficial. *Detective Martinez was rebuked by his superior officer for drawing conclusions about the murder after only a cursory examination of the crime scene.*

debilitating (adjective)   Weakening; sapping the strength of. *One can't help but marvel at the courage Steven Hawking displays in the face of such a debilitating disease as ALS.* debilitate (verb).

Word Origin   Latin celer = *swift. Also found in English* accelerate *and* celerity.

decelerate (verb)   To slow down. *Randall didn't decelerate enough on the winding roads, and he ended up smashing his new sports utility vehicle into a guard rail.* deceleration (noun).

decimation (noun)   Almost complete destruction. *Michael Moore's documentary* Roger and Me *chronicles the decimation of the economy of Flint, Michigan, after the closing of a General Motors factory.* decimate (verb).

decry (verb)   To criticize or condemn. *Cigarette ads aimed at youngsters have led many to decry the unfair marketing tactics of the tobacco industry.*

Take It to the Next Level

defamation (noun)   Act of harming someone by libel or slander. *When the article in* The National Enquirer *implied that she was somehow responsible for her husband's untimely death, Renata instructed her lawyer to sue the paper for defamation of character.* defame (verb).

defer (verb)   To graciously submit to another's will; to delegate. *In all matters relating to the children's religious education, Joy deferred to her husband, since he clearly cared more about giving them a solid grounding in Judaism.* deference (noun).

deliberate (verb)   To think about an issue before reaching a decision. *The legal pundits covering the O.J. Simpson trial were shocked by the short time the jury took to deliberate after a trial that lasted months.* deliberation (noun).

demagogue (noun)   A leader who plays dishonestly on the prejudices and emotions of his followers. *Senator Joseph McCarthy was a demagogue who used the paranoia and biases of the anti-communist 1950s as a way of seizing fame and considerable power in Washington.* demagoguery (noun).

Word Origin   Greek demos = *people. Also found in English* democracy, demographic, *and* endemic.

demographic (adjective)   Relating to the statistical study of population. *Three demographic groups have been the intense focus of marketing strategy: baby boomers, born between 1946 and 1964; baby busters, or the youth market, born between 1965 and 1976; and a group referred to as tweens, those born between 1977 and 1983.* demography (noun), demographics (noun).

demonstratively (adverb)   Openly displaying feeling. *The young congressman demonstratively campaigned for reelection, kissing every baby and hugging every senior citizen at the Saugerties Chrysanthemum festival.* demonstrative (adjective).

derisive (adjective)   Expressing ridicule or scorn. *Many women's groups were derisive of Avon's choice of a male CEO, since the company derives its $5.1 billion in sales from an army of female salespeople.* derision (noun).

derivative (adjective)   Imitating or borrowed from a particular source. *When a person first writes poetry, her poems are apt to be derivative of whatever poetry she most enjoys reading.* derivation (noun), derive (verb).

desiccate (verb)   To dry out, to wither; to drain of vitality. *The long drought thoroughly desiccated our garden; what was once a glorious Eden was now a scorched and hellish wasteland. A recent spate of books has debunked the myth that menopause desiccates women and affirmed, instead, that women often reach heights of creativity in their later years.* desiccant (noun), desiccation (noun).

despotic (adjective)   Oppressive and tyrannical. *During the despotic reign of Idi Amin in the 1970s, an estimated 200,000 Ugandans were killed.* despot (noun).

desultory (adjective)   Disconnected, aimless. *Tina's few desultory stabs at conversation fell flat as Guy just sat there, stony-faced; it was a disastrous first date.*

deviate (verb)   To depart from a standard or norm. *Having agreed upon a spending budget for the company, we mustn't deviate from it; if we do, we may run out of money before the year ends.* deviation (noun).

diatribe (noun)   Abusive or bitter speech or writing. *While angry conservatives dismissed Susan Faludi's* Backlash *as a feminist diatribe, it is actually a meticulously researched book.*

diffident (adjective)   Hesitant, reserved, shy. *Someone with a diffident personality is most likely to succeed in a career that involves little public contact.* diffidence (noun).

digress (verb)   To wander from the main path or the main topic. *My high school biology teacher loved to digress from science into personal anecdotes about his college adventures.* digression (noun), digressive (adjective).

PETERSON'S
getting you there

dirge (noun)   Song or hymn of grief. *When Princess Diana was killed in a car crash, Elton John resurrected his hit song "Candle in the Wind," rewrote it as "Good-bye England's Rose," and created one of the most widely heard funeral dirges of all time.*

disabuse (verb)   To correct a fallacy, to clarify. *I hated to disabuse Filbert, who is a passionate collector of musical trivia, but I had to tell him that the Monkees hadn't played their own instruments on almost all of their albums.*

disburse (verb)   To pay out or distribute (funds or property). *Jaime was flabbergasted when his father's will disbursed all of the old man's financial assets to Raymundo and left him with only a few sticks of furniture.* disbursement (noun).

discern (verb)   To detect, notice, or observe. *With difficulty, I could discern the shape of a whale off the starboard bow, but it was too far away to determine its size or species.* discernment (noun).

discordant (adjective)   Characterized by conflict. *Stories and films about discordant relationships that resolve themselves happily are always more interesting than stories about content couples who simply stay content.* discordance (noun).

discourse (noun)   Formal and orderly exchange of ideas, a discussion. *In the late twentieth century, cloning and other feats of genetic engineering became popular topics of public discourse.* discursive (adjective).

Word Origin   Latin credere = *to believe. Also found in English* credential, credible, credit, credo, credulous, *and* incredible.

discredit (verb)   To cause disbelief in the accuracy of some statement or the reliability of a person. *Although many people still believe in UFOs, among scientists the reports of "alien encounters" have been thoroughly discredited.*

discreet (adjective)   Showing good judgment in speech and behavior. *Be discreet when discussing confidential business matters—don't talk among strangers on the elevator, for example.* discretion (noun).

discrete (adjective)   Separate, unconnected. *Canadians get peeved when people can't seem to distinguish between Canada and the United States, forgetting that Canada has its own discrete heritage and culture.*

disparity (noun)   Difference in quality or kind. *There is often a disparity between the kind of serious, high-quality television people say they want and the low-brow programs they actually watch.* disparate (adjective).

Word Origin	Latin *simulare* = *to resemble. Also found in English* semblance, similarity, simulacrum, simultaneous, *and* verisimilitude.

dissemble (verb)   To pretend, to simulate. *When the police asked whether Nancy knew anything about the crime, she dissembled innocence.*

dissipate (verb)   To spread out or scatter. *The windows and doors were opened, allowing the smoke that had filled the room to dissipate.* dissipation (noun).

dissonance (noun)   Lack of music harmony; lack of agreement between ideas. *Most modern music is characterized by dissonance, which many listeners find hard to enjoy. There is a noticeable dissonance between two common beliefs of most conservatives: their faith in unfettered free markets and their preference for traditional social values.* dissonant (adjective).

distillation (noun)   Something distilled, an essence or extract. In chemistry, a process that drives gas or vapor from liquids or solids. *Sharon Olds's poems are powerful distillations of motherhood and other primal experiences. In Mrs. Hornmeister's chemistry class, our first experiment was to create a distillation of carbon gas from wood.* distill (verb).

diverge (verb)   To move in different directions. *Frost's poem "The Road Not Taken" tells of the choice he made when "Two roads diverged in a yellow wood."* divergence (noun), divergent (adjective).

diversify (verb)   To balance by adding variety. *Any financial manager will recommend that you diversify your stock portfolio by holding some less-volatile blue-chip stocks along with more growth-oriented technology issues.* diversification (noun), diversified (adjective).

Take It to the Next Level

divest (verb)   To rid (oneself) or be freed of property, authority, or title. *In order to turn around its ailing company and concentrate on imaging, Eastman Kodak divested itself of peripheral businesses in the areas of household products, clinical diagnostics, and pharmaceuticals.* divestiture (noun).

divulge (verb)   To reveal. *The people who count the votes for the Oscar awards are under strict orders not to divulge the names of the winners.*

dogmatic (adjective)   Holding firmly to a particular set of beliefs with little or no basis. *Believers in Marxist doctrine tend to be dogmatic, ignoring evidence that contradicts their beliefs or explaining it away.* dogma (noun), dogmatism (noun).

dolt (noun)   A stupid or foolish person. *Due to his frequent verbal blunders, politician Dan Quayle was widely considered to be a dolt.*

Word Origin	Latin dormire = *to sleep. Also found in English* dormitory.

dormant (adjective)   Temporarily inactive, as if asleep. *An eruption of Mt. Rainier, a dormant volcano in Washington state, would cause massive, life-threatening mud slides in the surrounding area. Bill preferred to think that his sex drive was dormant rather than extinct.* dormancy (noun).

dross (noun)   Something that is trivial or inferior; an impurity. *As a reader for the* Paris Review, *Julia spent most of her time sifting through piles of manuscripts to separate the extraordinary poems from the dross.*

dubious (adjective)   Doubtful, uncertain. *Despite the chairman's attempts to convince the committee members that his plan would succeed, most of them remained dubious.* dubiety (noun).

dupe (noun)   Someone who is easily cheated. *My cousin Ravi is such a dupe; he actually gets excited when he receives those envelopes saying "Ravi Murtugudde, you may have won a million dollars," and he even goes so far as to try claiming his prize.*

eccentricity (noun)   Odd or whimsical behavior. *Rock star Michael Jackson is now better known for his offstage eccentricities—such as sleeping in an oxygen tank, wearing a surgical mask, and building his own theme park—than for his onstage performances.* eccentric (adjective).

edifying (adjective)   Instructive, enlightening. *Ariel would never admit it to her high-brow friends, but she found the latest self-help best-seller edifying and actually helpful.* edification (noun), edify (verb).

Word Origin	Latin facere = *to do. Also found in English* facility, factor, facsimile, *and* faculty.

efficacy (noun)   The power to produce the desired effect. *While teams have been enormously popular in the workplace, there are some who now question their efficacy and say that "one head is better than ten."* efficacious (noun).

effrontery (noun)   Shameless boldness. *The sports world was shocked when a pro basketball player had the effrontery to choke the head coach of his team during a practice session.*

elaborate (verb)   To expand upon something; develop. *One characteristic of the best essayists is their ability to elaborate ideas through examples, lists, similes, small variations, and even exaggerations.* elaborate (adjective), elaboration (noun).

elegy (noun)   A song or poem expressing sorrow. *Thomas Gray's "Elegy Written in a Country Churchyard," one of the most famous elegies in Western literature, mourns the unsung, inglorious lives of the souls buried in an obscure, rustic graveyard.* elegiac (adjective).

embellish (verb)   To enhance or exaggerate; to decorate. *The long-married couple told their stories in tandem, with the husband outlining the plot and the wife embellishing it with colorful details.* embellished (adjective).

Take It to the Next Level

PETERSON'S
getting you there

embezzle (verb)   To steal money or property that has been entrusted to your care. *The church treasurer was found to have embezzled thousands of dollars by writing phony checks on the church bank account.* embezzlement (noun).

emollient (noun)   Something that softens or soothes. *She used a hand cream as an emollient on her dry, work-roughened hands.* emollient (adjective).

empirical (adjective)   Based on experience or personal observation. *Although many people believe in ESP, scientists have found no empirical evidence of its existence.* empiricism (noun).

emulate (verb)   To imitate or copy. *The British band Oasis is quite open about their desire to emulate their idols, the Beatles.* emulation (noun).

encomium (noun)   A formal expression of praise. *For many filmmakers, winning the Palm d'Or at the Cannes Film Festival is considered the highest encomium.*

enervate (verb)   To reduce the energy or strength of someone or something. *The stress of the operation left her feeling enervated for about two weeks.* enervation (noun).

engender (verb)   To produce, to cause. *Countless disagreements over the proper use of national forests and parklands have engendered feelings of hostility between ranchers and environmentalists.*

enhance (verb)   To improve in value or quality. *New kitchen appliances will enhance your house and increase the amount of money you'll make when you sell it.* enhancement (noun).

enigmatic (adjective)   Puzzling, mysterious. *Alain Resnais' enigmatic film* Last Year at Marienbad *sets up a puzzle that is never resolved: A man meets a woman at a hotel and believes he once had an affair with her—-or did he?* enigma (noun).

enmity (noun)   Hatred, hostility, ill will. *Long-standing enmity, like that between the Protestants and Catholics in Northern Ireland, is difficult to overcome.*

ensure (verb) To make certain; to guarantee. *In order to ensure a sufficient crop of programmers and engineers for the future, the United States needs to raise the quality of its math and science schooling.*

> **Word Origin** Latin aequus = *equal. Also found in English* equality, equanimity, *and* equation.

equable (adjective) Steady, uniform. *While many people can't see how Helena could possibly be attracted to "Boring Bruno," his equable nature is the perfect complement to her volatile personality.*

equivocate (verb) To use misleading or intentionally confusing language. *When Pedro pressed Renee for an answer to his marriage proposal, she equivocated by saying, "I've just got to know when your Mercedes will be out of the shop!"* equivocal (adjective), equivocation (noun).

epicure (noun) Someone who appreciates fine wine and fine food, a gourmand. *M.F.K. Fisher, a famous epicure, begins her book* The Gastronomical Me *by saying, "There is a communion of more than bodies when bread is broken and wine is drunk."* epicurean (adjective).

epithet (noun) Term or words used to characterize a person or thing, often in a disparaging way. *In her recorded phone conversations with Linda Tripp, Monica Lewinsky is said to have referred to President Clinton by a number of epithets, including "The Creep" and "The Big He."* epithetical (adjective).

> **Word Origin** Latin radix = *root. Also found in English* radical.

eradicate (verb) To destroy completely. *American society has failed to eradicate racism, although some of its worst effects have been reduced.* eradication (noun).

erudition (noun) Extensive knowledge, usually acquired from books. *When Dorothea first saw Mr. Casaubon's voluminous library she was awed, but after their marriage she quickly realized that erudition is no substitute for originality.* erudite (adjective).

Take It to the Next Level

PETERSON'S
getting you there

esoterica (noun)   Items of interest to a select group. *The fish symposium at St. Antony's College in Oxford explored all manner of esoterica relating to fish, as is evidenced in presentations such as "The Buoyant Slippery Lipids of the Escolar and Orange Roughy" or "Food on Board Whale Ships—from the Inedible to the Incredible."* esoteric (adjective).

espouse (verb)   To take up as a cause; to adopt. *No politician in America today will openly espouse racism, although some behave and speak in racially prejudiced ways.*

estimable (adjective)   Worthy of esteem and admiration. *After a tragic fire raged through Malden Mills, the estimable mill owner, Aaron Feuerstein, restarted operations and rebuilt the company within just one month.* esteem (noun).

eulogy (noun)   A formal tribute usually delivered at a funeral. *Most people in Britain applauded Lord Earl Spencer's eulogy for Princess Diana, not only as a warm tribute to his sister Diana but also as a biting indictment of the Royal Family.* eulogize (verb).

euphemism (noun)   An agreeable expression that is substituted for an offensive one. *Some of the more creative euphemisms for "layoffs" in current use are: "release of resources," "involuntary severance," "strengthening global effectiveness," and "career transition program."* euphemistic (adjective).

| **Word Origin** | Latin acer = *sharp. Also found in English* acerbity, acrid, *and* acrimonious. |

exacerbate (verb)   To make worse or more severe. *The roads in our town already have too much traffic; building a new shopping mall will exacerbate the problem.*

excoriation (noun)   The act of condemning someone with harsh words. *In the small office we shared, it was painful to hear my boss's constant excoriation of his assistant for the smallest faults—a misdirected letter, an unclear phone message, or even a tepid cup of coffee.* excoriate (verb).

exculpate (verb) To free from blame or guilt. *When someone else confessed to the crime, the previous suspect was exculpated.* exculpation (noun), exculpatory (adjective).

executor (noun) The person appointed to execute someone's will. *As the executor of his Aunt Ida's will, Phil must deal with squabbling relatives, conniving lawyers, and the ruinous state of Ida's house.*

exigent (adjective) Urgent, requiring immediate attention. *A two-year-old is likely to behave as if her every demand is exigent, even if it involves simply retrieving a beloved teddy bear from under the couch.* exigency (noun).

expedient (adjective) Providing an immediate advantage or serving one's immediate self-interest. *When the passenger next to her was strafed by a bullet, Sharon chose the most expedient means to stop the bleeding; she whipped off her pantyhose and made an impromptu, but effective, tourniquet.* expediency (noun).

extant (adjective) Currently in existence. *Of the seven ancient "Wonders of the World," only the pyramids of Egypt are still extant.*

Word Origin	Latin tenere = *to hold. Also found in English* retain, tenable, tenant, tenet, *and* tenure.

extenuate (verb) To make less serious. *Karen's guilt is extenuated by the fact that she was only 12 when she committed the theft.* extenuating (adjective), extenuation (noun).

extol (verb) To greatly praise. *At the party convention, one speaker after another took to the podium to extol the virtues of their candidate for the presidency.*

extraneous (adjective) Irrelevant, nonessential. *One review of the new Chekhov biography said the author had bogged down the book with far too many extraneous details, such as the dates of Chekhov's bouts of diarrhea.*

Take It to the Next Level

PETERSON'S
getting you there

extrapolate (verb)   To deduce from something known, to infer. *Meteorologists were able to use old weather records to extrapolate backward and compile lists of El Niño years and their effects over the last century.* extrapolation (noun).

extricate (verb)   To free from a difficult or complicated situation. *Much of the humor in the TV show* I Love Lucy *comes in watching Lucy try to extricate herself from the problems she creates by fibbing or trickery.* extricable (adjective).

facetious (adjective)   Humorous in a mocking way; not serious. *French composer Erik Satie often concealed his serious artistic intent by giving his works facetious titles such as "Three Pieces in the Shape of a Pear."*

facilitate (verb)   To make easier or to moderate. *When the issue of racism reared its ugly head, the company brought in a consultant to facilitate a discussion of diversity in the workplace.* facile (adjective), facility (noun).

fallacy (noun)   An error in fact or logic. *It's a fallacy to think that "natural" means "healthful"; after all, the deadly poison arsenic is completely natural.* fallacious (adjective).

fatuous (adjective)   Inanely foolish; silly. *Once backstage, Elizabeth showered the opera singer with fatuous praise and embarrassing confessions, which he clearly had no interest in hearing.*

fawn (verb)   To flatter in a particularly subservient manner. *Mildly disgusted, Pedro stood alone at the bar and watched Renee fawn over the heir to the Fabco Surgical Appliances fortune.*

feckless (adjective)   Weak and ineffective; irresponsible. *Our co-op board president is a feckless fellow who has let much-needed repairs go unattended while our maintenance fees continue to rise.*

feint (noun)   A bluff; a mock blow. *It didn't take us long to realize that Gaby's tears and stomachaches were all a feint, since they appeared so regularly at her bedtime.*

ferret (verb)   To bring to light by an extensive search. *With his repeated probing and questions, Fritz was able to ferret out the location of Myrna's safe deposit box.*

finesse (noun)   Skillful maneuvering; delicate workmanship. *With her usual finesse, Charmaine gently persuaded the Duncans not to install a motorized Santa and sleigh on their front lawn.*

florid (adjective)   Flowery, fancy; reddish. *The grand ballroom was decorated in a florid style. Years of heavy drinking had given him a florid complexion.*

Word Origin	Latin fluere = *to flow. Also found in English* affluent, effluvia, fluid, *and* influx.

flourish (noun)   An extraneous embellishment; a dramatic gesture. *The napkin rings made out of intertwined ferns and flowers were just the kind of flourish one would expect from Carol, a slavish follower of Martha Stewart.*

fluctuation (noun)   A shifting back and forth. *Investment analysts predict fluctuations in the Dow Jones Industrial Average due to the instability of the value of the dollar.* fluctuate (verb).

foil (verb)   To thwart or frustrate. *I was certain that Jerry's tendency to insert himself into everyone's conversations would foil my chances to have a private word with Helen.*

foment (verb)   To rouse or incite. *The petty tyrannies and indignities inflicted on the workers by upper management helped foment the walkout at the meat-processing plant.*

forestall (verb)   To hinder or prevent by taking action in advance. *The pilot's calm, levelheaded demeanor during the turbulence forestalled any hysteria among the passengers of Flight 268.*

fortuitous (adjective)   Lucky, fortunate. *Although the mayor claimed credit for the falling crime rate, it was really caused by a series of fortuitous accidents.*

Take It to the Next Level

PETERSON'S

getting you there

foster (verb)   To nurture or encourage. *The white-water rafting trip was supposed to foster creative problem solving and teamwork between the account executives and the creative staff at Apex Advertising Agency.*

fracas (noun)   A noisy fight; a brawl. *As Bill approached the stadium ticket window, he was alarmed to see the fracas that had broken out between a group of Giants fans and a man wearing a Cowboys jersey and helmet.*

functionary (noun)   Someone holding office in a political party or government. *The man shaking hands with the governor was a low-ranking Democratic Party functionary who had worked to garner the Hispanic vote.*

gainsay (verb)   To contradict or oppose; deny, dispute. *Dot would gainsay her married sister's efforts to introduce her to eligible men by refusing to either leave her ailing canary or give up her thrice-weekly bingo nights.*

garble (verb)   To distort or slur. *No matter how much money the Metropolitan Transit Authority spends on improving the subway trains, the public address system in almost every station seems to garble each announcement.* garbled (adjective).

garrulous (adjective)   Annoyingly talkative. *Claude pretended to be asleep so he could avoid his garrulous seatmate, a self-proclaimed expert on bonsai cultivation.*

Word Origin	Latin genus = *type or kind; birth. Also found in English* congenital, genetic, genital, genre, genuine, *and* genus.

generic (adjective)   General; having no brand name. *Connie tried to reduce her grocery bills by religiously clipping coupons and buying generic brands of most products.*

gist (noun)   The main point, the essence. *Although they felt sympathy for the victim's family, the jurors were won over by the gist of the defense's argument: There was insufficient evidence to convict.*

192

gouge (verb)   To cut out, to scoop out with one's thumbs or a sharp instrument; to overcharge, to cheat. *Instead of picking the lock with a credit card, the clumsy thieves gouged a hole in my door. The consumer watchdog group accused the clothing stores of gouging customers with high prices.*

guile (noun)   Deceit, duplicity. *In Margaret Mitchell's* Gone With the Wind, *Scarlett O'Hara uses her guile to manipulate two men and then is matched for wits by a third, Rhett Butler.* guileful (adjective).

gullible (adjective)   Easily fooled. *Terry was so gullible she actually believed Robert's stories of his connections to the Czar and Czarina.* gullibility (noun).

hackneyed (adjective)   Without originality, trite. *When someone invented the phrase, "No pain, no gain," it was clever and witty, but now it is so commonly heard that it seems hackneyed.*

harrow (verb)   To cultivate with a harrow; to torment or vex. *During grade school, my sister was harrowed mercilessly for being overweight.* harrowing (adjective) nerve-wracking, traumatic. *Jon Krakauer's harrowing book* Into Thin Air *chronicles the tragic consequences of leading groups of untrained climbers up Mt. Everest.*

haughty (adjective)   Overly proud. *The fashion model strode down the runway, her hips thrust forward and a haughty expression, something like a sneer, on her face.* haughtiness (noun).

hierarchy (noun)   A ranking of people, things, or ideas from highest to lowest. *A cabinet secretary ranks just below the president and vice president in the hierarchy of the government's executive branch.* hierarchical (adjective).

Word Origin | Greek homos = *same. Also found in English* homologous, homonym, *and* homosexual.

homogeneous (adjective)   Uniform, made entirely of one thing. *It's hard to think of a more homogenous group than those eerie children in* Village of the Damned, *who all had perfect features, white-blond hair, and silver, penetrating eyes.*

Take It to the Next Level

PETERSON'S
getting you there

hoodwink (verb) To deceive by trickery or false appearances; to dupe. *That was my cousin Ravi calling to say that he's been hoodwinked again, this time by some outfit offering time shares in a desolate tract of land in central Florida.*

hone (verb) To improve and make more acute or affective. *While she was a receptionist, Norma honed her skills as a stand-up comic by trying out jokes on the tense crowd in the waiting room.*

iconoclast (noun) Someone who attacks traditional beliefs or institutions. *Comedian Dennis Miller relishes his reputation as an iconoclast, though people in power often resent his satirical jabs.* iconoclasm (noun), iconoclastic (adjective).

idolatry (noun) The worship of a person, thing, or institution as a god. *In communist China, admiration for Mao resembled idolatry; his picture was displayed everywhere, and millions of Chinese memorized his sayings and repeated them endlessly.* idolatrous (adjective).

idyll (noun) A rustic, romantic interlude; poetry or prose that celebrates simple pastoral life. *Her picnic with Max at Fahnstock Lake was not the serene idyll she had envisioned; instead, they were surrounded by hundreds of other picnickers blaring music from their boom boxes and cracking open soda cans.* idyllic (adjective).

illicit (adjective) Illegal, wrongful. When Janet caught her 13-year-old son and his friend downloading illicit pornographic photos from the World Wide Web, she promptly pulled the plug on his computer.

illuminate (verb) To brighten with light; to enlighten or elucidate; to decorate (a manuscript). *The frosted-glass sconces in the dressing rooms at Le Cirque not only illuminate the rooms but make everyone look like a movie star. Alice Munro is a writer who can illuminate an entire character with a few deft sentences.*

immaterial (adjective) Of no consequence, unimportant. *"The fact that your travel agent is your best friend's son should be immaterial," I told Rosa; "If he keeps putting you on hold and acting nasty, just take your business elsewhere."*

194

immaculate (adjective)   Totally unblemished, spotlessly clean. *The cream-colored upholstery in my new Porsche was immaculate—that is, until a raccoon came in through the window and tracked mud across the seats.*

Word Origin   Latin mutare = *to change. Also found in English* immutable, mutant, *and* mutation.

immutable (adjective)   Incapable of change. *Does there ever come an age when we realize that our parents' personalities are immutable, when we can relax and stop trying to make them change?*

impartial (adjective)   Fair, equal, unbiased. *If a judge is not impartial, then all of her rulings are questionable.* impartiality (noun).

impassivity (noun)   Apathy, unresponsiveness. *Dot truly thinks that Mr. Right will magically show up on her door step, and her utter impassivity regarding her social life makes me want to shake her!* impassive (adjective).

imperceptible (adjective)   Impossible to perceive, inaudible, or incomprehensible. *The sound of footsteps was almost imperceptible, but Donald's paranoia had reached such a pitch that he immediately assumed he was being followed.*

imperturbable (adjective)   Marked by extreme calm, impassivity, and steadiness. *The proper English butler in Kazuo Ishiguro's novel* The Remains of the Day *appears completely imperturbable even when his father dies or when his own heart is breaking.*

impetuous (adjective)   Acting hastily or impulsively. *Ben's resignation was an impetuous act; he did it without thinking, and he soon regretted it.* impetuosity (noun).

Word Origin   Latin placare = *to please. Also found in English* complacent, placate, *and* placid.

implacable (adjective)   Unbending, resolute. *The state of Israel is implacable in its policy of never negotiating with criminals.*

Take It to the Next Level

implosion (noun)   To collapse inward from outside pressure. *While it is difficult to know what is going on in North Korea, no one can rule out a violent implosion of the North Korean regime and a subsequent flood of refugees across its borders.* implode (verb).

incessant (adjective)   Unceasing. *The incessant blaring of the neighbor's car alarm made it impossible for me to concentrate on my upcoming Bar exam.*

inchoate (adjective)   Only partly formed or formulated. *At editorial meetings, Nancy had a habit of presenting her inchoate book ideas before she had a chance to fully determine their feasibility.*

Word Origin	Latin *caedere* = *to cut. Also found in English* concise, decide, excise, incision, *and* precise.

incise (verb)   To carve into, to engrave. *My wife felt nostalgic about the old elm tree since we had incised our initials in it when we were both in high school.*

incisive (adjective)   Admirably direct and decisive. *Ted Koppel's incisive questions have made many politicians squirm and stammer.*

incongruous (adjective)   Unlikely. *Art makes incongruous alliances, as when punk rockers, Tibetan folk musicians, gospel singers, and beat poets shared the stage at the Tibet House benefit concert.* incongruity (noun).

incorrigible (adjective)   Impossible to manage or reform. *Lou is an incorrigible trickster, constantly playing practical jokes no matter how much his friends complain.*

incursion (noun)   A hostile entrance into a territory; a foray into an activity or venture. *It is a little-known fact that the Central Intelligence Agency organized military incursions into China during the 1950s. The ComicCon was Barbara's first incursion into the world of comic strip artists.*

indefatigable (adjective)   Tireless. *Eleanor Roosevelt's indefatigable dedication to the cause of human welfare won her affection and honor throughout the world.* indefatigability (noun).

196

indelicate (adjective)   Blunt, undisguised. *No sooner had we sat down to eat than Mark made an indelicate remark about my high salary.*

inevitable (adjective)   Unable to be avoided. *Once the Japanese attacked Pearl Harbor, U.S. involvement in World War II was inevitable.* inevitability (noun).

infer (verb)   To conclude, to deduce. *Can I infer from your hostile tone of voice that you are still angry about yesterday's incident?* inference (noun).

inimical (adjective)   Unfriendly, hostile; adverse or difficult. *Relations between Greece and Turkey have been inimical for centuries.*

inimitable (adjective)   Incapable of being imitated, matchless. *John F. Kennedy's administration dazzled the public, partly because of the inimitable style and elegance of his wife, Jacqueline.*

inopportune (adjective)   Awkward, untimely. *When Gus heard raised voices and the crash of breaking china behind the kitchen door, he realized that he'd picked an inopportune moment to visit the Fairlights.*

inscrutability (noun)   Quality of being extremely difficult to interpret or understand, mysteriousness. *I am still puzzling over the inscrutability of the package I received yesterday, which contained twenty pomegranates and a note that said simply "Yours."* inscrutable (adjective).

insensible (adjective)   Unaware, incognizant; unconscious, out cold. *It's a good thing that Marty was insensible to the titters and laughter that greeted his arrival in the ballroom. In the latest episode of police brutality, an innocent young man was beaten insensible after two cops stormed his apartment.*

insipid (adjective)   Flavorless, uninteresting. *Most TV shows are so insipid that you can watch them while reading or chatting without missing a thing.* insipidity (noun).

Take It to the Next Level

PETERSON'S
getting you there

insinuate (verb)   Hint or intimate; to creep in. *During an extremely unusual broadcast, the anchor man insinuated that the Washington bureau chief was having a nervous breakdown. Marla managed to insinuate herself into the Duchess of York's conversation during the "Weight Watchers" promotion event.* insinuation (noun).

insolence (noun)   An attitude or behavior that is bold and disrespectful. *Some feel that news reporters who shout accusatory questions at the president are behaving with insolence toward his high office.* insolent (adjective).

insoluble (adjective)   Unable to be solved, irresolvable; indissoluble. *Fermat's last theorem remained insoluble for over 300 years until a young mathematician from Princeton solved it in 1995. If you are a gum chewer, you probably wouldn't like to know that insoluble plastics are a common ingredient of most popular gums.*

insular (adjective)   Narrow or isolated in attitude or viewpoint. *New Yorkers are famous for their insular attitudes; they seem to think that nothing important has ever happened outside of their city.* insularity (noun).

intercede (verb)   To step in, to moderate; to mediate or negotiate on behalf of someone else. *After their rejection by the co-op board, Kevin and Sol asked Rachel, another tenant, to intercede for them at the next board meeting.* intercession (noun).

interim (noun)   A break or interlude. *In the interim between figure-skating programs, the exhausted skaters retreat to the "kiss and cry" room to wait for their scores.*

interpolate (verb)   To interject. *The director's decision to interpolate topical political jokes into his production of Shakespeare's* Twelfth Night *was not viewed kindly by the critics.* interpolation (noun).

intransigent (adjective)   Unwilling to compromise. *Despite the mediator's attempts to suggest a fair solution to the disagreement, the two parties were intransigent, forcing a showdown.* intransigence (noun).

198

intrinsically (adverb)   Essentially, inherently. *There is nothing intrinsically difficult about upgrading a computer's microprocessor, yet Al was afraid to even open up the hard drive.* intrinsic (adjective).

Word Origin	Latin unda = wave. Also found in English undulate.

inundate (verb)   To overwhelm; to flood. *When America Online first announced its flat-rate pricing, the company was inundated with new customers, and thus began the annoying delays in service.* inundation (noun).

invective (noun)   Insulting, abusive language. *I remained unscathed by his blistering invective because in my heart I knew I had done the right thing.*

invigorate (verb)   To give energy to, to stimulate. *As her car climbed the mountain road, Lucinda felt herself invigorated by the clear air and the cool breezes.* invigoration (noun).

irascible (adjective)   Easily provoked into anger, hot-headed. *Soup chef Al Yeganah, the model for Seinfeld's "Soup Nazi," is an irascible man who flies into a temper if his customers don't follow his rigid procedure for purchasing soup.* irascibility (noun).

jeopardize (verb)   To put in danger. *Terrorist attacks on civilians jeopardize the fragile peace in the Middle East.* jeopardy (noun).

jocular (adjective)   Humorous, amusing. *Listening to the CEO launch into yet another uproarious anecdote, Ted was frankly surprised by the jocular nature of the "emergency" board meeting.* jocularity (noun).

labyrinthine (adjective)   Extremely intricate or involved; circuitous. *Was I the only one who couldn't follow the labyrinthine plot of the movie L.A. Confidential? I was so confused I had to watch it twice to see "who did it."*

laconic (adjective)   Concise to the point of terseness; taciturn. *Tall, handsome, and laconic, the actor Gary Cooper came to personify the strong, silent American, a man of action and few words.*

Take It to the Next Level

199

PETERSON'S
getting you there

lambaste (verb)   To give someone a dressing-down; to attack someone verbally; to whip. *Once inside the locker room, the coach thoroughly lambasted the team for their incompetent performance on the football field.*

Word Origin	Latin laus = *praise. Also found in English* applaud, laud, laudatory, *and* plaudit.

laudable (adjective)   Commendable, praiseworthy. *The Hunt's Point nonprofit organization has embarked on a series of laudable ventures pairing businesses and disadvantaged youth.*

lethargic (adjective)   Lacking energy; sluggish. *Visitors to the zoo are surprised that the lions appear so lethargic, but, in the wild, lions sleep up to 18 hours a day.* lethargy (noun).

levy (verb)   To demand payment or collection of a tax or fee. *The environmental activists pushed Congress to levy higher taxes on gasoline, but the automakers' lobbyists quashed their plans.*

lien (noun)   A claim against a property for the satisfaction of a debt. *Nat was in such financial straits when he died that his Fishkill property had several liens against it and all of his furniture was being repossessed.*

limn (verb)   To outline in distinct detail; to delineate. *Like many of her novels, Edith Wharton's* The Age of Innocence *expertly limns the tyranny of New York's upper-class society in the 1800s.*

loquacity (noun)   Talkativeness, wordiness. *While some people deride his loquacity and his tendency to use outrageous rhymes, no one can doubt that Jesse Jackson is a powerful orator.* loquacious (adjective).

Word Origin	Latin lux = *light. Also found in English* elucidate, pellucid, *and* translucent.

lucid (adjective)   Clear and understandable. *Hawking's* A Short History of the Universe *is a lucid explanation of a difficult topic, modern scientific theories of the origin of the universe.* lucidity (noun).

200

magnanimous (adjective) Noble, generous. *When media titan Ted Turner pledged a gift of $1 billion to the United Nations, he challenged other wealthy people to be equally magnanimous.* magnanimity (noun).

maladroit (adjective) Inept, awkward. *It was painful to watch the young congressman's maladroit delivery of the nominating speech.*

malinger (verb) To pretend illness to avoid work. *During the labor dispute, hundreds of employees malingered, forcing the company to slow production and costing it millions in profits.*

malleable (adjective) Able to be changed, shaped, or formed by outside pressures. *Gold is a very useful metal because it is so malleable. A child's personality is malleable, and is often deeply influenced by things her parents say and do.* malleability (noun).

Word Origin	Latin mandare = *entrust, order. Also found in English* command, demand, *and* remand.

mandate (noun) Order, command. *The new policy on gays in the military went into effect as soon as the president issued his mandate about it.* mandate (verb), mandatory (adjective).

marginal (adjective) At the outer edge or fringe; of minimal quality or acceptability. *In spite of the trend toward greater paternal involvement in child-rearing, most fathers still have a marginal role in their children's lives. Jerry's GRE scores were so marginal that he didn't get accepted into the graduate schools of his choice.*

marginalize (verb) To push toward the fringes; to make less consequential. *Hannah argued that the designation of a certain month as "Black History Month" or "Gay and Lesbian Book Month" actually does a disservice to minorities by marginalizing them.*

martial (adjective) Of, relating to, or suited to military life. *My old teacher, Miss Woody, had such a martial demeanor that you'd think she was running a boot camp instead of teaching fifth grade. The military seized control of Myanmar in 1988, and this embattled country has been ruled by martial law since then.*

Take It to the Next Level

Word Origin	Latin medius = *middle. Also found in English* intermediate, media, *and* medium.

mediate (verb)   To reconcile differences between two parties. *During the baseball strike, both the players and the club owners expressed willingness to have the president mediate the dispute.* mediation (noun).

mercenary (adjective)   Doing something only for pay or for personal advantage. *People have criticized the U.S. motives in the Persian Gulf War as mercenary, pointing out that the U.S. would not have come to Kuwait's defense had it grown carrots rather than produced oil.* mercenary (noun).

mercurial (adjective)   Changing quickly and unpredictably. *The mercurial personality of Robin Williams, with his many voices and styles, made him a natural choice to play the part of the ever-changing genie in Aladdin.*

metamorphose (verb)   To undergo a striking transformation. *In just a century, book publishers have metamorphosed from independent, exclusively literary businesses to minor divisions in multimedia entertainment conglomerates.* metamorphosis (noun).

meticulous (adjective)   Very careful with details. *Watch repair calls for a craftsperson who is patient and meticulous.*

mettle (noun)   Strength of spirit; stamina. *Linda's mettle was severely tested while she served as the only female attorney at Smith, Futterweitt, Houghton, and Dobbs.* mettlesome (adjective).

mimicry (noun)   Imitation, aping. *The continued popularity of Elvis Presley has given rise to a class of entertainers who make a living through mimicry of "The King."* mimic (noun and verb).

minatory (adjective)   Menacing, threatening. *As soon as she met Mrs. Danforth, the head housemaid at Manderlay, the young bride was cowed by her minatory manner and quickly retreated to the morning room.*

mince (verb) To chop into small pieces; to speak with decorum and restraint. *Malaysia's prime minister, Mahathir Mohamad, is not a man known to mince words; he has accused satellite TV of poisoning Asia and has denounced the Australian press as "congenital liars."*

Word Origin	*Greek* anthropos = *human. Also found in English* anthropology, anthropoid, anthropomorphic, *and* philanthropy.

misanthrope (noun) Someone who hates or distrusts all people. *In the beloved Christmas classic,* It's a Wonderful Life, *Lionel Barrymore plays Potter, the wealthy misanthrope who is determined to make life miserable for everyone, and particularly for the young, idealistic George Bailey.* misanthropic (adjective), misanthropy (noun).

miscreant (adjective) Unbelieving, heretical; evil, villainous. *After a one-year run playing Iago in* Othello, *and then two years playing Bill Sikes in* Oliver, *Sean was tired of being typecast in miscreant roles.* miscreant (noun).

mitigate (verb) To make less severe; to relieve. *There's no doubt that Wallace committed the assault, but the verbal abuse Wallace had received helps to explain his behavior and somewhat mitigates his guilt.* mitigation (noun).

monopoly (noun) A condition in which there is only one seller of a certain commodity. *Wary of Microsoft's seeming monopoly of the computer operating-system business, rivals are asking for government intervention.* monopolistic (adjective).

monotonous (adjective) Tediously uniform, unchanging. *Brian Eno's "Music for Airports" is characterized by minimal melodies, subtle textures, and variable repetition, which I find rather bland and monotonous.* monotony (noun).

morose (adjective) Gloomy, sullen. *After Chuck's girlfriend dumped him, he lay around the house for a couple of days, refusing to come to the phone and feeling morose.*

Take It to the Next Level

PETERSON'S
getting you there

mutation (noun)   A significant change; in biology, a permanent change in hereditary material. *Most genetic mutations are not beneficial, since any change in the delicate balance of an organism tends to be disruptive.* mutate (verb).

Word Origin   Latin frangere = *to break. Also found in English* fraction, fractious, fracture, frangible, infraction, *and* refract.

nadir (noun)   Lowest point. *Pedro and Renee's marriage reached a new nadir last Christmas Eve when Pedro locked Renee out of the house upon her return from the supposed "business trip."*

nascent (adjective)   Newly born, just beginning. *While her artistry was still nascent, it was 15-year-old Tara Lipinski's technical wizardry that enabled her to win a gold medal in the 1998 Winter Olympics.* nascence (noun).

noisome (adjective)   Putrid, fetid, noxious. *We were convinced that the noisome odor infiltrating every corner of our building was evidence of a mouldering corpse.*

notorious (adjective)   Famous, especially for evil actions or qualities. *Warner Brothers produced a series of movies about notorious gangsters such as John Dillinger and Al Capone.* notoriety (noun).

Word Origin   Latin durus = *hard. Also found in English* durable *and* endure.

obdurate (adjective)   Unwilling to change; stubborn, inflexible. *Despite the many pleas he received, the governor was obdurate in his refusal to grant clemency to the convicted murderer.*

oblivious (adjective)   Unaware, unconscious. *Karen practiced her oboe solo with complete concentration, oblivious to the noise and activity around her.* oblivion (noun), obviousness (noun).

obscure (adjective)   Little known; hard to understand. *Mendel was an obscure monk until decades after his death, when his scientific work was finally discovered. Most people find the writings of James Joyce obscure; hence the popularity of books that explain the many odd references and tricks of language in his work.* obscure (verb), obscurity (noun).

obsolete (adjective)   No longer current; old-fashioned. *W. H. Auden said that his ideal landscape would contain water wheels, grain mills, and other forms of obsolete machinery.* obsolescence (noun).

obstinate (adjective)   Stubborn, unyielding. *Despite years of government effort, the problem of drug abuse remains obstinate.* obstinacy (noun).

obtuse (adjective)   Dull-witted, insensitive; incomprehensible, unclear, or imprecise. *Amy was so obtuse she didn't realize that Alexi had proposed marriage to her. French psychoanalyst Jacques Lacan's collection of papers, Ecrits, is notoriously obtuse, yet it has still been highly influential in linguistics, film theory, and literary criticism.*

obviate (verb)   Preclude, make unnecessary. *Truman Capote's meticulous accuracy and total recall obviated the need for note-taking when he wrote his account of a 1959 murder,* In Cold Blood.

odium (noun)   Intense feeling of hatred, abhorrence. *When the neighbors learned that a convicted sex offender was now living in their midst, they could not restrain their odium and began harassing the man whenever he left his house.* odious (adjective).

opprobrium (noun)   Dishonor, disapproval. *Switzerland recently came under public opprobrium when it was revealed that Swiss bankers had hoarded the gold the Nazis had confiscated from their victims.* opprobrious (adjective).

orthodox (adjective)   In religion, conforming to a certain doctrine; conventional. *George Eliot's relationship with George Lewes, a married journalist, offended the sensibilities of her more orthodox peers.* orthodoxy (noun).

Take It to the Next Level

PETERSON'S
getting you there

ossified (adjective)   In biology, to turn into bone; to become rigidly conventional and opposed to change. *His harsh view of co-education had ossified over the years so that he was now the only teacher who sought to bar girls from the venerable boys' school.* ossification (noun).

ostentatious (adjective)   Overly showy, pretentious. *To show off his new wealth, the financier threw an ostentatious party featuring a full orchestra, a famous singer, and tens of thousands of dollars' worth of food.* ostentation (noun).

ostracize (verb)   To exclude from a group. *In Biblical times, those who suffered from the disease of leprosy were ostracized and forced to live alone.* ostracism (noun).

paean (adjective)   A joyous expression of praise, gratitude, or triumph. *Choreographer Paul Taylor's dance "Eventide" is a sublime paean to remembered love, with couple after loving couple looking back as they embrace an unknown future.*

parody (noun)   An imitation created for comic effect; a caricature. *While the creators of the 1970s comedy series* All in the Family *intended Archie Bunker to be a parody of closed-mindedness in Americans, large numbers of people adopted Bunker as a working-class hero.*

parse (verb)   To break a sentence down into grammatical components; to analyze bit by bit. *In the wake of the sex scandal, journalists parsed every utterance by administration officials regarding the president's alleged promiscuity. At $1.25 million a day,* Titanic *is the most expensive movie ever made, but director James Cameron refused to parse the film's enormous budget for inquisitive reporters.*

partisan (adjective)   Reflecting strong allegiance to a particular party or cause. *The vote on the president's budget was strictly partisan: Every member of the president's party voted yes, and all others voted no.* partisan (noun).

pastoral (adjective)   Simple and rustic, bucolic, rural. *While industry grew and the country expanded westward, the Hudson River School of painters depicted the landscape as a pastoral setting where humans and nature could coexist.*

patron (noun)   A special guardian or protector; a wealthy or influential supporter of the arts. *Dominique de Menil used her considerable wealth to become a well-known patron of the arts; she and her husband owned a collection of more than 10,000 pieces ranging from cubist paintings to tribal artifacts.* patronize (verb).

peccadillo (noun)   A minor offense, a lapse. *What Dr. Sykes saw as a major offense—being addressed as Marge rather than Doctor—Tina saw as a mere peccadillo and one that certainly should not have lost her the job.*

pedantic (adjective)   Academic, bookish. *The men Hillary met through personal ads in the* New York Review of Books *were invariably pasty-skinned pedantic types who dropped the names of nineteenth-century writers in every sentence.* pedantry (noun).

pedestrian (adjective)   Unimaginative, ordinary. *The new Italian restaurant received a bad review due to its reliance on pedestrian dishes such as pasta with marinara sauce or chicken parmigiana.*

Word Origin	Latin fides = *faith. Also found in English* confide, confidence, fidelity, *and* infidel.

perfidious (adjective)   Disloyal, treacherous. *Although he was one of the most talented generals of the American Revolution, Benedict Arnold is remembered today as a perfidious betrayer of the patriot cause.* perfidy (noun).

peripatetic (adjective)   Moving or traveling from place to place; always on the go. *In Barbara Wilson's* Trouble in Transylvania, *peripatetic translator Cassandra Reilly is on the road again, this time to China by way of Budapest, where she plans to catch the TransMongolian Express.*

permeate (verb)   To spread through or penetrate. *Little by little, the smell of gas from the broken pipe permeated the house.*

personification (noun)   The embodiment of a thing or an abstract idea in human form. *Many people view Theodore Kaczynski, the killer known as the Unabomber, as the very personification of evil.* personify (verb).

Take It to the Next Level

PETERSON'S

getting you there

pervasive (adjective)   Spreading throughout. *As news of the disaster reached the town, a pervasive sense of gloom could be felt everywhere.* pervade (verb).

philistine (noun)   Someone who is smugly ignorant and uncultured. *A true philistine, Meg claimed she didn't read any book that wasn't either recommended by Oprah Winfrey or on the best-seller list.* philistine (adjective).

pith (noun)   The core, the essential part; in biology, the central strand of tissue in the stems of most vascular plants. *After spending seventeen years in psychoanalysis, Frieda had finally come face to face with the pith of her deep-seated anxiety.* pithy (adjective).

placate (verb)   To soothe or appease. *The waiter tried to placate the angry customer with the offer of a free dessert.* placatory (adjective).

placid (adjective)   Unmarked by disturbance; complacent. *Dr. Kahn was convinced that the placid exterior presented by Frieda in her early analysis sessions masked a deeply disturbed psyche.* placidity (noun).

plaintive (adjective)   Expressing suffering or melancholy. *In the beloved children's book* The Secret Garden, *Mary is disturbed by plaintive cries echoing in the corridors of gloomy Misselthwaite Manor.*

plastic (adjective)   Able to be molded or reshaped. *Because it is highly plastic, clay is an easy material for beginning sculptors to use.* plasticity (noun).

plausible (adjective)   Apparently believable. *The idea that a widespread conspiracy to kill the president has been kept secret by all the participants for over thirty years hardly seems plausible.* plausibility (noun).

platitude (noun)   A trite remark or saying; a cliché. *How typical of June to send a sympathy card filled with mindless platitudes like "One day at a time," rather than calling the grieving widow on the phone.* platitudinous (adjective).

plummet (verb)   To dive or plunge. *On October 27, 1997, the stock market plummeted by 554 points and left us all wondering if the bull market was finally over.*

polarize (adjective) To separate into opposing groups or forces. *For years, the abortion debate polarized the American people, with many people voicing views at either extreme and few people trying to find a middle ground.* polarization (noun).

ponderous (adjective) Unwieldy and bulky; oppressively dull. *Unfortunately, the film director weighed the movie down with a ponderous voice-over narrated by the protagonist as an old man.*

poseur (noun) Someone who pretends to be what he isn't. *Gerald had pretensions for literary stardom with his book proposal on an obscure World War II battle, yet most agents soon realized that the book would never be written and categorized him as a poseur.*

positivism (noun) A philosophy that denies speculation and assumes that the only knowledge is scientific knowledge. *David Hume carried his positivism to an extreme when he argued that our expectation that the sun will rise tomorrow has no basis in reason and is purely a matter of belief.* positivistic (adjective).

pragmatism (noun) A belief in approaching problems through practical rather than theoretical means. *Roosevelt's attitude toward the economic troubles of the Depression was based on pragmatism: "Try something," he said; "If it doesn't work, try something else."* pragmatic (adjective).

precedent (noun) An earlier occurrence that serves as an example for a decision. *In a legal system that reveres precedent, even defining the nature of a completely new type of dispute can seem impossible.* precede (verb).

precept (noun) A general principle or law. *One of the central precepts of Tai Chi Ch'uan is the necessity of allowing ki (cosmic energy) to flow through one's body in slow, graceful movements.*

precipitate (verb) To spur or activate. *In the summer of 1997, the selling off of the Thai baht precipitated a currency crisis that spread throughout Asia.*

Latin claudere = *to close. Also found in English* conclude, include, recluse, *and* seclude.

preclude (verb)   To prevent, to hinder. *Unfortunately, Jasmine's appointment at the New Age Expo precluded her attendance at our weekend Workshop for Shamans and Psychics.* preclusive (adjective), preclusion (noun).

precursor (noun)   A forerunner, a predecessor. *The Kodak Brownie camera, a small boxy camera made of jute board and wood, was the precursor to today's sleek 35mm cameras.* precursory (adjective).

preponderance (noun)   A superiority in weight, size, or quantity; a majority. *In Seattle, there is a great preponderance of seasonal affective disorder, or SAD, a malady brought on by light starvation during the dark Northwest winter.* preponderate (verb).

presage (verb)   To foretell, to anticipate. *According to folklore, a red sky at dawn presages a day of stormy weather.*

prescience (noun)   Foreknowledge or foresight. *When she saw the characteristic eerie yellowish-black light in the sky, Dorothy had the prescience to seek shelter in the storm cellar.* prescient (adjective).

presumptuous (adjective)   Going beyond the limits of courtesy or appropriateness. *The senator winced when the presumptuous young staffer addressed him as "Ted."* presume (verb), presumption (noun).

prevaricate (verb)   To lie, to equivocate. *When it became clear to the FBI that the mobster had threatened the 12-year-old witness, they could well understand why he had prevaricated during the hearing.*

Latin primus = *first. Also found in English* primate, primitive, primogeniture, *and* primodial.

primacy (noun)   State of being the utmost in importance; preeminence. *The anthropologist Ruth Benedict was an inspiration to Margaret Mead for her emphasis on the primacy of culture in the formation of an individual's personality.* primal (adjective).

pristine (adjective)   Pure, undefiled. *As climbers who have scaled Mt. Everest can attest, the trails to the summit are hardly in pristine condition and are actually strewn with trash.*

probity (noun)   Goodness, integrity. *The vicious editorial attacked the moral probity of the senatorial candidate, saying he had profited handsomely from his pet project, the senior-citizen housing project.*

procure (verb)   To obtain by using particular care and effort. *Through partnerships with a large number of specialty wholesalers, W.W. Grainger is able to procure a startling array of products for its customers, from bear repellent for Alaska pipeline workers to fork-lift trucks and toilet paper.* procurement (noun).

prodigality (noun)   The condition of being wastefully extravagant. *Richard was ashamed of the prodigality of his bride's parents when he realized that the cost of the wedding reception alone was more than his father earned in one year.* prodigal (adjective).

proliferate (verb)   To increase or multiply. *Over the past fifteen years, high-tech companies have proliferated in northern California, Massachusetts, and other regions.* proliferation (noun).

prolixity (noun)   A diffuseness; a rambling and verbose quality. *The prolixity of Sarah's dissertation on Ottoman history defied even her adviser's attempts to read it.* prolix (adjective).

prophetic (adjective)   Auspicious, predictive of what's to come. *We often look at every event leading up to a new love affair as prophetic—the flat tire that caused us to be late for work, the chance meeting in the elevator, the horoscope that argued "a new beginning."* prophecy (noun), prophesy (verb).

propagate (verb)   To cause to grow; to foster. *John Smithson's will left his fortune for the founding of an institution to propagate knowledge, leaving open whether that meant a university, a library, or a museum.* propagation (noun).

Take It to the Next Level

PETERSON'S
getting you there

propitiating (adjective)   Conciliatory, mollifying or appeasing. *Management's offer of a five-percent raise was meant as a propitiating gesture, yet the striking workers were unimpressed.* propitiate (verb).

propriety (noun)   Appropriateness. *Some people expressed doubts about the propriety of Clinton's discussing his underwear on MTV.*

proximity (noun)   Closeness, nearness. *Neighborhood residents were angry over the proximity of the proposed sewage plant to the local elementary school.* proximate (adjective).

pundit (noun)   Someone who offers opinions in an authoritative style. *The Sunday morning talk shows are filled with pundits, each with his or her own theory about this week's political news.*

Word Origin	Latin *pungere = to jab, to prick. Also found in English* pugilist, punctuate, and puncture.

pungency (noun)   Marked by having a sharp, biting quality. *Unfortunately, the pungency of the fresh cilantro overwhelmed the delicate flavor of the poached flounder.* pungent (adjective).

purify (verb)   To make pure, clean, or perfect. *The new water-treatment plant is supposed to purify the drinking water provided to everyone in the nearby towns.* purification (noun).

quiescent (adjective)   In a state of rest or inactivity; latent. *Polly's ulcer has been quiescent ever since her mother-in-law moved out of the condo, which was well over a year ago.* quiescence (noun).

quixotic (adjective)   Foolishly romantic, idealistic to an impractical degree. *In the novel* Shoeless Joe, *Ray Kinsella carries out a quixotic plan to build a baseball field in the hopes that past baseball greats will come to play there.*

quotidian (adjective)   Occurring every day; commonplace and ordinary. *Most of the time, we long to escape from quotidian concerns, but in the midst of a crisis we want nothing more than to be plagued by such simple problems as a leaky faucet or a whining child.*

raconteur (noun)   An excellent storyteller. *A member of the Algonquin Round Table, Robert Benchley was a natural raconteur with a seemingly endless ability to turn daily life and its irritations into entertaining commentary.*

rancorous (adjective)   Marked by deeply embedded bitterness or animosity. *While Ralph and Kishu have been separated for three years, their relationship is so rancorous that they had to hire a professional mediator just to discuss divorce arrangements.* rancor (noun).

rapacious (adjective)   Excessively grasping or greedy. *Some see global currency speculators like George Soros as rapacious parasites who destroy economies and then line their pockets with the profits.* rapacity (noun).

rarefied (adjective)   Of interest or relating to a small, refined circle; less dense, thinner. *Those whose names dot the society pages live in a rarefied world where it's entirely normal to dine on caviar for breakfast or order a $2,000 bottle of wine at Le Cirque. When she reached the summit of Mt. McKinley, Deborah could hardly breathe in the rarefied air.*

raucous (adjective)   Boisterous, unruly and wild. *Sounds of shouts and raucous laughter drifted out of the hotel room where Felipe's bachelor party was being held.*

reactionary (adjective)   Ultra conservative. *Every day, over twenty million listeners tune in to hear Rush Limbaugh spew his reactionary opinions about "feminazis" and environmental "fanatics."* reactionary (noun).

recede (verb)   To draw back, to ebb, to abate. *Once his hairline began to recede, Hap took to wearing bizarre accessories, like velvet ascots, to divert attention from it.* recession (noun).

reclusive (adjective)   Withdrawn from society. *During the last years of her life, Garbo led a reclusive existence, rarely appearing in public.* recluse (noun).

Take It to the Next Level

PETERSON'S
getting you there

reconcile (verb) To make consistent or harmonious. *Roosevelt's greatness as a leader can be seen in his ability to reconcile the differing demands and values of the varied groups that supported him.* reconciliation (noun).

recompense (noun) Compensation for a service rendered or to pay for damages. *The 5% of the estate that Phil received as executor of his Aunt Ida's will is small recompense for the headaches he endured in settling her affairs.* recompense (verb).

recondite (adjective) Profound, deep, abstruse. *Professor Miyaki's recondite knowledge of seventeenth-century Flemish painters made him a prized—if barely understood—member of the art history department.*

redemptive (adjective) Liberating and reforming. *While she doesn't attend formal church services, Carrie is a firm believer in the redemptive power of prayer.* redeem (verb), redemption (noun).

Word Origin	Latin frangere = *to break. Also found in English* fraction, fractions, fracture, frangible, infraction, and refract.

refractory (adjective) Stubbornly resisting control or authority. *Like a refractory child, Jill stomped out of the car, slammed the door, and said she would walk home, even though her house was 10 miles away.*

relevance (noun) Connection to the matter at hand; pertinence. *Testimony in a criminal trial may only be admitted to the extent that it has clear relevance to the question of guilt or innocence.* relevant (adjective).

reparation (noun) The act of making amends; payment of damages by a defeated nation to the victors. *The Treaty of Versailles, signed in 1919, formally asserted Germany's war guilt and ordered it to pay reparations to the allies.*

reproof (noun) A reprimand, a reproach or castigation. *Joe thought being grounded for one month was a harsh reproof for coming home late only once.* reprove (verb).

repugnant (adjective)   Causing dislike or disgust. *After the news broke about Mad Cow Disease, much of the beef-loving British public began to find the thought of a Sunday roast repugnant.*

requiem (noun)   A musical composition or poem written to honor the dead. *Many financial analysts think that the ailing typewriter company should simply say a requiem for itself and shut down; however, the CEO has other plans.*

repudiate (verb)   To reject, to renounce. *After it became known that Duke had been a leader of the Ku Klux Klan, most Republican leaders repudiated him.* repudiation (noun).

resilient (adjective)   Able to recover from difficulty. *A pro athlete must be mentally resilient, able to lose a game one day and come back the next with renewed enthusiasm and confidence.* resilience (noun).

resonant (adjective)   Full of special import or meaning. *I found the speaker's words particularly resonant because I, too, had served in Vietnam and felt the same mixture of shame and pride.* resonance (noun).

resplendent (adjective)   Glowing, shining. *In late December, midtown New York is resplendent with holiday lights and decorations.* resplendence (noun).

rite (noun)   Ceremony. *From October to May, the Patwin Indians of California's Sacramento Valley held a series of rites and dances designed to bring the tribe health and prosperity.*

rogue (noun)   A mischievously dishonest person; a scamp. *In Jane Austen's* Pride and Prejudice, *Wickham, a charming rogue, seduces Darcy's young sister Georgiana and later does the same thing with Kitty Bennett.*

ruffian (noun)   A brute, roughneck or bully. *In Dickens'* Oliver Twist, *Fagin instructs his gang of orphaned ruffians on the arts of picking pockets and shoplifting.*

rumination (noun)   The act of engaging in contemplation. *Marcel Proust's semi-autobiographical novel cycle,* Remembrance of Things Past, *is less a narrative than an extended rumination on the nature of memory.* ruminate (verb).

Take It to the Next Level

PETERSON'S
getting you there

sage (noun)   A person of great wisdom, a sagacious philosopher. *It was the Chinese sage Confucius who first taught what is now known the world over as "The Golden Rule."* sagacious (adjective), sagacity (noun).

Word Origin *Latin* salus = *health. Also found in English* salubrious, salutation, *and* salute.

salutary (adjective)   Restorative, healthful. *I find a short dip in an icy stream to be extremely salutary, although the health benefits of my bracing swims are, as yet, unclear.*

sanction (verb)   Support or authorize. *Even after a bomb exploded on the front porch of his home, the Reverend Martin Luther King Jr. refused to sanction any violent response and urged his angry followers to love their enemies.* sanctify (verb), sanction (noun).

sap (verb)   To exhaust, to deplete. *The exhaustive twelve-city reading tour so sapped the novelist's strength that she told her publicist that she hoped her next book would be a flop! While Uganda is making enormous economic strides under President Yoweri Musevini, rebel fighting has sapped much of the country's resources.*

satiate (verb)   To fulfill to or beyond capacity. *Judging by the current crop of films featuring serial killers, rape, ritual murder, gunslinging, and plain old-fashioned slugfests, the public appetite for violence has not yet been satiated.* satiation (noun), satiety (noun).

saturate (verb)   To drench or suffuse with liquid or anything that permeates or invades. *The hostess's furious dabbing at the tablecloth was in vain, since the spilt wine had already saturated the damask cloth.* saturation (noun), saturated (adjective).

scrutinize (verb)   To study closely. *The lawyer scrutinized the contract, searching for any detail that could pose a risk for her client.* scrutiny (noun).

scurvy (adjective)   Shabby, low. *I couldn't believe that Farouk was so scurvy as to open up my computer files and read my e-mail.*

Word Origin	*Latin* sequi = *to follow. Also found in English* consequence, sequel, *and* subsequent.

sequential (adjective) Arranged in an order or series. *The courses required for the chemistry major are sequential; you must take them in the prescribed order since each course builds on the previous ones.* sequence (noun).

sedulous (adjective) Diligent, industrious. *Those who are most sedulous about studying this vocabulary list are likely to breeze through the antonyms sections of their GRE exam.*

sidereal (adjective) Relating to the stars or the constellations. *Jacqueline was interested in matters sidereal and was always begging my father to take the dusty old telescope out of our garage.*

signatory (noun) Someone who signs an official document or petition along with others. *Alex urged me to join the other signatories and add my name to the petition against toxic sludge in organic foods, but I simply did not care enough about the issue. The signatories of the Declaration of Independence included John Adams, Benjamin Franklin, John Hancock, and Thomas Jefferson.*

sinuous (noun) Winding, circuitous, serpentine. *Frank Gehry's sinuous design for the Guggenheim Museum in Bilbao, Spain, has led people to hail the museum as the first great building of the twenty-first century.* sinuosity (noun).

specious (adjective) Deceptively plausible or attractive. *The infomercial for "Fat-Away" offered mainly specious arguments for a product that is, essentially, a heavy-duty girdle.*

spontaneous (adjective) Happening without plan or outside cause. *When the news of Kennedy's assassination hit the airwaves, people everywhere gathered in a spontaneous effort to express their shock and grief.* spontaneity (noun).

Take It to the Next Level

spurious (adjective) False, fake. *The so-called Piltdown Man, supposed to be the fossil of a primitive human, turned out to be spurious, though who created the hoax is still uncertain.*

splice (verb) To unite by interweaving separate strands or parts. *Amateur filmmaker Duddy Kravitz shocked and angered his clients by splicing footage of tribal rituals into his films of their weddings and bar mitzvahs.*

squander (verb) To use up carelessly, to waste. *Those who had made donations to the charity were outraged to learn that its director had squandered millions on fancy dinners, first-class travel, and an expensive apartment for entertaining.*

stanch (verb) To stop the flow. *When Edison began to bleed profusely, Dr. Munger stanched the blood flow by applying direct pressure to the wound.*

stint (verb) To limit, to restrain. *The British bed and breakfast certainly did not stint on the breakfast part of the equation; they provided us with fried tomatoes, fried sausages, fried eggs, smoked kippers, fried bread, fried mushrooms, and bowls of a cereal called "Wheatabix" (which tasted like cardboard).* stinting (adjective).

stolid (adjective) Impassive, unemotional. *The popular animated television series* King of the Hill *chronicles the woes of a stolid, conservative Texan confronting changing times.* stolidity (noun).

subordination (noun) The state of being subservient or treated as less valuable. *Heather left the naval academy because she could no longer stand the subordination of every personal whim or desire to the rigorous demands of military life.* subordinate (verb).

Word Origin Latin poena = *pain. Also found in English* impunity, penal, penalty, *and* punishment.

subpoena (noun)   An order of a court, legislation or grand jury that compels a witness to be present at a trial or hearing. *The young man's lawyer asked the judge to subpoena a boa constrictor into court on the grounds that the police had used the snake as an "instrument of terror" to coerce his confession.*

subside (verb)   To settle or die down. *The celebrated lecturer had to wait ten minutes for the applause to subside before he began his speech.*

subsidization (noun)   The state of being financed by a grant from a government or other agency. *Without subsidization, the nation's passenger rail system would probably go bankrupt.* subsidize (verb).

substantiated (adjective)   Verified or supported by evidence. *The charge that Nixon had helped to cover up crimes was substantiated by his comments about it on a series of audiotapes.* substantiate (verb), substantiation (noun).

subsume (verb)   To encompass or engulf within something larger. *In Alan Dershowitz's* Reversal of Fortune, *he makes it clear that his work as a lawyer subsumes his personal life.*

subterranean (adjective)   Under the surface of the earth. *Subterranean testing of nuclear weapons was permitted under the Nuclear Test Ban Treaty of 1963.*

summarily (adverb)   Quickly and concisely. *No sooner had I voiced my concerns about the new ad campaign than my boss put her hand on my elbow and summarily ushered me out of her office.*

superficial (adjective)   On the surface only; without depth or substance. *Her wound was only superficial and required no treatment except a light bandage. His superficial attractiveness hides the fact that his personality is lifeless and his mind is dull.* superficiality (noun).

Take It to the Next Level

PETERSON'S
getting you there

superimpose (verb) To place or lay over or above something. *The artist stirred controversy by superimposing portraits of certain contemporary politicians over images of such reviled historical figures as Hitler and Stalin.*

supersede (verb) To displace, to substitute or supplant. *"I'm sorry," the principal announced, "but today's afternoon classes will be superseded by an assembly on drug and alcohol abuse."*

supine (adjective) Prone. *One always feels rather vulnerable when wearing a flimsy paper gown and lying supine on a doctor's examining table.*

supposition (noun) Assumption, conjecture. *While most climate researchers believe that increasing levels of greenhouse gases will warm the planet, skeptics claim that this theory is mere supposition.* suppose (verb).

surge (noun) A gush; a swelling or sweeping forward. *When Mattel gave the Barbie Doll a makeover in the late eighties, coming out with dolls like doctor Barbie and astronaut Barbie, the company experienced a surge in sales.*

| **Word Origin** | *Latin* tangere = *to touch. Also found in English* contact, contiguous, tactile, tangent, *and* tangible. |

tangential (adjective) Touching lightly; only slightly connected or related. *Having enrolled in a class on African-American history, the students found the teacher's stories about his travels in South America only of tangential interest.* tangent (noun).

tedium (noun) Boredom. *For most people, watching even a fifteen-minute broadcast of Earth as seen from space would be an exercise in sheer tedium.* tedious (adjective).

temperance (noun) Moderation or restraint in feelings and behavior. *Most professional athletes practice temperance in their personal habits; too much eating or drinking and too many late nights, they know, can harm their performance.*

temperate (adjective) Moderate, calm. *The warm gulf streams are largely responsible for the temperate climate of the British Isles.*

220

tenuous (adjective)   Lacking in substance; weak, flimsy, very thin. *His tenuous grasp of the Spanish language was evident when he addressed Señor Chavez as "Señora."*

terrestrial (adjective)   Of the earth. *The movie* Close Encounters of the Third Kind *tells the story of the first contact between beings from outer space and terrestrial creatures.*

throwback (noun)   A reversion to an earlier type; an atavism. *The new Volkswagen Beetle, with its familiar bubble shape, looks like a throwback to the sixties, but it is actually packed with modern high-tech equipment.*

tiff (noun)   A small, almost inconsequential quarrel or disagreement. *Megan and Bruce got into a tiff when Bruce criticized her smoking.*

tirade (noun)   A long, harshly critical speech. *Reformed smokers, like Bruce, are prone to delivering tirades on the evils of smoking.*

torpor (noun)   Apathy, sluggishness. *Stranded in an airless hotel room in Madras after a 27-hour train ride, I felt such overwhelming torpor that I doubted I would make it to Bangalore, the next leg of my journey.* torpid (adjective).

tout (verb)   To praise highly, to brag publicly. *A much happier Eileen is now touting the benefits of Prozac, but, to tell you the truth, I miss her witty, self-lacerating commentaries.*

Word Origin | Latin tractare = *to handle. Also found in English* intractable, tractate, *and* traction.

tractable (adjective)   Obedient, manageable. *When he turned 3, Harrison suddenly became a tractable, well-mannered little boy after being, quite frankly, an unruly little monster!*

tranquillity (noun)   Freedom from disturbance or turmoil; calm. *Seeking the tranquillity of country life, she moved from New York City to rural Vermont.* tranquil (adjective).

Take It to the Next Level

221

PETERSON'S
getting you there

transgress (verb)   To go past limits; to violate. *If Iraq has developed biological weapons, then it has transgressed the UN's rules against manufacturing weapons of mass destruction.* transgression (noun).

transmute (verb)   To change in form or substance. *Practitioners of alchemy, a forebear of modern chemistry, tried to discover ways to transmute metals such as iron into gold.* transmutation (noun).

treacherous (adjective)   Untrustworthy or disloyal; dangerous or unreliable. *Nazi Germany proved to be a treacherous ally, first signing a peace pact with the Soviet Union, then invading. Be careful crossing the rope bridge; parts of the span are badly frayed and treacherous.* treachery (noun).

tremor (noun)   An involuntary shaking or trembling. *Michael still manages to appear calm and at ease despite the tremors caused by Parkinson's disease. Brooke felt the first tremors of the 1989 San Francisco earthquake while she was sitting in Candlestick Park watching a Giants baseball game.*

trenchant (adjective)   Caustic and incisive. *Essayist H. L. Mencken was known for his trenchant wit and was famed for mercilessly puncturing the American middle class (which he called the "booboisie").*

Word Origin	Latin trepidus = *alarmed. Also found in English* intrepid.

trepidation (noun)   Fear and anxiety. *After the tragedy of TWA flight 800, many previously fearless flyers were filled with trepidation whenever they stepped into an airplane.*

turbulent (adjective)   Agitated or disturbed. *The night before the championship match, Martina was unable to sleep, her mind turbulent with fears and hopes.* turbulence (noun).

turpitude (noun)   Depravity, wickedness. *Radical feminists who contrast women's essential goodness with men's moral turpitude can be likened to religious fundamentalists who make a clear distinction between the saved and the damned.*

222

tyro (noun)   Novice, amateur. *For an absolute tyro on the ski slopes, Gina was surprisingly agile at taking the moguls.*

unalloyed (adjective)   Unqualified, pure. *Holding his newborn son for the first time, Malik felt an unalloyed happiness that was unlike anything he had ever experienced in his 45 years.*

undermine (verb)   To excavate beneath; to subvert, to weaken. *Dot continued to undermine my efforts to find her a date by showing up at our dinner parties in her ratty old sweat suit.*

unfeigned (adjective)   Genuine, sincere. *Lashawn responded with such unfeigned astonishment when we all leapt out of the kitchen that I think she had had no inkling of the surprise party.*

univocal (adjective)   With a single voice. *While they came from different backgrounds and classes, the employees were univocal in their demands that the corrupt CEO resign immediately.*

unstinting (adjective)   Giving with unrestrained generosity. *Few people will be able to match the unstinting dedication and care that Mother Theresa lavished on the poor people of Calcutta.*

| **Word Origin** | Latin urbs = *city. Also found in English* suburb *and* urban. |

urbanity (noun)   Sophistication, suaveness and polish. *Part of the fun in a Cary Grant movie lies in seeing whether the star can be made to lose his urbanity and elegance in the midst of chaotic or kooky situations.* urbane (adjective).

usurious (adjective)   Lending money at an unconscionably high interest rate. *Some people feel that Shakespeare's portrayal of the Jew, Shylock, the usurious money lender in* The Merchant of Venice, *has enflamed prejudice against the Jews.* usury (adjective).

Take It to the Next Level

PETERSON'S
getting you there

Word Origin Latin validus = *strong. Also found in English* invalid, invaluable, prevail, *and* value.

validate (verb) To officially approve or confirm. *The election of the president is formally validated when the members of the Electoral College meet to confirm the verdict of the voters.* valid (adjective), validity (noun).

vapid (adjective) Flat, flavorless. *Whenever I have insomnia, I just tune the clock radio to Lite FM, and soon those vapid songs from the seventies have me floating away to dreamland.* vapidity (noun).

venal (adjective) Corrupt, mercenary. *Sese Seko Mobuto was the venal dictator of Zaire who reportedly diverted millions of dollars in foreign aid to his own personal fortune.* venality (noun).

veneer (noun) A superficial or deceptive covering. *Beneath her folksy veneer, Samantha is a shrewd and calculating businessperson just waiting for the right moment to pounce.*

venerate (verb) To admire or honor. *In Communist China, Mao Tse-Tung is venerated as an almost godlike figure.* venerable (adjective), veneration (noun).

veracious (adjective) Truthful, earnest. *Many people still feel that Anita Hill was entirely veracious in her allegations of sexual harassment during the Clarence Thomas confirmation hearings.* veracity (noun).

verify (verb) To prove to be true. *The contents of Robert L. Ripley's syndicated "Believe it or Not" cartoons could not be verified, yet the public still thrilled to reports of "the man with two pupils in each eye," "the human unicorn," and other amazing oddities.* verification (noun).

Word Origin Latin verus = *true. Also found in English* verisimilitude, veritable, *and* verity.

veritable (adjective) Authentic. *A French antiques dealer recently claimed that a fifteenth-century child-sized suit of armor that he purchased in 1994 is the veritable suit of armor worn by heroine Joan of Arc.*

224

vindictive (adjective)   Spiteful. *Paula embarked on a string of petty, vindictive acts against her philandering boyfriend, such as mixing dry cat food with his cereal and snipping the blooms off his prize African violets.*

viscid (adjective)   Sticky. *The 3M company's "Post-It," a simple piece of paper with one viscid side, has become as commonplace—and as indispensable—as the paper clip.*

viscous (adjective)   Having a gelatinous or gooey quality. *I put too much liquid in the batter, and so my Black Forest cake turned out to be a viscous, inedible mass.*

vitiate (verb)   To pollute, to impair. *When they voted to ban smoking from all bars in California, the public affirmed their belief that smoking vitiates the health of all people, not just smokers.*

vituperative (adjective)   Verbally abusive, insulting. *Elizabeth Taylor won an award for her harrowing portrayal of Martha, the bitter, vituperative wife of a college professor in Edward Albee's* Who's Afraid of Virginia Woolf? vituperate (verb).

volatile (adjective)   Quickly changing; fleeting, transitory; prone to violence. *Public opinion is notoriously volatile; a politician who is very popular one month may be voted out of office the next.* volatility (noun).

volubility (noun)   Quality of being overly talkative, glib. *As Lorraine's anxiety increased, her volubility increased in direct proportion, so during her job interview the poor interviewer couldn't get a word in edgewise.* voluble (adjective).

Word Origin	Latin vorare = *to eat. Also found in English* carnivorous, devour, *and* omnivorous.

voracious (adjective)   Gluttonous, ravenous. *"Are all your appetites so voracious?" Wesley asked Nina as he watched her finish off seven miniature sandwiches and two lamb kabob skewers in a matter of minutes.* voracity (noun).

wag (noun)   Wit, joker. *Tom was getting tired of his role as the comical wag who injected life into Kathy's otherwise tedious parties.* waggish (adjective).

Take It to the Next Level

whimsical (adjective)   Based on a capricious, carefree, or sudden impulse or idea; fanciful, playful. *Dave Barry's* Book of Bad Songs *is filled with the kind of goofy jokes that are typical of his whimsical sense of humor.* whim (noun).

xenophobia (noun)   Fear of foreigners or outsiders. *Slobodan Milosevic's nationalistic talk played on the deep xenophobia of the Serbs, who after 500 years of brutal Ottoman occupation had come to distrust all outsiders.*

zenith (noun)   Highest point. *Compiling the vocabulary list for the* Insider's Guide to the GRE *was the zenith of my literary career: after this, there was nowhere to go but downhill.*

Chapter

6

Analytical Writing Review

Analytical 101: Fundamental Essay Writing Skills

The two-essay Analytical section is the first section you encounter after surviving the interminable form-filling-out pre-GRE shenanigans. It does not have much in common with its Math and Verbal siblings. The Analytical section is scored differently, structured differently, and takes longer to complete than both other sections combined. This last point can be somewhat frustrating if your Analytical score is not relevant to your particular graduate program, since you will have to spend the first 75 minutes of the test mucking about and wasting valuable brainpower units in a section that's not important to you. If this is the case, conserve your energy for the sections that matter, but don't blow off the section either.

> **Note**
>
> If you are an international student or if English is your second language, your Analytical score might be scrutinized by universities to determine how fluent you are in English.

Immediately after you complete your GRE CAT, your Quantitative and Verbal scores appear on the screen. The Analytical score takes two to six weeks longer to get, since your essays must be sent off to "GRE-Land," where they are read and graded by professional readers. These readers might be English graduate students, former English teachers, or educational professionals of one ilk or another. Whatever their background, the professional readers share some traits in common:

1. They are experts in the essay-writing format and are well-qualified to make judgments about the effectiveness of a particular essay.

2. They use a shared rubric to evaluate both essays and decide upon a single score for each test-taker.

3. All the ones who give out the lowest scores are members of Mrs. Smith's 8ᵗʰ grade class at Lawrence Middle School.

Tip

The ugly-sounding term *rubric* often rears its head when the topic of essay grading comes up. A rubric is little more than a set of rules, or standards, regarding a topic like essay-writing. Since essay-grading is inherently subjective, a rubric helps codify certain general points that every good essay should have. Standards like "Every essay should have a clear, well-articulated point of view" and "A well-written essay will contain a series of concise supporting details that back up the argument" are two examples that usually appear on an essay-writing rubric. Although a rubric helps professional readers standardize the essay-grading process, there is still room for interpretation and differences of opinion.

The third point might not be factually accurate (it's more of an outright lie), but the other two points are true. Both essays are read, evaluated, and given a score from 0 to 6 by two different readers. A 6 is the highest score, while a 0 means you didn't make much sense or use real words. You can get half-point scores if one reader gives you a 4 while another gives you a 5; if that's the case, you end up with a 4.5 on that test. If two readers disagree by a lot, then a third reader is brought in to help resolve the disagreement.

A 4 or 5 are both good scores, a 3's a bit dodgy, and a 1 or 2 show you have some deficiencies in the essay-writing arena. The goal of this section is to give you the knowledge needed to score at least a 4 on the essay. A 5 or 6 is also a possibility, but the primary goal is to keep your score above a 3. Level 2 Analytical, which begins on page 245, focuses on scoring a 6.

The Issue Essay

For an idea of what the issue will be, look no further than the official GRE Web site, www.gre.org. Every possible issue topic is listed there (the current link is www.gre.org/issuetop.html, but this might change if the site gets redesigned). There are more than 200 topics listed, so writing sample essays for each one would not be the best use of your time. Then again, it wouldn't hurt to practice writing a couple of sample essays from this list if you feel your essay-writing skills need work.

Looking over the list, you will see that most topics are broad statements that leave themselves open for interpretation. A statement like, "A nation should be ruled by its telemarketers" is the kind of open-ended topic that just dares you to agree or disagree with it.

228

The first essay begins by presenting you with two issues, not just one. You get to choose which issue you would like to gab about. You might get two topics similar to the ones below:

1. The creation of a theater company, however small, increases the attractiveness of a city to visitors. The theater company demonstrates that a city is committed to artistic endeavors, and such a commitment is usually associated with good governance.

2. Quick decisions lead to success in today's business world.

Alert!

Since the idea of being sued is always unappealing, the two sample topics listed here are NOT from the official list. They're not even close to any of the topics listed there, thank goodness. Rest assured that the methods and strategies discussed throughout the section will work on all the topics from the official list, even though these two sample topics are NOT—N.O.T.—from the official list.

It's nice to have a choice of two topics to write about, but don't waste too much time deciding which one you want to discuss. The clock starts counting down once the topics appear, so you want to decide as quickly as possible. Every second you spend thinking about the topic you don't choose is time completely wasted. You want to maximize the amount of time you have for the topic you do choose, so read the two choices and then ask yourself, "Which topic can I write about more?" Getting words onto the screen is key, so make a decision about which topic you feel more loquacious about. If you're the kind of person who reads the *Wall Street Journal*, choose the second topic. If you're someone who flips through the *Wall Street Journal* searching for comics and movie reviews, the first topic is probably better for you.

Once you pick a topic, you need to decide whether you want to agree or disagree with the initial statement. Each topic sentence presents one side of an issue, and it's up to you to "present your perspective on an issue" (that's the official moniker for this part of the Analytical section). It doesn't matter whether you choose to agree or disagree, since there's no single "right" answer to these topics. All that matters is how well you explain your side of the argument with supporting details arranged in a logical manner.

Let's say you choose the first topic sentence, and feeling cantankerous you decide to disagree with the opinion that theater companies increase the attractiveness of a city. With about 43 minutes remaining, take about 5 minutes to brainstorm some ideas that will help support this viewpoint. Jot these points down on scratch paper, and try to decide where you want to place them in the essay. There is a fine balance between spending time formulating your essay outline and getting down to actually writing it. The more planning you do, the better your essay will appear in terms of organization. Countering this attribute is the fact that a well-planned essay of only two paragraphs is not as good as a four-paragraph essay with some continuity problems. Five minutes is a good amount of time to plan. After that, start clacking those keys.

As stated on page 28, your typing speed is a factor in the Analytical section, since getting words into the computer can be a time-consuming process. Take the test on page 28 to see how many words you should be able to type for the first essay. If you are a speedy typist, you can give yourself a little more time to brainstorm ideas and organize your thoughts. If you are an average typist, shoot for a four- to five-paragraph essay. If you are a very slow, hunt-and-peck, are-these-letters-moving-around-on-me? kind of typist, you'll need to improve your speed. You want to be able to write at least 400 words for the first essay. Start keeping a journal on your computer, write letters to your friends, type out a manifesto, but do something to increase your speed so that your slow typing no longer becomes an issue that can affect your score.

X-Ref

Take the time now and jot down some ideas about how theaters do not make a city more attractive to visitors. You might have some ideas similar to the ones below, but the topic is broad enough that there are many different ways to craft an essay arguing that this is not true.

1. The introduction of a local theater company has little or no impact at all on a city's attractiveness to visitors. (Main idea, first sentence)

2. Local theater is not something that most visitors think about when considering a city—pollution, crime, economic vitality all bigger factors.

3. Tourist attractions can increase a city's attractiveness, BUT

    —How much of a draw is a "local" theater?

    —Except for NYC Broadway, what place is known for its plays?

    —One-of-a-kind natural wonders, or museums of one type of another, these are things that increase a city's attractiveness.

—In this light, local theater is about as important as a local grocer. Everyone likes having one, but it's not some kind of tourist draw or city enhancement.

4. Also, some lousy governments have presided over great art, so connection between governance and pursuit of artistic excellence pretty flimsy.

The last statement attacks the link connecting artistic endeavor with good governance, but the other statements don't have anything to do with it. Statement 4 might make it into the essay, but it's not crucial that it does. If this essay were untimed, it would help to mount a comprehensive attack on all salient points that you want to disagree with, but hey! This is Essay Writing under Pressure, and no one expects you to be able to cover all bases with the paltry amount of time available.

Statement 1 provides your perspective on the issue, placing you firmly in the "I've listened to the original statement and I disagree" camp. Make sure you very clearly state whether you are for or against the original issue, and do so in the first one or two sentences. The readers are not going to spend four hours on every essay. It's more accurate to say that they will spend less than 10 minutes on both essays combined, in which case you want to have your position very clearly stated right away, in plain view and for everyone to see. Mentally, a reader can then place a check alongside the rubric standard that says, "Every essay should have a clear, well-articulated point of view."

Your first paragraph could look like something like this:

Although a local theater company can have many positive effects on a community, it is unlikely that such a company will have any impact on how visitors view that city. There are many different ways people consider a city not their own. While there are certainly some people who use theater as part of their criteria, this number is probably very small. It is much more likely that most visitors will use other factors to decide whether or not a city is attractive to them, and the existence of a local theater will not even be an issue.

One paragraph down, three to go.

Having stated your position, you must now back it up. The readers will expect your second paragraph to back up your position using specific details, so don't disappoint them. Flesh out Statement 2, and use precise examples whenever possible. Cite specific examples that work in your favor. The point is to be convincing by using facts to state your point. You can't just say, "C'mon! Believe me! I know what I'm talkin' about!"

Sample Second Paragraph

(A) Looking back over the past ten years, many of the Most popular cities in the U.S. became popular for reasons that had nothing to do with theater. (B) Seattle became known as a place where the trendiest rock-and-roll music was created. (C) That was good enough for a lot of young people. (D) Silicon Valley was the center of the Internet explosion, and people flocked there in search of great jobs, not great Shakespeare. (E) Several older cities revitalized their image with large public renovations like the Harbor project in Baltimore. (F) Baltimore's harbor area now contains restaurants, malls, an aquarium, and various other tourist attractions. (G) No local theater, though, showing how it was not factor.

Admittedly, this is not the greatest second paragraph the world has ever seen. Sentence A capitalizes the word *Most* for no reason. Sentences B and C could probably be combined to form one single good sentence instead of two choppy sentences. Sentence D is a bit vague on details, with phrases like *Silicon Valley* and *Internet explosion* tossed around with little explanation. Sentence E has the word *Harbor* capitalized incorrectly.

Sentences E, F, and G are all culled from the author's brief visit to Baltimore last year, so a bold statement like G is not known to be definitively true. They are just the author's recollections from a brief three-day visit two years ago that were dredged up from memory to help bolster a point on the standardized test. Someone could go to Baltimore or do research in a library to determine whether or not local theater was a factor in the Baltimore harbor renaissance. However, that someone is not going to be the reader of your essay, since this individual has only a couple of minutes to read through your essays, assign a grade, and then move on to the next. In other words, while you can't—and shouldn't—lie outright, you can use broad, plausible facts to prove your point. Looking over the statements made in the second paragraph, you can see that all of them are a nice blend of specificity (naming the actual city) and generalization ("people flocked there in search of great jobs").

For all its faults, this second paragraph uses a host of supporting details to back up the initial perspective stated in the first paragraph. That is exactly what you want a second paragraph to do in order to get a good score on this essay. If this were an untimed essay, you would be expected to correct mistakes like improperly capitalized words, and you might also be expected to provide actual data. For instance, an untimed essay should provide actual census figures for the growth rate (and unemployment rate) in Silicon Valley between 1990 and 2000, and it should probably give a more precise geographical location than just "Silicon Valley."

But this isn't an untimed essay, is it? The people reading this essay don't expect exact facts. They are looking for a slew of supporting details that back up the original position, and that's just what the second paragraph gives them. The paragraph covers three different areas of the country and shows how local theater was not a factor in making them attractive to visitors.

With the first paragraph firmly supported by the second, it's time to change tack.

Your third paragraph should be the "I understand the other side of the argument, I just don't agree with it" paragraph. Somewhere in your essay the readers want to see that you understand both sides of the issue, and the third paragraph's as good a place as any. So throw the opposition a bone, but then show how this little point still does not alter the fact that your initial position is the superior one.

Sample Third Paragraph

(H) Of course people do enjoy going to the theater occasionally, so having a local theater company would make a city more attractive for some. (I) But who, exactly? (J) You would think a 'local' theater would benefit the local population the most, and that visitors would hardly notice it. (K) Most people who come in from out of town want to go see large, unique tourist attractions like Graceland or an exceptional natural wonder like Pike's Peak. (L) The local theater is there to raise the artistic consciousness of the community, not attract visitors from another city who may well have a local theater scene of their own.

Again, this paragraph is not flawless, nor does it have to be. All it must do is show that you are a balanced person able to see both sides of an issue, and that you have reasons for rejecting the opposing side in favor of your own. Sentence H is the proverbial bone, and the rest of the paragraph does its best to explain why this viewpoint is not as strong as your own. This is done by making broad, plausible statements with a dash of specificity if possible. Sentence L works fine as, "Most people who come in from out of town want to go see large, unique tourist attractions or exceptional natural wonders." It works better by including precise examples, since this helps reinforce the point and it shows the reader that you can cite specific examples if you have to. Think of it as your way of saying, "If I had time,

PETERSON'S
getting you there

I would bore you with precise details, but I only have time for a few right now."

Specific examples like this help mask some other, vaguer claims. For instance, what exactly does the "artistic consciousness of the community" in Sentence E mean? The precise meaning is up for grabs, but it sure sounds good, doesn't it? Readers skimming their way through this essay won't pause, place their chin in their hand, and deeply reflect upon the exact meaning of that phrase. Instead, they'll just go "uh-huh" absently and keep on blazing through the text. You will get the benefit of the doubt due to the time constraints of the format.

With three paragraphs in the bag, it's time to check the clock. If you have less than 5 minutes left, you should hammer out a concluding sentence or two for paragraph four and then glance over the rest of your essay. Try to catch any obvious grammatical errors, and try to work on the overall flow of the essay, making sure that one paragraph flows well into another. You could use this time to combine Sentences B and C in the second paragraph, for instance.

If you finish three paragraphs and have around 10 minutes left, then you can use the word-processing format to your advantage in the following ways:

1. Write a 2- to 3-sentence final paragraph that restates your take on the initial proposition.

2. Look through everything you've written and catch any blatant grammatical mistakes.

3. Now, try to slip in another paragraph between the third paragraph and the final one. Your conclusion is already in place, so you don't have to worry about ending your essay properly. You can use the remaining time to create a fourth paragraph that piles on more detail to support your belief. You might attack the "good governance" angle at this point, which is something you haven't really addressed in the rest of your essay.

4. When the clock hits 1 minute to go, stop work on the fourth paragraph and make sure the transition between it and your final paragraph is smooth. If you only had a chance to write two sentences in the fourth paragraph, then just tack your two-sentence conclusion to the end of it. However, if you were able to write 3–5 sentences in the fourth paragraph, don't combine the final paragraph with the fourth.

234

If you had to write out your essay, you wouldn't be able to go back and insert an entire paragraph into the rest of the text. Yet the computer format allows you to do that, so you should take advantage of it. Writing the final paragraph first fulfills the rubric standard, "restates original position clearly," a basic requirement in essay-writing. You can then use the remaining time to expound upon your perspective on the issue. No one except you will know that you didn't write the entire essay out in perfect linear fashion. All they will see is a well-organized five-paragraph essay.

Sample Last Paragraph to Write First

Local theater has benefits, but these benefits serve mainly the community itself and remain unknown or of no concern to outsiders. Therefore, the creation of a local theater company is unlikely to have any impact on whether or not a city is attractive to outside visitors.

Then, squeeze in a fourth paragraph above that can go something like:

(M) Furthermore, while the connection between theater and city attractiveness is fairly slim, the connection between art and good government is even more so. (N) A city might provide public funds to help a local theater get started. (O) Although some would like this, others would call it bad government, since that was tax money that could be spent elsewhere, like in a public school or to provide more police officers. (P) In this light, the connection between theater and government would be considered bad government since public funds are being spent poorly.

This fourth paragraph has mistakes just like the others before it, but it still achieves its purpose, which is to show your ability to approach the issue from more than one angle. Sentence N sets up a "what-if" hypothesis, and then Sentence O shows how this could be considered poor government. Sentence O is a bit unwieldy, but that's OK, since the phrase "like in a public school or to provide more police officers" shows that you could be more specific . . . if only you had more time (fake sigh). Since you don't have enough time, the essay has to stay as is.

Grouping all the sample paragraphs together gives you a good blueprint on how to achieve a solid score on the first Analytical essay. You don't have to follow this blueprint exactly, but it wouldn't hurt you if you did. Whether or not you add any variations, make sure that your first essay clearly contains the following points:

PETERSON'S
getting you there

Key Points to Include on the First Essay

1. **A Clearly Stated Position.** Don't send the readers on a scavenger hunt to see how you feel about the issue. Make sure your point of view is clearly stated. Basically, you will either disagree or agree with the initial topic sentence. The safest place to state your point of view is the first paragraph.

2. **A Cartload of Plausible Supporting Details.** You can't use the phrase "because I say so" to back up your argument. You need to come up with believable reasons that justify your position. The more specific they are, the better, but the format of the time-intensive essay will prevent you from using hard data. You could memorize an almanac or census book if you like, but this is probably not a good use of your time. Instead, paint with broad strokes with phrases like, "many people enjoy fine seafood" and "computer skills are becoming increasingly important in the modern world." Both of these statements are believable, even though they contain no hard facts.

3. **Demonstrate That You Can See Other Side's Point of View, Even Though You Disagree with It.** Sadly, actual debate is very rare, at least on television. On TV, most shows put two implacable enemies on screen together, and then watch both sides use every sophistic trick in the book to browbeat their opponent and win the argument. It might make for entertaining TV, but it's a lousy discourse. Such an extreme, unbending position is the exact opposite of what you want in your essay. Take a sentence or two to show how you understand the opponent's point of view, and then use the rest of the paragraph to explain why you feel this position is not as strong as the one you believe.

4. **Have a Clear Conclusion.** It's a basic point of every essay, and the readers will be looking for it. If possible, try to rephrase your original position. Don't use the exact same words as you did at the beginning of the essay.

Look at the some of the sample issues at the GRE Web site and decide how you would approach them using the information in the chart above. Would you agree or disagree? What facts would you use to support your case? How would you show that you understood the other side's view? If the Analytical score is important to you, give yourself 45 minutes and practice writing some sample essays. Use a computer to type out your response, since you want to practice your typing skills as well. Since there are about 240 topics listed, it is not very likely that a topic you practice on will be one of the ones you get for your actual GRE. Then again, stranger things have happened, and people do get lucky. If you glance over a bunch of the issue topics—say, about half of them—and think about how you would respond to them, you will be making your own luck.

The last thing to note is that you should take the entire 45 minutes on the essay. When it's over, stretch your fingers and get prepared for some more typing. The Argument essay is next on the menu.

The Argument Essay

The second essay is 15 minutes shorter than the first, and you are only given one topic. A lengthy list of possible topics can again be found at the GRE Web site, specifically at www.gre.org/argutop.html. Most topics are around 100 words in length and are written to resemble editorials, memos, letters, and reports from fictional people or businesses.

Read a bunch of these "arguments" to get a feel for what they are like. The first thing you should notice is that every argument has a point. Quite often, this point is the first sentence, although in other instances it is farther into the text. The point—which can also be called the *topic statement*, *main idea of the argument*, or *conclusion*—is a judgment or belief made by the author of the topic. This point can be something like, "Therefore, people should try to reduce their intake of salmon if they are concerned about mercury poisoning" or "It is obvious that higher salaries will lead to a higher number of new products."

Note

Words like *therefore*, *clearly*, and *thus* are big signposts that scream, "Main point up ahead!" These words are often used after a series of supporting details, and they act as a verbal transition between the supporting details and the main idea supported by the details. You should be familiar with them, as it is likely you used one of these exact words when restating your main point at the end of the first essay.

The main point of the argument is something that can be disputed. To help convince you of the main idea, the author surrounds the main idea with supporting details that back up the initial claim. These supporting details serve the same function here as the supporting details you created for the first essay: They provide facts that support the author's claim. Some arguments consist of one supporting idea, which is fleshed out and described in detail for the rest of the paragraph. Other arguments make 3–4 different points, each of which supports the main point. If you scan

PETERSON'S

getting you there

through the sample passages provided online, you can find examples of both types, as well as many more that fall between these two poles.

The ability to dissect each argument into a main idea and its supporting details is the first step to doing well on the second essay. If you feel you need some practice at this, take a sheet of lined paper and write the following:

The main idea of this argument is: _____

_____

_____

The supporting details used to make this claim are:

1. _____

_____

2. _____

_____

3. _____

_____

Scroll through the GRE argument passages, pick one at random, and place it into the above template. Determine the main idea, and write out that sentence in the space provided. Then list the supporting details that back up the claim. Since some details might be connected, make a note like ↔ to show that two facts are linked. Repeat this exercise several times until you are able to spot a conclusion and its supporting details with little difficulty. It should help that you spent the first essay deciding on your own point of view and then backing it up with supporting details. For the second essay, the main point and supporting details have been given to you. You just have to determine which is which.

When you've sliced apart a bunch of essays, look with a skeptical eye at the conclusions and the supporting details used to prove them. How airtight are these arguments? Are any of these arguments going to be eligible for the Nobel prize in logic?

The answer is "No." A thousand times, no! Every single one of these arguments can be attacked and discredited in one way or another. To succeed on the second essay, your primary mission is to recognize these errors and write about them.

238

Find the Flaw

The second essay is officially called "Analyze an Argument," but you should think of it as a game called "Find the Flaw." Using this name will get you in the proper mindset. When you read the argument essay, you want to be much more critical than you usually are. When doing regular reading, people often give an author the benefit of the doubt and keep an open mind that what is being written could be valid. This means you might read an editorial, mentally shrug, and think, "Yes, I suppose that could be true."

You don't want to be so kind on the second essay. Once the clock starts ticking, your goal is to:

1. Read the argument

2. Determine the main point

3. Determine the supporting details

4. Brainstorm alternatives that attack either the main idea or a supporting detail

5. Write about these flaws in the argument

A run-through of these steps can be shown using this sample argument (which once again has NOT been plagiarized from the official site).

The following memorandum was written by the President of Dextrose Bank.

"The President of Sucrose Bank, our main competitor, recently mentioned that over half of Sucrose's new customers were people passing by who simply walked in the front door. With this in mind, a large portion of this year's marketing budget will be shifted to improving the exterior look of our bank. This will make our bank look more attractive to people passing by, and we should be able to attract new customers the same way Sucrose Bank did."

Having read the paragraph, Step 1 is complete. Now it's time to determine what the main point is. Some of you might think the main point is, "a large portion of this year's marketing budget will be shifted to improving the exterior look of our bank," since this is the big change at Dextrose Bank. However, keep in mind that a main point is a point of view. It's something that a particular person believes, but it's not a fact. The statement, "A large portion of this year's marketing budget . . ." is a fact. You can't agree or disagree, so it's not a point of view.

PETERSON'S
getting you there

Tip

Again, thinking about the first essay will help you determine the main point of the second essay. Recall how you decided whether to agree or disagree with the initial statement, since this subjective statement could be interpreted either way. The main idea of the argument essay will be a statement you could either agree or disagree with, although you want to do more disagreeing than agreeing.

The conclusion reached by the President of Dextrose Bank is that spending money on the exterior "will make our bank look more attractive to people passing by, and we should be able to attract new customers the same way Sucrose Bank did." This is the President's *belief*, but it's not a fact like "the temperature is currently 80 degrees."

Just for starters, some people might think the bank looks less attractive, and others might like the way the bank looks but not go in and start a new account because of it. Both of these scenarios call the President's conclusion into question. While the President's point may or may not be valid, it is still the conclusion, so Step 2 is complete. Once you have the conclusion, pretty much everything else becomes the supporting details used to justify the claim, so Step 3 falls into place as well.

Reading the argument and determining what's what should take no more than 3 minutes, leaving you with 27 minutes for the last two steps. With any essay (even a timed one), it's always a good idea to do a bit of brainstorming before you start writing. This essay's no exception, so spend about 3–5 minutes coming up with ways to show why the President's conclusion might not hold true.

You wouldn't have to write out every alternative. Just take quick notes to remind yourself. Once the clock reads 23 minutes to go, you should stop brainstorming and start writing. Your first sentence can be something like, "Although [Main Point . . . Blah Blah Blah] has some validity, it does not hold up to intense scrutiny. There are several ways that this conclusion can be proven wrong, such as. . . ." Then you put your essay-writing cap on and light the sucker up for all its flaws.

To do this, you need to come up with alternatives to what is assumed in the text. These alternatives require a little bit of creativity on your part, but once you practice on some sample passages, you'll get the hang of it. These alternatives—you can call them alternative reasons, outcomes, explanations, scenarios, and possibilities—are all designed to undercut a specific part of the original text. Look at the previous chart that shows the conclusion. The bank president assumes that the new look "will make our bank look more attractive," so Alternative #1 is created by simply stating

Finding Flaws in the Argument

Conclusion: "This will make our bank look more attractive to people passing by, and we should be able to attract new customers the same way Sucrose Bank did."

Alternative #1: What if people don't like the new look? This would discourage them from entering, the exact opposite of what is wanted.

Alternative #2: What if exterior appearance had nothing to do with Sucrose's success with walk-ins? If Sucrose was located near a busy, trendy supermarket, people might walk in and start an account there because it was convenient.

Supporting Detail: "With this in mind, a large portion of this year's marketing budget will be shifted to improving the exterior look of our bank."

Alternative #3: What if Dextrose has had success with radio and print ads? Taking money in the budget away from these successful marketing strategies might hurt the overall number of new customers. Walk-ins might increase, but they wouldn't counteract the number of customers lost by abandoning or cutting back on the proven methods of radio and print ads.

Alternative #4: What if there are better ways to spend money and attract walk ins? Dextrose Bank could leave the exterior as is, but throw a benefit concert featuring local musicians. This might generate a large crowd of people who then sign up as new customers.

Supporting Detail: "The President of Sucrose Bank, our main competitor, recently mentioned that over half of Sucrose's new customers were people passing by who simply walked in the front door."

Alternative #5: Putting it bluntly, what if the President of Sucrose Bank is lying? Suppose the Sucrose Bank president made those remarks knowing that his/her counterpart at Dextrose Bank would react strongly to them? If this is the case, then the Dextrose President has been played like a violin, and large amounts of Dextrose Bank marketing money are being spent to counter a claim that is not even true.

a different outcome. To flesh out Alternative #1, you could have something like the following paragraph.

(A) The President of Dextrose Bank believes that the new look will make the bank more attractive to passers by, but this is not necessarily true. (B) Some people might not like the new decor, and avoid the bank for that reason. (C) For example, suppose the bank spends a lot of money and plants a large number of flowers and bushes around the parking lot. (D) However, the state is in the midst of a severe drought. (E) Some people might think the bank looks nice, but others would believe that the bank is foolishly wasting water and money during a drought. (F) These people would be turned off by the expensive remodeling, considering it wasteful and boorish.

Sentence A is the set-up sentence. It clearly states which part of the argument you are going to attack. As you might expect, starting every paragraph with a simple set-up sentence is a good game plan. Sentence B states an alternative outcome, showing how this alternative leads to actions opposite of what the bank president assumes will happen. Sentences C and D are where you have to get a little creative. Basically, you need to think of a reason why people would not like a new exterior for a bank. The sample above goes the "ecological conservationist" route, setting up a mythical drought that the cads at the bank care nothing about. Sentences E and F explain why the eco-conservationists are now less likely to open an account at Dextrose Bank now that the exterior has been expensively remodeled.

The "eco-conservationist" route is not the only explanation you can give. You could also say, "Suppose the renovations to the exterior require large parts of the bank building (including the bank sign) to be covered in scaffolding and other construction materials. This might make it hard for people new to the area to realize that the building under construction was a bank. Since newly moved people are more likely to need a new account, the work on the exterior would hurt Dextrose's ability to sign these people up." This isn't perfect, but perfection isn't required for a 30-minute essay. You just need to show that you can break down an argument and come up with alternatives.

Alert!

The essay does not require you to go out and actually find an eco-conservationist who supports your opinion. You do not need to have a sentence that shows the national membership figures for the Sierra Club.

242

All you have to do is come up with a plausible (there's that word again!) alternative that shows how the initial point might be wrong. Once you explain your alternative, you have done what is needed for the second essay. Now you need some more of it, so it's time to start another paragraph and attack something else from the original argument.

If you are wondering why the emphasis is on finding flaws in the argument, the answer is simple. The GRE readers aren't going to be kind to an essay that states, "After looking over the argument, everything the speaker claims is true." Anyone who doesn't understand the argument can write this, so it doesn't really show that you did any thinking. The readers want evidence of some mental work on your part. This is why you must attack the argument, pulling it apart and coming up with alternative possibilities that subvert the main point.

However, you can recycle the old "I understand both sides of the issue, but they're wrong" concept from the first essay. This is done below with Alternative #3.

> (G) The Dextrose Bank President has decided to shift "a large portion of this year's marketing budget . . . to improving the exterior look of our bank." (H) A new exterior might indeed bring in some new customers, since a bold new exterior might increase walk-in interest. (I) However, the shift in marketing money might not be the best for the overall number of new customers. (J) Suppose the shift in money means that the bank can no longer do many print and radio ads? (K) If these ads were very successful, their decline might mean fewer new customers come in after reading or hearing an ad. (L) This means that the number of walk-in new customers increases, but the number of radio and print new customers drops.
> (M) Overall, this might lead to a decline in the total number of new customers, and Dextrose Bank will be worse off.

Sentence G is a set-up sentence that uses quotes to show exactly what part of the argument is going to be scrutinized. Sentence H shows, "Hey, dude, I can totally see where you're coming from." The other side of the issue has now been given a little credit. The rest of the paragraph proceeds to show why this point of view is flawed. Sentence I is a transition sentence, as you go from agreeing to disagreeing. The next four sentences follow the same blueprint as the first paragraph. Sentences J and K create a hypothetical situation—which you can totally make up so long as it's somewhat believable—and Sentences L and M show how this hypothetical situation will lead to an outcome exactly opposite of what the Dextrose Bank President assumes will happen. Not every sentence in this second paragraph is stellar, and if you had time, you might not want to use both radio and print ads. Using only one would simplify the paragraph and still get the point across. But you don't have time, so it doesn't matter. The second paragraph is fine as it is for a 30-minute "Analyze the Argument" essay.

After two paragraphs, you might not have much time left. Following the template of the first essay, write a brief closing and then use any remaining time to hammer out more alternatives. Your closing might be something like the following:

> The Dextrose Bank President's plan to gain more new walk-in customers might work. However, if it doesn't, it could be because of one of the reasons listed above, since the President's plan is by no means foolproof.

The above closes out the essay nicely. The vague phrase "it could be because of one of the reasons listed" works quite well, because you wouldn't be expected to list every one of the reasons in the closing. You can now use all the time remaining to add as many reasons as you can type.

When the clock starts flashing 3 minutes, finish up the sentence you are writing and then look over the essay for any grammatical mistakes. Correct any mistakes you can find until the clock winds down. Once the time is up, the essay will vanish, and the Analytical portion of the GRE will be over.

. . . And One More Thing

The following words were used in this chapter. They are all college-level vocabulary words that might appear on the Verbal portion of the GRE. If you didn't know the meaning of these words, add them to your vocabulary lists now. The best way to improve your vocabulary is to learn new words in the context of reading, so find the definitions of all the words below and then look back and find them throughout the chapter:

cad	*proverbial*
cantankerous	*renaissance*
endeavor	*rubric*
interminable	*scrutiny* (three different times!)
loquacious	*sophistic*
moniker	

Take It to
the Next Level

Acing the Essays

The fundamentals of sound essay writing are covered earlier in this chapter. If you follow those basic steps—clearly stated main idea in first paragraph of first essay, finding the flaw in the argument for the second essay, and so forth—you should get a decent score on the Analytical portion of the GRE. However, if you are an English major or someone shooting to get into a highly competitive program that stresses writing skills, a *decent* score might not be all that you want. Anything less then a 5 might not be enough; you want a 5.5 or ideally a 6.

There's no way to guarantee you a perfect score. Essays are just too subjective, and one reader's idea of an excellent essay might differ from what another reader thinks a perfect essay should look like. But there are a host of different strategies you can use to transform a good essay into a superior essay, and these strategies will be covered in this chapter.

Mixing It up on the First Essay

Since the first essay is longer and requires more mental work than the second, it stands to reason that this essay affects your overall Analytical score more than the second essay. The first essay is also more open-ended, which gives you a greater range of creativity on this essay than on the second. For the second essay, the goal is to "analyze the argument," and this limits your responses since you must stay focused on the argument given. This set-up is good news for you, because it means that you can demonstrate your snazzy writing skills on the essay that counts more toward your overall score.

Before delving into specific techniques to improve your essay, the general theme you should shoot for is to write a "standard essay, but with frills." Think of a perfect score of 6 as a 4 + 2. The 4 comes from having all the basic requirements needed in an essay, such as a main idea supported by details. Every essay needs the basics, and yours is no exception. Yet most students are familiar with the basic essay format, so just writing a standard essay might not be enough to get you a 6. That's where the "+2" idea comes in. The extra 2 points comes from distinguishing your essay in some way. Your overall goal is to make your essay different in a way that shows you are capable of writing more than a standard essay.

> The "4 + 2" concept seems to imply that simply writing a basic essay will never get you a score higher than a 4. This is not its purpose, nor is the implication true. If you totally nail a basic essay—a clear main idea, great set of supporting details, excellent organization on the paragraph and sentence level, and good overall grammar—you could easily earn a 6 that way. In the end, it all depends on the reader. The point behind the "4 + 2" concept is to emphasize that adding advanced writing flourishes will help separate your essay from the standard essays. If you add these flourishes well, it will greatly increase your chance of getting a 5 or 6 since you will be demonstrating your advanced writing ability.

Note

How you decide to make your essay stand out from the pack is up to you. Here are three different methods that you can use:

1. Tweak the Basic Format

It's a simple fact that repetition leads to boredom for most people. You have to think that GRE readers get tired of seeing the same essays over and over again. This doesn't mean they'll start giving out bad grades to standard essays. It means that they might perk up a bit if your essay plays with the basic format a bit.

For instance, the basic essay starts with the main idea clearly stated in the first paragraph. So tweak the format by placing your main idea in the second paragraph. Use the first paragraph to "set the scene," vividly describing an imaginary scenario that will back up your claim. Or start the paragraph off with a good quote, provided the quote could then be used to back up your point. Do something that captures the reader's attention while remaining relevant to the discussion at hand.

Page 229 earlier in this chapter listed two fictitious essay topics. The first one has already been discussed, so we will use the second topic to take it to the next level.

Sample Topic:
Quick decisions lead to success in today's business world.

Setting the scene with an imaginary scenario. (agrees with the topic)

> The owners of Murpu Labs face a quandary. Over the past six months, they've worked long hours developing a new software program that makes it easier to transfer video images over the Internet. This market is currently underserved, and large profits are available for a company that fulfills customer demands in this area. Yet the Murpu software still has some bugs to be worked out. With start-up money drying up, the company owners find themselves pondering the question, 'Do we release the flawed software or not?'

> Murpu's owners should stop deliberating and start selling, since speedy decisions are crucial in today's business world.

If you have knowledge of an actual business that hesitated and lost, by all means use it. Using a historical anecdote here would be even better, since it would give your argument the weight of some real historical events behind it. However, a lack of precise business history will not hurt the stylistic effects of the anecdotal first paragraph. You just create a fictitious company and place them in the situation you want them to be stuck in. The point is to give the first paragraph some punch by creating a specific situation, one that draws the readers in and has them wondering how they would act if they were running Murpu Labs.

The sentence that starts the second paragraph, "Murpu's owners should stop deliberating and start selling, since speedy decisions are crucial in today's business world" ties into the first paragraph and shows just where you stand on the topic. It's your viewpoint, cleverly placed in the second paragraph, not the first. You can then expound upon this theme for the rest of the second paragraph.

Since you started out with software as your business model, you can make that the I-see-the-other-side-of-the-coin angle for the third paragraph, too.

> Speedy decisions are critical in the fast-paced computer software world, but it's true that other business areas are not so time-intensive. Banking, and institutional lending in general, are two areas in which deliberate decision making are well established. Yet technology has a way of speeding up the pace of the world, and even such ancient sectors as banking might find themselves pushed to make decisions more rapidly than they would have in the past.

247

Tip

In the sample essay outlined earlier, only one paragraph is devoted to showing the other side's point and then shooting it down. You can alter this standard essay format by creating every paragraph in the "I see your side, but mine's stronger" mold. Each paragraph would start off with you stating your opponent's viewpoint, but would then explain why your side of the argument is better. This is a little tougher to pull off in a short amount of time, which is why it would make your essay stand out.

The above paragraph shows how you can alter the initial outline of an essay just a bit, and still keep the rest of it the same. As always, you use vague yet plausible facts that cannot be disputed. The phrase "institutional lending in general" sounds very good and could mean such a huge range of things it's not even funny. In a time-intensive essay where readers can't pause and deeply ponder, it fits wonderfully.

Instead of starting out with a scenario, you could also begin with a quote.

Starting things off with a quote. (disagrees with the topic)

> Edward Young once wrote, "Be wise with speed; a fool at forty is a fool indeed." Although the English poet and dramatist lived over three hundred years ago, Young's words are still relevant today. They highlight the fact that rash decisions are often bad decisions, and such foolishness leaves people open to embarrassment and other unwanted consequences.
>
> Quick decisions can also translate to bad business, which is why they should be avoided in today's business world.

Now, the main problem with this set-up is that you have to have the quote from Edward Young floating around in your head in order to use it on the Analytical section. There are three ways to go about achieving this.

Starting with a quote or adding fictitious scenarios are just two ways to tweak the basic essay format. Anything you do that demonstrates you can write more than just a standard essay will improve your chances of garnering a high score on the Analytical portion of the GRE. Admittedly, you have to be able to pull off the altered essay format successfully, so don't add change just for change's sake. Adopting a writing style that is obviously artificial will not help your cause, so never strain or stretch to place a quote just to give your essay a quote. If tweaking the essay format in some way feels good to you, do it. Your instincts are better than you might think, and a more natural writing style can greatly benefit your essay, as you will see in the following section.

Three Ways to Have Snappy Quotes Floating around in Your Head

1. **Be the Kind of Person Who Likes to Memorize Quotes.** Many English majors like nothing more than to snap off a few lines of Shakespeare to prove their point. You might find this habit annoying in the real world, but in GRE-Land it's quite a useful habit. Even if you're not an English major, many people have proverbs (like "Haste makes waste"), Biblical quotes, and snippets of famous speeches floating around in their grey matter. These quotes can all be used if the situation warrants it.

   One caveat is that you want to use quotes that are as "literary" as possible. Shakespeare is good but John Dryden is better, since a Dryden quote shows that you have knowledge of famous literature that goes beyond the basics. If you need help remembering this idea, think of the acronym FIBTS: Faulkner Is Better Than Seuss.

2. **Start a List of Cool Quotes You Like.** This method works best if you are someone who reads literature on a regular basis. If you do, you should come across neat phrases that make you think to yourself, "Hey! That sentence rocks!" Start a quote list where you write down these good phrases. The list will help you remember the quote, and you can always refresh your memory by rereading the list from time to time.

3. **Memorize a Bunch of Quotes for the GRE.** This might not be the best use of your time, but to achieve it, all you need is a book of famous quotes and a computer connected to the Internet. Use the computer to scroll around and view all the different GRE essay topics, and use the quote book to rummage for quotes that you think would work well for each topic. This idea is part of a larger plan to prep for the essay section, and it will be discussed in greater detail starting on page 251.

2. Use Your Voice

Writing in your voice is the best way to help distinguish your essay from others, but it's the hardest one to achieve. There's no way to really teach voice, either, since a person's voice must come from the individual. However, the idea of voice can be discussed and described, and you can take it from there and run with it as long as you can.

Take It to the Next Level

PETERSON'S
getting you there

Tip

In writing, "voice" refers to an author's distinctive style of using words. Many established writers have such a unique voice that you can determine when a piece of writing is theirs after a couple of sentences. Suppose you read the words, "Round about there/In the Valley of Crair/Lived an old Hoobavax/By the name of Snare" and were asked to determine the writer. You would probably guess the well-known children's author Dr. Seuss, since these words are written in the *voice* of Dr. Seuss.

Take a moment and think about your own writing. Look over some old journal entries, term papers, poems, or short stories, if you have any laying around. Is your writing very serious, or do you include humor whenever possible? Do you prefer a short, terse journalistic style full of short sentences in small paragraphs, or do you tend toward lengthy paragraphs with long, highly developed sentences? No answer is better than another. The overarching goal is to differentiate your essay from the pack (in a good way), and using a style that's your own is an excellent way to do this.

Like everything, using your voice has some qualifiers attached to it. Not every type of voice can be used for an essay. For an example of an inappropriate voice, suppose you like to write in a style similar to the French writer Celine. Your essay would be a mishmash of thoughts connected by ellipses . . . like hearing a story through a strobe light . . . every other phrase making its way through—others, blacked out . . . Mon Dieu! That's a terrible style to use for an essay. The reader will not say,"Hmm, an homage to Celine!" The response will be more along the lines of, "This clown doesn't know when to use a period." As you can see, some styles are just too radical to use on the essay format. If you are gunning for a 6, you probably have enough of a writing background to know when you've crossed the line from strong voice into experimental text creation.

On a personal note, I like to make jokes while writing. (I won't go so far and claim they are funny.) I could have written an essay without humor, but I didn't see the point in doing so. While the entire text wasn't a stand-up routine, I told about one joke per paragraph, for both essays. My conclusion on the first essay was even a joke. I did this because that's the kind of writer I am. My score on the Analytical portion was a 6, which is good news for you because you probably wouldn't want to be reading a book from someone who scored a 3. You can say I received a 6 because:

1. I'm a professional writer.

2. I used my own voice, and this helped distinguish my essay from others.

3. I told jokes and the bored readers thought my jokes were funny, or at least helped break up the monotony of their task.

There might an element of truth to all three points, but the second point is the one you should concern yourself with. Don't feel you have to shackle the way you write in order to conform to the standard essay. Make all the standard essay points as necessary, and then garnish them with sentences that are your own.

While the strategy of using your own voice is a good one, it's not something that is easily taught. For more concrete assistance, look no further than the last technique, which pretty much reeks of realpolitik.

3. Just Prepare Ahead of Time

You know you have to write 2 essays, and you know where all the sample topics are located. It doesn't take a rocket scientist—or person aspiring to go to rocket scientist graduate school—to put two and two together and realize you can look over the topics and prepare ahead of time.

The question is not whether you should prepare ahead of time, but how much preparation do you wish to do? Writing out roughly 500 sample essays would not be the best use of your time. Besides, other people have already done this for you. If you're interested in seeing what some sample essays look like, you check out *ARCO GRE CAT Answers to the Real Essay Questions*. You don't want to use the essays as they appear in the book, since this is wrong for many different reasons. Instead, looking over the sample essays will give you an idea of what kinds of supporting details you could use for each essay. It will also give you a chance to look over different essay formats. Seeing different ways that supporting details are used should help you brainstorm ideas of your own, while reviewing different formats should make it easier for you to organize your own essay.

Note

These books are by Peterson's as well, although there might be similar titles by other publishers. The books listed here are the ones rated highest by the author and publisher, but that's merely a coincidence.

The importance of spending about 5 minutes brainstorming before writing your essay is covered on pages 229–230 earlier in this chapter. This brainstorming will be a lot better and take less time if you have already thought about the topic previously. So even if you don't want to use the sample essay book, you should still look over some sample topics and

Take It to the Next Level

PETERSON'S
getting you there

mentally sketch out how you would approach them. Take about 5 minutes for each topic and ask yourself, "Would I agree or disagree with the topic sentence? What type of supporting details would I like to use?" You don't have to write your answers down, although you can if you like. The main goal is to acquaint yourself with the topic beforehand, and come up with a rudimentary idea about how you would want to approach an essay on the subject. This can help you in several ways:

1. If you have a choice between a topic you've thought about and one that you haven't, the decision to choose the one you've thought about should come very rapidly.

2. If you get a topic you've seen before, you won't waste any time deciding whether to agree or disagree since you already thought about how to approach that topic. This should also make coming up with supporting details much quicker and easier, leaving you with more time to get words into the computer.

3. Even if you get two topics that you haven't thought about already, your brainstorming skills will be greatly improved with all the practice. This should translate to less time needed to decide whether to agree or disagree, as well as greater ease at coming up with good supporting details.

Doing the 5-minute brainstorm exercise on several topics is something everyone should do. If you want to be more gung-ho, there are other things you can do, but these might not be the optimal use of your time.

You could do research to come up with hard facts to use on every essay, but it's not a good idea for two reasons. For one thing, it would take a massive amount of time for very little payoff. Also, if you did include something very specific, it might tip the reader off to the fact that you prepared beforehand. There's nothing illegal about this, but it's not going to earn you any Brownie points. It's much better to appear like you *just happened* to get that particular topic, and you *just happened* to come up with the set of supporting details that you did.

The Second Essay

The second essay doesn't give you as much writing wiggle room as the first. That essay is more of a writing assignment, while the second essay is closer to an exercise in logical thinking. Sure, you still have to write, but you don't have to formulate an argument from scratch. You just have to comment on an argument given to you.

Other Ways to Prep for the Essay Beforehand

1. **Prepare a Quote List.** As stated earlier on page 248, placing a relevant quote is a nice addition to any essay. When brainstorming on a sample topic, ask yourself, "Is there a quote I can think of that would help prove my point?" If you can't think of one right away, you could always do some searching in a book of quotations like Bartlett's. Even if this exercise doesn't land you the quote you want, looking through a book of quotes is often pretty cool.

2. **Have Some Snazzy Vocabulary Words Ready to Go.** You can compile a list of advanced words that could be brought into play on your essay. For example, in the paragraph where you show that you can acknowledge the other side's point of view, you might have a sentence like, "Although this might happen, the chances of this occurring are actually very small." Instead of *small*, use *infinitesimal*. It means the same thing, but the GRE readers will note your use of advanced vocabulary. Other good words like *specious*, *verify*, *quandary* (seen earlier in this chapter), *ratiocination*, and *blinkered* can crop up in many point-of-view essays.

If you are already compiling a list of vocabulary words for the GRE Verbal section, you don't need to make two lists. Simply keep those advanced words in mind when writing your GRE essays.

Two of the three strategies you used on the first essay work on the second one, but the "Tweaking the Essay Format" technique doesn't really apply to the second essay. With only 30 minutes, you need to attack the argument and uncover the flaws. A basic essay with distinct paragraphs attacking specific points is the best way to do this. If you can add a quote to help make your point, bully for you. However, adding a complex organizational layer might obscure the points you are trying to make, so keeping it simple works best. If you want to take a risk and write the entire second essay as a Socratic dialogue, go right ahead, but this approach will likely be too radical for most readers. A simple format showing complex thoughts is better than a complex format obscuring complex thoughts.

Using your own voice can work on the second paragraph, but in a limited manner. Again, for the second essay your overall goal is to expose flaws in the original argument, not display your writing chops. If you can show a little personality, by all means do so. It would certainly look good if elements of your writing style displayed in the first essay appear in the second essay as well. That will show the GRE readers that the writing is definitely yours, and not something you crafted ahead of time with the help of others.

The third strategy, preparing beforehand, is the one that works best for the second essay. It is easily the best thing you can do to write a better second essay. The second essay requires you to acquire and display a certain skill—determining the flaws of a short argument—and the foremost way to get better at this skill is through practice on real topics.

> To help you analyze arguments, you can peruse the book *ARCO GRE CAT Answers to the Real Essay Questions*. This will give you an idea of how to create and write about alternative scenarios that undermine the conclusions and supporting details of an argument.

Tip

You do not need to write out entire essays, although you can write out some if you feel like it. Focus instead on honing your brainstorming skills to the point where you can take any 100-word argument, easily spot the conclusion and supporting details, and then start churning out alternatives that show the logical flaws. This can be a completely mental exercise where you spend roughly 5 minutes just thinking about every argument.

You have 240 arguments to work on, but you probably won't need that many to get proficient at finding the flaws in an argument. Once you have this skill under your belt, the hardest part of the second essay is done. When test day comes, you might get lucky and encounter an argument you've worked on, but even if you don't, it should be easy for you to read the text and begin formulating alternatives. You then place as many of these alternatives into a basic essay format as time allows, and give yourself a few minutes at the very end to check over your grammar and perhaps tighten up a few sentences.

A second essay with a host of strong alternatives is an excellent complement to a first essay that shows some originality in content and structure. While this combo can't guarantee you a 6—nothing can, for that matter—it does present a strong case to the GRE readers that you are someone who really knows her stuff on the GRE Analytical section.

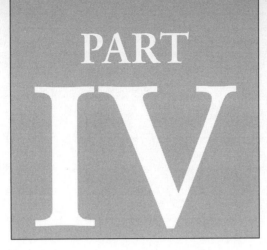

PART IV

Three Practice GREs

PART IV

Chapter

7

Preface to Practice Tests

Putting Ideas and Concepts into Practice

NOTE: Don't start on any of the following three tests until you have read this section.

The study materials in this book should have your head swirling with information. Although this might lead to strange dreams featuring QC problems, on the whole it's a positive thing. The following 3 practice tests will give you a chance to put some of the knowledge flitting around in your noggin to good use.

These tests should be used to give you a chance to test-drive the new strategies and ideas previously presented within this book. It's important you don't just jump to these questions and start answering them willy-nilly before reading all that came before. If you do this, odds are good you will only help reinforce the faults you had before you started studying for the GRE. To truly maximize your GRE score, these tests must be approached with the attitude that you will use them to try out the various different points and ideas covered so far. Doing this will help you absorb the material discussed and make you a better GRE test-taker.

Make sure you take only one test at a time, and then look over the explanations to the answers. Everyone will want to read the explanations for the questions that they miss, but it's also a good idea to look the answers for the other questions as well. The explanations can give you ideas about different ways you can approach a problem; learning about these different approaches will earn you points toward your Superior Test-Taker merit badge. Many people who score poorly on standardized tests do so because they are locked into the mindset that there is only one way to answer every problem. It's as if every problem is a locked door, and only a single correct key can unlock it.

Note

It's doesn't matter if you take these tests under timed conditions or not, although a good plan would be to take the first two untimed and the third one timed. Your real practice with timed GRE sections will come with the exams, not the CD, since these mimic the adaptive format.

If you get nothing else from this book, you should learn that this mode of thinking is incorrect. There are skeleton keys (general facts you can use to come to the right answer), lock-picking equipment (strategies like estimating and process of elimination), and if worse comes to worse, you can just try kicking the door down with your boot (guessing as time runs out). These won't work every time, but they'll work more times than you might think.

Do your best, and remember that the goal is to learn something from every missed question, and even from some that you answered correctly.

Practice Test

1

Quantitative

28 Questions—45 Minutes

General Information

1. The test has 28 questions. If you decide to take this exam under timed conditions, you have 45 minutes to complete the section.

2. All numbers used are *real* numbers.

3. All angle measurements can be assumed to be positive unless otherwise noted.

4. All figures lie in the same plane unless otherwise noted.

5. Drawings that accompany questions are intended to provide information useful in answering the question. The figures are drawn closely to scale unless otherwise noted.

Directions: For questions 1–14, Column A and Column B will have one quantity each. Your goal is to compare the quantities in each column and choose

    A if the quantity in Column A is greater
    B if the quantity in Column B is greater
    C if the two quantities are equal
    D if the relationship between the two quantities cannot be determined from the information in the problem

On some questions, information about one or both quantities will be given. This information will be centered above the two columns.

	Column A	**Column B**

1. $b = 6$

The number of minutes in b hours · The number of degrees in the sum of the angles of a square

2.

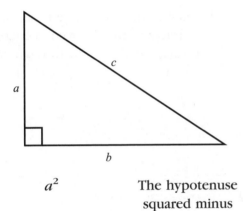

a^2 · The hypotenuse squared minus itself

3. A square has a side that is b inches long.

b^2 · The number of inches along the perimeter of the square

4. $|x| = 3, |y| = 4$

$y - x$ · 1

5. The sum of the three smallest prime numbers · $\sqrt{49} + \sqrt{8}$

6.

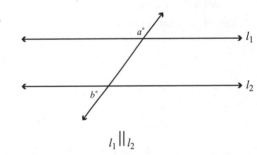

$l_1 \parallel l_2$

$\dfrac{a^2 + ab + a}{a}$ · 180

	Column A	Column B		Column A	Column B

7. Jackie, Beth, and Allison each have different cars and park in a three spot parking lot behind their house.

The number of possible different arrangements of their cars in the three spots	7

8. Twice the circumference of a circle divided by two times its diameter | π

9. One is less than a, and a is less than b.

$$\left[\frac{a^2 b}{2} - 12a\right]\left(\frac{1}{a}\right) \qquad 3\left[b\left(\frac{a}{6} - \frac{1}{3b}\right) - 4\right]$$

10. A triangle has one side of length 4 and another of length 10.

5	The length of the third side of the triangle

11. The median of the even integers 10 through 18 inclusive | The mean of the even integers 10 through 18 inclusive

12.

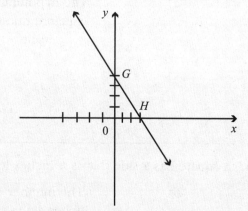

The length of $\overline{GH}$	The slope of $\overline{GH}$ times -4

	Column A	**Column B**

13. A and B are distinct digits.

$|A + A + B|$ 		 28

---

14. The local pet store has 73 cats and dogs. 40 of them are female, and 35 are dogs. There are 9 less male cats than male dogs.

The number of female cats

The number of male dogs

Directions: Select the best answer for each of the following questions.

15. If $-x^2 = 2x - 15$, then what does x equal?

　I. -3

　II. 3

　III. 5

　A. I only
　B. II only
　C. I and III only
　D. II and III only
　E. I, II, and III

16.

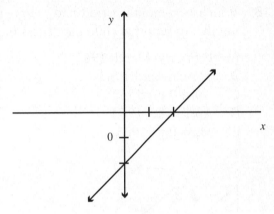

The linear equation that accurately corresponds to line r is

A. $y + 2 = -2x$
B. $y - 2 = -2x$
C. $y + 2 = -x$
D. $y - 2 = -x$
E. $y + 2 = x$

Questions 17–18 refer to the following graph.

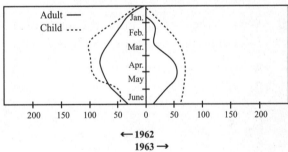

Comparison of Reported Incidences of Flu in the First Half of 1962 and 1963 in Tucker County

17. Which month had the fewest reported incidences of flu?

A. January 1962
B. June 1962
C. January 1963
D. February 1963
E. April 1963

18. Which two-month period had the greatest number of reported child incidences of flu?

    A. February–March 1962
    B. March–April 1962
    C. April–May 1962
    D. April–May 1963
    E. May–June 1963

19.

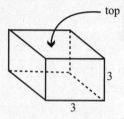

If the area of the top of the rectangular box is 15, what is the surface area of the entire figure?

    A. 69
    B. 72
    C. 78
    D. 85
    E. 90

20. What is the median minus the mode of the following number set {4, 16, 7, 2, 7, 10}?

    A. −3
    B. 0
    C. 3
    D. 5
    E. 9

Questions 21–23 are based on the following graphs.

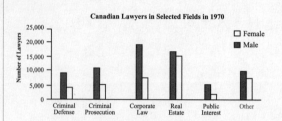

	1st	2nd	3rd	4th
Civil	482	401	525	510
Criminal	672	701	775	580

Breakdown of Cases Tried in Canadian Provincial Courts in 1970

Types of Law

Civil Includes: Corporate Law, Real Estate, Public Interest, Other

Criminal Includes: Criminal Defense, Criminal Prosecution

21. In which quarter was the ratio of criminal to civil cases the greatest?

    A. 1st quarter, 1970
    B. 2nd quarter, 1970
    C. 3rd quarter, 1970
    D. 4th quarter, 1970
    E. 1st quarter, 1971

22. Which of the following best approximates the ratio of female lawyers in Canada in 1970 practicing Civil Law to Criminal Law?

    A. 1:2
    B. 4:1
    C. 1:3
    D. 5:1
    E. 1:4

262

23. Which field of law in Canada had the greatest number of practitioners in 1970?

   A. Criminal Law
   B. Civil Law
   C. Corporate Law
   D. Real Estate Law
   E. Public Interest Law

24.

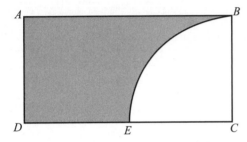

In the figure above the non-shaded region is a quarter circle. If the area of rectangle $ABCD$ is the sum of 12 and $\overline{AB} = 4$, what is the length of arc $BE + \overline{ED}$?

   A. $\dfrac{3}{2}\pi + 1$

   B. $2\pi + 1$

   C. $\dfrac{5}{2}\pi + 1$

   D. $6\pi + 2$

   E. $8\pi + 2$

25. What is the length of the longest distance between two corners of a rectangular box with sides 2, 3, and 4?

   A. $2\sqrt{7}$
   B. 5
   C. $\sqrt{29}$
   D. $\sqrt{33}$
   E. 6

26. The average fifth grader scored a 15 on the GST test. The average sixth grader scored 18 on the GST test. There are half as many sixth graders as fifth graders. What is the overall average score?

   A. 15.5
   B. 16
   C. 16.5
   D. 17
   E. 17.5

27.

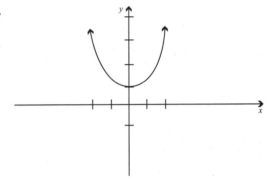

Which function is graphed above?

   A. $y = x^2 - 1$
   B. $x = y^2 - 1$
   C. $y = x^2 + 1$
   D. $x = y^2 + 1$
   E. $y^2 = x^2 + 1$

28.

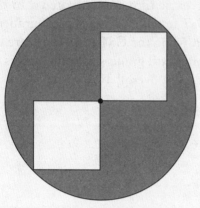

The two figures in the circle are squares, each with one corner at the center of the circle and one corner touching the circumference. If the radius of the circle is 4, what is the area of the shaded region?

A. $2(\pi - 1)$
B. $6(\pi - 1)$
C. $8(\pi - 1)$
D. $12(\pi - 1)$
E. $16(\pi - 1)$

Verbal

30 Questions—30 Minutes

Antonyms

Directions: Each question contains a word printed in capital letters, followed by five answer choices. Choose the answer choice that contains the word or phrase most nearly OPPOSITE in meaning to the word in capital letters.

1. ZEAL :

A. enthusiasm
B. apathy
C. antagonism
D. pride
E. neutrality

2. HETEROGENEOUS :

A. orthodox
B. abnormal
C. uniform
D. translucent
E. deficient

264

3. FEALTY :

  A. disloyalty
  B. turbidity
  C. probity
  D. fidelity
  E. substantiality

4. ARCHAIC :

  A. lusterless
  B. odious
  C. clichéd
  D. customary
  E. novel

5. ASSUAGE :

  A. pillory
  B. satiate
  C. blandish
  D. ameliorate
  E. provoke

6. MERCURIAL :

  A. emotionally stable
  B. bitterly rancorous
  C. embarrassingly sordid
  D. constantly morose
  E. extremely melodramatic

7. OPPROBRIUM :

  A. contempt
  B. platitude
  C. commendation
  D. prescience
  E. ennui

8. TYRO :

  A. miscreant
  B. curmudgeon
  C. virtuoso
  D. dilettante
  E. misogynist

9. SOPORIFIC :

  A. stimulant
  B. exigent
  C. torpor
  D. sophomoric
  E. jejune

Analogies

Directions: In each question, there is an initial pair of words or phrases that are related in some manner. Select the answer choice containing the lettered pair that best expresses a relationship similar to the initial pair.

10. PRATTLE : BABBLE ::

  A. battle : fight
  B. digest : eat
  C. engage : withdraw
  D. misconstrue : grasp
  E. mettle : disassociate

11. FAWN : FLATTER ::

  A. praise : criticize
  B. divulge : tell
  C. burgeon : grow
  D. bolster : disapprove
  E. misquote : lie

12. DENOUEMENT : STORY ::

   A. prologue : novel
   B. sunset : day
   C. intermission : play
   D. sidewalk : bistro
   E. traffic : thoroughfare

13. FEDERALISM : POLITICAL ORDER ::

   A. class : student
   B. dictatorship : anarchy
   C. colleague : cohort
   D. insomnia : sleep disorder
   E. extrinsic : external

14. SPURIOUS : TRUE ::

   A. sporadic : anomalous
   B. ingenious : innovative
   C. hilarious : witty
   D. insipid : flavorful
   E. base : dishonest

15. ERSATZ : ARTIFICAL ::

   A. natural : polluted
   B. abstruse : facile
   C. caustic : astute
   D. nascent : incipient
   E. ribald : naïve

16. DIATRIBE : EULOGY ::

   A. recommendation : commendation
   B. impugnation : chastisement
   C. rebuke : reproof
   D. verity : axiomatic
   E. remonstration : encomium

17. HAGIOGRAPHY : VENERATES ::

   A. polemic : attacks
   B. vendetta : scares
   C. complaint : angers
   D. report : obscures
   E. truism : enunciates

Sentence Completions

Directions: Each sentence below contains one or two blanks, with each blank corresponding to an omitted word. Find the answer choice that has the word or set or words that best fits the meaning of the sentence as a whole.

18. Although _____ continues on minor points, the _____ themes of the General's plan have been accepted.

   A. discussion..peripheral
   B. debate..central
   C. dissension..cultural
   D. discovery..main
   E. agreement..basic

19. Recent advances in research methodologies in neuroscience have created excitement in academic circles and have _____ greater interest in funding new research projects in the field.

   A. stymied
   B. intensified
   C. magnified
   D. engendered
   E. multiplied

20. Although the boom appeared to still be in full swing, in the latter years of the decade, most economic indicators pointed to _____ times ahead.

- A. leaner
- B. profitable
- C. healthy
- D. daring
- E. aberrant

21. Though often crude and overly _____, early theories of biogenesis were important for the _____ of the question of life's origin.

- A. dramatic..institutionalization
- B. hypothetical..clarification
- C. inscrutable..illumination
- D. schematic..extermination
- E. simplistic..advancement

22. The lawyer's argumentation was _____ and factually misleading, but these problems in his closing argument were masked by his _____ and superior mastery of language.

- A. spurious..elusiveness
- B. debonair..equivocations
- C. duplicitous..dissembling
- D. specious..eloquence
- E. spectacular..suaveness

23. The professor became _____ after attempting to explain the important concept multiple different ways, but her visible frustration only made the student less likely to _____ the material.

- A. mystified..assimilate
- B. belligerent..understand
- C. stupefied..comprehend
- D. vexed..grasp
- E. agitated..eschew

Reading Comprehension

Directions: Questions follow each passage. After reading the passage, determine the best answer for each question based on the passage's content.

Passage 1

Line   The nature and structure of dark matter is a primary topic in contemporary cosmology, the sub-discipline of astronomy in which the universe is studied

(5)   as a whole. Dark matter has aroused great interest in cosmological circles, because current theories of the evolution of the universe require the hypothesis that dark matter constitutes nearly

(10)   three-fourths of the matter in the universe. This hypothesis, if true, makes understanding dark matter of signal importance to understanding the universe.

(15)   Dark matter is matter that does not interact with electromagnetic waves— that is, it does not emit or absorb light. In contrast, light or regular matter does interact with electromagnetic waves and

(20)   therefore does emit and absorb light. When astronomers look into space with electromagnetic sensitive telescopes (or other forms of light sensitive telescopes), they can detect light matter but not dark

(25)   matter. This is how dark matter earned its moniker. Astronomers are not able to "see" it with conventional telescopes.

The existence of dark matter in a particular region of space must be

(30)   inferred from the dark matter's gravitational interaction with light matter. Like light matter, dark matter gravitationally attracts all matter and so sustains a gravitational field. As an astronomer

(35)   studies a galaxy, he or she can infer the presence of dark matter if the galaxy's motion requires gravitational interactions greater than those afforded by the galaxy's light matter.

(40)   Our understanding of dark matter does not extend much beyond this rudimentary model of matter that is gravitationally interactive but electromagnetically non-interactive. Since most

(45)   astronomical probing of the universe employs light-sensitive instruments, knowledge of dark matter comes only indirectly. Thus, we are left to theoretical hypotheses about dark matter until more

(50)   fecund methods of investigating dark matter are developed.

24. The author's tone toward the future advancement of our understanding of dark matter is

A.   deeply pessimistic.
B.   moderately skeptical.
C.   guardedly hopeful.
D.   tenaciously idealistic.
E.   basically theoretical.

25. According to the passage, dark matter

I. gravitationally interacts with light matter.
II. does interact with electromagnetic waves.
III. is similar to light matter in its gravitational properties.

A. I only
B. III only
C. I and II only
D. I and III only
E. I, II, and III

26. It can be inferred from the third paragraph that

A. light matter sustains a gravitational field.
B. regular matter is more stable than dark matter.
C. astronomers infer the presence of light matter if a galaxy's dark matter does not fully account for gravitational interactions.
D. dark matter is of primary importance in contemporary cosmology.
E. theoretical hypotheses about dark matter are becoming more refined.

Passage 2

Line   Though the discipline of historiography purports to be an empirical endeavor free of the biases of political persuasion and temperament, the actual writing of
(5)   history is often reduced to the role of ideology's handmaiden. Histories of the French Revolution serve as a prime example of this historiographic tendency. A survey of the histories written on the
(10)   French Revolution produces an impressive array of narratives of late eighteenth century France. Within this diverse crowd of narratives the causes, inner workings, and final consequences of the
(15)   Revolution all have differing assignments.

To the flagship conservative, Edmund Burke, writing contemporaneously with the events, the Revolution was a sudden
(20)   and radical manipulation of the French nation by a small class of *philosophes*, literati, and the newly-monied. In Burke's view, these so-termed aspirants to power successively harnessed methods of mass
(25)   persuasion to incite revolt and to ultimately destroy the basic institutions of French society and in their place erect a historical novelty, the newly christened French Republic. In an instructive
(30)   contrast, Alex de Tocqueville, a French provincial aristocrat, writing a few decades after Burke, saw the Revolution as a logical consequence and unfolding of the reforms set in motion by the *ancien*
(35)   *regime*. On this account, the Revolution was a continuation of the "administrative revolution" begun by Louis XVI. In this light, the French Republic was the reasonable outgrowth of the evolution of
(40)   French society that stretched far back in the eighteenth century, as opposed to a monstrous and cataclysmic break with France's past.

Both of these figures, through their
(45)   respective historical fame, have come to embody loaded historical mythoi themselves, but the contrast between their understanding and interpretation of the events of the French Revolution is
(50)   still illuminating with respect to historiography. The complexity of large-scale historical events resists simplification into incontrovertible datum in the service of one narrative over another. This obtuse

(55) reality complicates the historian's attempt to simply ply her trade, but nonetheless is a facet of historiography that must be addressed if history is to be written with intellectual honesty.

27. The passage would most appropriately be titled

    A. "The French Revolution: Two Competing Views."
    B. "Contemporary Issues in Historiography."
    C. "Challenges in Intellectually Honest Historiography."
    D. "Methodologies in Intellectual Historiography."
    E. "Historiography's Dark Secret."

28. The second paragraph's role in the passage as a whole is to

    A. present a view contrary to the one presented in the introductory paragraph.
    B. conceptually link the first and third paragraphs.
    C. illustrate with examples the thesis of the passage.
    D. offer a complimentary interpretation to the one given in the first paragraph.
    E. attack the topic sentence of the first paragraph.

29. In line 28, the author states that in Burke's view, the French Republic was a "historical novelty." This implies that Burke believed the French Republic

    A. bore close resemblance to its historical predecessor.
    B. shared some resemblance to its historical predecessor.
    C. bore no resemblance to its historical predecessor.
    D. was the logical outgrowth of its historical predecessor.
    E. had minimal institutional continuity with its historical predecessor.

30. The author employs the idea that there are "diverse narratives" (line 12–13) of the French Revolution to support the contention that historiography

    A. is merely a function of the historian's biases.
    B. can be influenced by the historian's ideology.
    C. is not a science.
    D. is the discipline of sophisticated story telling.
    E. can be manipulated by diverse interests.

270

Answers and Explanations

The following notes are intended to show you one way in which the correct answer can be determined. If you found the right answer using another method, good for you! The more strategies you have at your disposal, the better off you will be.

Quantitative

1. **C** For Column A, the number of minutes in 6 hours (since $h = 6$) can be found by multiplying: (6)(60 minutes) = 360 minutes, or 360. For Column B, you must know that a square has four right angles, all of which equal 90 degrees. This means Column B works out to: (4)(90) = 360.

   This first problem is fairly straightforward, and even though there was a variable involved, definite real numbers were found for both columns. Be aware that this will change as the questions get harder. On later problems, the use of variables will lead to column quantities that have more than one possible answer, so even though these problems will resemble this earlier one, finding the correct answer will not be as straightforward.

2. **D** Since they are a simple shape with a ton of special cases and associated rules, triangles make many appearances on the standard GRE. On question 2, the triangle has a right angle, meaning the Pythagorean theorem can be applied. Start with the basic Pythagorean theorem:

   $$a^2 + b^2 = c^2$$

   $$a^2 + b^2 - b^2 = c^2 - b^2 \text{ (This subtracts } b^2 \text{from both sides)}$$

   $$a^2 = c^2 - b^2$$

   Column A can be written as either a^2 or $c^2 - b^2$. As for Column B, the hypotenuse is length c, so the square of the hypotenuse minus itself would be $c^2 - c$. Comparing this to Column A, you

271

can see that both have an initial c^2 that is then subtracted by either b^2(Column A) or c (Column B). The problem boils down to how c compares with b^2. Frankly, there's no way to know. The variable b could be smaller than one, in which case its square would be even smaller. Depending on which numbers you plug in, Column A or Column B might be greater.

3. D The perimeter of the square is $4h$, but you do not know how this relates to h^2. If, $h = 1$ then Column B is greater, but if $h = 10$, then Column A is greater. Note that if you confuse the area of a square with its perimeter, you will find the two columns are equal, leading you to pick the incorrect answer (C).

4. D You might jump to say that the answer is (C), but that would be a little hasty. The absolute value sign (those two bars on either side) means that x could be either 3 or -3, and that y could equal either 4 or -4. Remember that $|y - x| \neq |y| - |x| = 1$. We actually do not know what $|y - x|$ equals. It could be seven, or it could be one. The answer, then, is (D).

5. A For people rusty with their math terminology, this question looks much more difficult that it really is. The three smallest prime numbers are 2, 3, and 5, and their sum is 10. As for Column B, the square root of 49 is 7. You probably don't know the square root of 8 off the top of your head, but you do know that the square root of 9 is 3. This means the square root of 8 must be something less than 3. *Seven + something less than 3 = something a little less than 10.* Therefore, Column A is greater.

6. A In looking at the figure, we can reason that $a + b = 180$ since the lines are parallel. Thus, we need to manipulate Column A so that we can compare it to $a + b$. In the numerator, we can factor out an a and then eliminate it in the following manner:

$$\frac{a^2 + ab + a}{a} = \frac{a(a + b + 1)}{a} = \frac{\cancel{a}(a + b + 1)}{\cancel{a}} = a + b + 1$$

This leaves us with $a + b + 1$, which is 1 greater than Column B's $a + b = 180$. Therefore, Column A is greater.

7. B A good way to attack a problem like this is to sketch it out. If J is space 1 then there are two possibilities: JBA and JAB. If (B) is in space 1, BJA and BAJ. If (A) is in space 1, AJB and ABJ. That is six distinct arrangements. Can you get anymore? Try to put J in space 2, AJB or BJA. You already have both of those counted.

Try any other arrangement, and you will see that it is a repeat. (B) is greater.

8. C This one is tricky, but not if you recall that π is defined as the ratio of the circumference divided by the diameter. If you didn't recall this, you still could have tried to find an equation that related all three entities, such as $C = 2\pi r = \pi d \rightarrow \pi = \dfrac{C}{d}$. As for Column B it can be manipulated like this, $\dfrac{2C}{2d} = \dfrac{C}{d} = \pi$. The columns are equal, so the answer is (C).

9. D This requires straightforward arithmetic work.

Column A	**Column B**
$\left[\dfrac{a^2b}{2} - 12a\right]\left(\dfrac{1}{a}\right)$	$3\left[b\left(\dfrac{a}{6} - \dfrac{1}{3b}\right) - 4\right]$
$= \dfrac{ab}{2} - 12$	$= 3b\left(\dfrac{a}{6} - \dfrac{1}{3b}\right) - 12$
	$= \dfrac{ab}{2} - 1 - 12$

You can cancel out the -12, since both columns share it. Column A and B share the first term, but Column B is the first term -1. Since we are dealing with positive numbers here, that makes Column A greater.

10. B The only way that your triangle could be a triangle is if the third side is greater than 6. If it is not, then the three sides would not connect, making an enclosed figure with 3 angles and 3 sides. This is readily apparent if you attempt to make a triangle with sides 1, 4, and 10. Thus, (B) is greater.

11. C The number set is {10, 12, 14, 16, 18}, so, the median is 14. The mean of any evenly spaced number set is always the median, so the mean is also 14 (you could also just sum the numbers and divide by 5).

12. B This one is greatly simplified if you realize that you are looking at a right triangle here, and you know two of its sides, namely 3 and 4. Using the Pythagorean theorem or recognizing it is a 3:4:5 triangle, you can determine the third side is 5. That is the value of Column A. For Column B, the slope of $\overline{GH}$ can be determined by simply counting the rise (4) and the run (3) and putting the former over the latter, $-\frac{4}{3}$. Now multiply it,

$\left(-\frac{4}{3}\right)(-4) = \frac{16}{3} = 5\frac{1}{3}$, which is greater than 5.

13. B The greatest that Column A could be is $9 + 9 + 8 = 26$, since A and B are distinct digits, so the answer then is (B).

14. A A good way to approach this problem is make a table filling in the information you do know and from that trying to determine the information you need to answer the question.

If there are 73 total animals and 35 dogs, then there are 38 cats. If there are 40 females, then there are 33 males. If x is the number of male cats, then the number of male dogs is $x + 9$, since it states there are 9 less male cats than dogs.

The total number of male animals is 33, so $x + (x + 9) = 33 \rightarrow 2x = 24 \rightarrow x = 12$. There are 12 male cats and 21 $(x + 9)$ male dogs. The total number of cats is 38, so that means there are 26 female cats.

15. C There are two ways to find the answer. One way is to plug in the answer choices and see which ones work or solve the binomial expression. You can also solve the equation:

$$-x^2 = -2x - 15 \rightarrow$$
$$-x^2 + x^2 = -2x - 15 + x^2 \rightarrow$$
$$0 = x^2 - 2x - 15 \rightarrow$$
$$0 = (x - 5)(x + 3) \rightarrow$$
$$x = -3, 5$$

16. E The first thing to do is to convert each answer choice into $y = mx + b$ form. From the graph, you can figure that the slope is -1, and the y-intercept is -2. Now you can simply look for the equation with these characteristics, and (E) is it.

17. C Eyeball the graph to see which months have both adult and children graphs near the zero line in the middle. Both Januaries do, but 1963 is clearly a smaller total number. Thus, (C) is correct.

18. B If you notice that March–April 1962 is the only time the child flu incidence exceeds 100, this one will be straightforward: answer choice (B).

19. C If the area of the top of the box is 15, then the third side is of length 5 since this length times 3 must yield an area of 15. Now

274

that you know all three lengths you just need to add up the areas of all six sides. Four of the sides have an area of 15, which sums to 60. The two end sides have an area of 9, which sums to 18. Add these together and you get (C).

20. B Begin by determining the median and the mode. The mode is simply the number that occurs the most times in the set. That is clearly 7. The median is the number that is in the middle if you line them up from least to greatest. The two middle numbers are 7, so halfway between them is still just 7. The median minus the mode then is $7 - 7 = 0$.

21. B Look to the number chart to find this one. The ratio we are looking for is criminal/civil. Remember that you are looking for the quarter that has the greatest ratio and not the quarter with the largest numbers. Look for numbers whose difference is great, and then compare. The 2nd quarter in 1970 is the answer, choice (B).

22. B You need to be careful on this one. It has a number of steps, but none of them are hard. First, estimate how many female criminal lawyers there are (approximately 10,000). Now estimate how many female civil lawyers there are (approximately 20,000). So the ratio is, 20,000 to 10,000, which reduces to 2:1 or (B).

23. C As the graph headings make clear, (A) and (B) are not fields of law but are types of law. With that obstacle out of the way, you merely need to add up the bar graph pairs to see which is the greatest.

24. A Since you know the area of the rectangle and one of the sides, you can deduce the length of the second side $\left(\overline{BC} = 3\right)$. This side also happens to be the radius of the quarter circle. Thus the circumference of the full circle is $C = 2\pi(3) = 6\pi$. But you only need a quarter of the circumference, which is $6\pi\left(\frac{1}{4}\right) = \frac{3}{2}\pi$. Now $\overline{CD} = 4$ and $\overline{EC} = 3$, so $\overline{ED} = 1$. So, (A) is the answer.

25. C The longest distance between two corners in a rectangular box—though sounding difficult to find—is actually rather easy to compute. Simply square all three sides, sum them, then take the square root of this sum and you have it. Here it would be:

$$2^2 + 3^2 + 4^2 =$$
$$4 + 9 + 16 = 29$$

whose square root is (C). The other way to do this problem is to draw the figure and start using the Pythagorean theorem. You need to find the diagonal of one of the rectangular sides, and then create another triangle using that diagonal, the remaining side, and a hypotenuse, which just happens to be the diagonal from one corner of the box to another. You end up with the same answer, (C).

26. B The overall average is the sum of all the scores of all the classes divided by the total number of students. You do not have either of those numbers, so you have to arrive at the overall average in some other fashion. A weighted average would do the trick here. Since there are twice as many fifth graders, you weight their average with a coefficient of two and the sixth grade average with a coefficient of one.

$$\frac{(2)(15) + (1)(18)}{3} = \frac{48}{3} = 16$$

27. C On this graph there are two x values for every y value; thus, it is the x variable that should be squared. Furthermore, when $x = 0$ on this graph, $y = 1$, so you need an equation that reflects this. That is true of (C).

28. E You can find the area of the circle since you know the radius ($a = gpr^2 = 16\pi$). If you find the area of the two squares then you can subtract from the area of the circle to find the area of the shaded region. The diagonal of each square is the radius of the circle, so this number is 4. From this you can deduce that the sides of the square are $2\sqrt{2}$. Thus the area of each square is 8. Incidentally, you know that the squares are congruent because the length of their diagonal is the same. This makes the area in the two squares 16. The area of the circle minus the area of the squares is $16\pi - 16$, which is equivalent to (E).

Verbal

Antonyms

1. **B** To have *zeal* is to have great *enthusiasm*. The opposite of zeal is *apathy*, choice (B).

2. **C** *Heterogeneous* is the antonym of *homogeneous*. Homogeneous means "to be uniform in kind or quality; similar." Choice (C) comes closest to this.

3. **A** *Fealty* is loyalty. Thus, if you know the definition, this antonym is straightforward, *disloyalty*, choice (A).

4. **E** Something *archaic* is old or antiquated. A good pre-guess then would be *new*. In looking down the list of answer choices, only (E), *novel*, fits our pre-guess. In this context, novel is not a noun, which you can tell since all choices and the stem word are adjectives. The adjective *novel* means new, original, or unique.

5. **E** To *assuage* is to *pacify* or to *satiate*. Choices (B) and (D) are synonyms, not antonyms. The opposite of assuaging an issue is to *provoke* it, answer choice (E). Note that even if you didn't know what the stem word meant, if you had two answer choices that mean almost the same thing, (B) and (D), it's a good guess that neither of them will be right since there's no way they could both be right.

6. **A** If you did not know the definition of *mercurial*, you might have recalled that mercury was once used in thermometers to gauge temperatures. The mercury goes up and down in a thermometer, and in similar fashion, *mercurial* means to have an unstable or fast-changing mood. The opposite of this is (A).

7. **C** *Opprobrium* means severe scorn, so you are looking for a word that means something like *approval* or *praise*. Choice (C), *commendation*, fits the bill.

8. **C** This is a tough word. *Tyro* means beginner or novice. Thus a good pre-guess would be experienced. None of the words fit with our pre-guess except (C), *virtuoso*. A virtuoso is a master of a medium or instrument.

9. **A** Something that is *soporific* is sleep inducing. The opposite of this then would be something that would wake you up. *Stimulant*, choice (A), fits.

Analogies

10. **A** The stem relationship is definitional: To *prattle* is to *babble*. To *battle* is to *fight*, so (A) fits. Do any of the others? No. "To *digest* is to *eat*" does not work because after you eat something, you then digest it. These events come in sequence, but they don't mean the same thing.

11. **C** Here the relationship between the stem words is one of degree. To *fawn* is to *flatter* excessively. In similar fashion, to *burgeon* is to *grow* quickly. Choice (B) does not share the same relationship of degree because it is a relationship of definition (to *divulge* something is to *tell* it). Choice (E) might have also seemed attractive, but remember to *misquote* is not the same thing as *lying*.

12. **B** The *denouement* is the end/falling action of the *story*. Which answer pair has the same relationship? Choice (B), a *sunset*, is the end of a *day*. If you didn't know the meaning of denouement, you should be very wary of answer choices (A) and (C), which have second words meant to catch people shopping for connections.

13. **D** *Federalism* is a form/kind of *political order*. Going through the answer choices, a *class* is composed of *students*, a *dictatorship* is not a kind of *anarchy*, a *colleague* might be in a *cohort*, *insomnia* is a kind of *sleep disorder*, and something *extrinsic* is *external* to a thing. Clearly, (D) is the only pair that shares the same relationship.

14. **D** What is the stem relationship? To be *spurious* is to not be *true*. Thus, we have a relationship of opposites. The only answer choice that shares this relationship is (D), since to be *insipid* is to not be *flavorful*.

15. **D** Remember, always begin with the stem relationship. It is definitional, as something *ersatz* is *artificial*. If you did not know the definition of *ersatz*, you could have eliminated (A) and (C) since neither has a necessary relationship. Of choices (B), (D), and (E), only (D)—to be *nascent* is to be *incipient*—has the definitional relationship.

16. **E** A *diatribe* is harsh verbal attack, and a *eulogy* is a speech of praise or remembrance. Thus, the words are antonyms. The stem relationship is a *diatribe* is the opposite of a *eulogy*. To *remonstrate* is to reprove, or stand in opposition to, while an *encomium* is warm praise. Thus a *remonstration* is the opposite of an *encomium*.

278

17. A The stem relationship is one of definition, a *hagiography venerates* its subject. In (A), a *polemic attacks* its subject. A *vendetta* may or may not *scare* its object. The same is true for a *complaint*. The other choices do not have a strong relationship. Choice (A) is the answer. If you have trouble with the vocabulary, you could look at (C) and (D) and eliminate these choices for having weak links.

Sentence Completions

18. B On two blank questions, it's easiest to consider one blank at a time. Attacking the second blank first makes most sense since you know that it is in contrast to *minor points* (the trigger word *Although* should tip your hand). What is a contrast to a *minor point*? A major one. You should go look for something like *major* or *important*. That eliminates (A) and (C). Into the first blank, *debate* clearly fits best of the remaining choices, as a debate is more likely to have *themes* than an agreement or discovery. So, (B) is the answer.

19. D The blank is a word that goes along with *created excitement*, and so it is definitely positive. What is a positive verb that flows with greater interest? *Created* is a good pre-guess. Check the answer choices, and (D), *engendered*, fits your pre-guess quite well.

20. A The "*although*" at the beginning of the sentence clues you into the fact that this is a contrast sentence. The good times spoken of in the present are contrasted with what is in the blank. What is a contrast with good times? Tough times. Choice (A) works well.

21. E It should be easy to eliminate some answer choices with the first blank since it has to fit with *crude*. Choice (C) certainly does not fit and possibly (A) also. The second blank is a positive word since the logic of the sentence is that *though* the early theories were *crude*, they were still helpful. Thus we can eliminate (A) and (D). Choice (E) works best.

22. D Here the first blank seems more assailable. You know that it has to pair with *factually misleading*. Choices (B) and (E) do not, so eliminate them. As for the second blank, you know two things: It pairs with *superior mastery of language*, and it *masks* the *problems* mentioned in the first part of the sentence. Thus, it must be something fairly positive. Choices (A) and (C) do not meet these requirements, but (D) does.

23. D A pre-guess on the second blank would be a good place to start. Something like *understand* works. Checking the answer choices, we can eliminate (E). The first blank goes along with the professor being *visibly frustrated*. Choice (B) is out because it does not fit the context. Choices (A) and (C) are okay choices, but (D) definitely works best in the first blank.

Reading Comprehension

24. C The author's tone toward the advancement of our understanding of dark matter is most clearly seen in the last sentence of the passage. There, the author looks forward to a time when "more fecund methods of investigating dark matter are developed." That is an expression of hope, but not unqualifiedly so (just read the first part of that sentence to see that). Thus, (C) is the best answer.

25. D Here, you just have to go through each proposition and see which ones the passage relates to.

Option I—the passage makes clear that this is true. Check the third and fourth paragraph for verification of this.

Option II—the passage states the exact opposite of this.

Option III—lines 31–33, "Like light matter, dark matter gravitationally attracts all matter." III then is true. Choice (D) then is correct.

26. A To start, reread the entire third paragraph. You have to go through the answer choices to see which is a correct inference from the third paragraph. For choice (A), the third paragraph reads, "Like light matter, dark matter gravitationally attracts all matter and so sustains a gravitational field." If dark matter sustains a gravitational field and dark matter is like light matter in this respect, then it can be inferred that light matter sustains a gravitational field. For choice (B), the third paragraph does not mention anything about the comparative stability of light and dark matter. Choice (C) has it backward, as astronomers infer the existence of dark matter from insufficient light matter. Choice (D) is true, but is stated in the first paragraph, not the third. For (E), the third paragraph does not discuss theoretical hypotheses about dark matter. Choice (A) is the correct answer.

27. C On a question like this, you have to go through the answer choices to see which is best. The title, of course, should reflect the tone and content of the passage, so you are looking for the

280

title that best does this. Choice (A) could be the title of the second paragraph, but not of the entire passage. Choice (B) sounds appealing but there is no indication in the passage that the issues discussed are just ones for the present time. Choice (C) captures the tone and content of the passage and so is a likely candidate. Choice (D) is also appealing except for the phrase *Intellectual Historiography*, which does not appear in the passage. Choice (E) is much too extreme in its tone. Choice (C) is the best choice.

28. C Reread the second paragraph (or at least skim it) and consider its relation to the rest of the passage. Then, proceed to the question. Notice that the second paragraph contains two contrasting examples. The answer choice should reflect this. The basic thesis of the passage is that there are multiple narratives in historiography of the same events. The content of the second paragraph illustrates this thesis. Thus, (C) is correct.

29. C Go and read the relevant text and be careful to have in mind what Burke's view is, which is that the Revolution produced a result that was a radical departure from the past. On this view the phrase *historical novelty* clearly implies the newness and uniqueness of the French Republic. Choice (C) fits this well. Choice (E) might have seemed attractive but recall that institutional continuity was never mentioned in the passage. That should make you wary of that choice. Choice (D) is the view of de Tocqueville, not Burke. So, (C) is the best choice.

30. B This question relates to the main idea and tone of the passage. The correct answer will reflect both.

Main idea: Historiography can be influenced by ideology and so intellectually honest historiography should be mindful of this.

Tone: Guarded optimism that with care historiography can be intellectually honest

Choice (A) is too extreme. Choice (B) fits well with both. As for (C), though the passage states, "historiography purports to be an empirical endeavor free of . . . biases" the passage neither defines what it is to be a science nor states that historiography is not one. Choice (D) is cynical, and the tone of the passage is not (just read the last sentence of the passage). Choice (E) is also cynical, more so than the passage is. So, (B) is the best choice.

Practice Test

2

1.

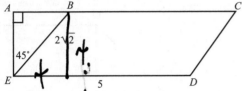

BCDE is a parallelogram. What is its area?

A. $\sqrt{10}$
B. 10
C. $10\sqrt{2}$
D. $10\sqrt{5}$
E. $10\sqrt{10}$

2. If $\&x = [x - (x - 1)](x + 2)$ then $\&(\&(2)) =$

A. 4
B. 6
C. 12
D. 18
E. 24

3. The price of Company *X*'s stock started the day at \$40 per share, rose to \$90 per share, and then fell to \$45 per share. Compared to the price at the beginning of the day, the final price of the stock was a

A. 10% increase.
B. 10% decrease.
C. 12.5% increase.
D. 12.5% decrease.
E. 50% decrease.

4. If $3c + 6d = 24$ and $4a + 3d = 18$, what does *a* equal in terms of *c*?

A. $\dfrac{9}{2} - \dfrac{3}{4}c$
B. $\dfrac{3}{8}c + \dfrac{3}{2}$
C. $\dfrac{3}{11}c + \dfrac{12}{11}$
D. $\dfrac{1}{2}c + 4$
E. $\dfrac{3}{4}c + 5$

Questions 5–6 refer to the following graph.

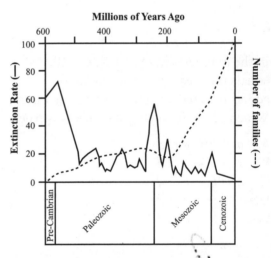

5. How many millions of years ago did the extinction rate reach its highest value?

A. 200
B. 245
C. 500
D. 560
E. 600

6. In which era did the extinction rate and number of families have the same value the most number of times?

   A. Pre-Cambrian
   B. Paleozoic
   C. Mesozoic
   D. Cenozoic
   E. Silurian

7. Which of the following numbers would have a remainder of zero if it were divided by 3 or 6 and 9?

   A. 1,024
   B. 1,323
   C. 1,506
   D. 1,632
   E. 1,764

8. In the number set {15, 10, 7, 12, 10, 18} a equals the mean, b equals the mode, c equals the median, and d equals the range. Which of the following statements is true?

   A. $a < b = c < d$
   B. $a > b < c > d$
   C. $a = b = c > d$
   D. $a > b < c = d$
   E. $a < b < c < d$

9.

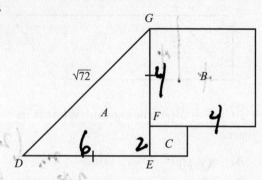

The area of square B is 16 meters squared and $\overline{DE} = \overline{EG}$ What is the area of square C in meters squared?

   A. 1
   B. 2
   C. 4
   D. 6
   E. 9

Questions 10–12 refer to the following graphs.

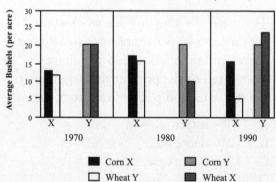

Bushels of Wheat Per Acre Versus Bushels of Corn Per Acre in County X and Y

10. Which county and crop had the smallest percentage change from 1970 to 1990?

   A. County X, Corn
   B. County Y, Corn
   C. County X, Wheat
   D. County Y, Wheat
   E. None of the above

11. How much on average would ten acres of corn in County Y in 1980 produce?

   A. 100 bushels
   B. 120 bushels
   C. 150 bushels
   D. 200 bushels
   E. 220 bushels

12. What is the ratio of bushels of corn produced per acre to bushels of wheat produced per acre in County Y in 1980?

   A. 1:1
   B. 2:1
   C. 3:1
   D. 3:2
   E. 3:4

13. How many distinct integers less than 100 can be formulated with the digits 2, 4, and 6?

   A. 9
   B. 11
   C. 12
   D. 14
   E. 15

14.

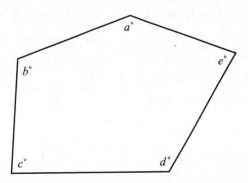

For the 5-sided polygon above $a + b = 160$ degrees and $d - b = 30$. How many degrees is $c + e + b$?

   A. 70
   B. 125
   C. 350
   D. 300
   E. 325

15. What is the sum of the consecutive integers from 15 to 55 (inclusive)?

   A. 1405
   B. 1435
   C. 1465
   D. 1500
   E. 1587

Column A	Column B	Column A	Column B

16. The circumference of a circle with a diameter equal to 2 | The perimeter of a square that has one side equal to $1\frac{1}{2}$ | **20.** The circumference of a circle with a diameter of 7 | The perimeter of a rectangle with an area of 24

17.
$$\frac{\left(\frac{1}{3}\right)\left(\frac{1}{4}\right)}{\left(\frac{2}{3}\right)\left(\frac{2}{4}\right)} \qquad \frac{\left(\frac{2}{3}\right)\left(\frac{1}{5}\right)}{\left(\frac{2}{5}\right)\left(\frac{1}{3}\right)}$$

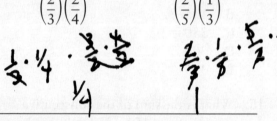

21. z is a one-digit even integer. The square root of z is also an integer.

$z + z + z \qquad\qquad z^2$

18. $\overline{AB} = \overline{CD}$

A ●——— B ●——— C ●——— D ●
  $r+s$ $2t+3r$ $s+3t$

$\overline{BC}$ \qquad\qquad 10t

22. \$16,000 is invested at 5% simple annual interest.

Interest accrued after eight months \qquad Six hundred dollars

19. $3 - 2x > 5$

$x^2 \qquad\qquad 2$

286

	Column A	Column B

23. The ratio of a to b is three fourths.

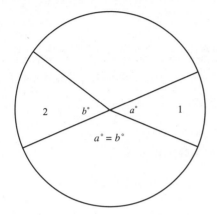

The area of sector 1	Seventy-five percent of sector 2

24. | The greatest common factor of 24 and 120 | The least common multiple of 8 and 6 |
|---|---|

25. m and n are integers.

$(m + n)(m + n)$ $\qquad$ $(m + 2n)(m - n)$

	Column A	Column B

26. $x^2 - 4y^2 + 7 = 7$

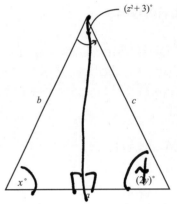

$c^2 + a^2$	$a^2 + b^2$

(handwritten:) $x^2 = 4y^2$

$x = 2y$

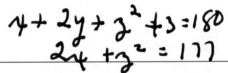

(handwritten:) $x + 2y + z^2 + 3 = 180$

$2x + z^2 = 177$

27. C and D are integers, and $C > D$.

The number of integers from D to C inclusive	$\dfrac{C^2 - CD + 2C}{4C - 3C}$

28. $\{x, y, x + 4, z, y + 3\}$

This number set is ordered from least to greatest, and x, y, and z are distinct integers.

$z - 5$ $\qquad$ x

Verbal

30 Questions—30 Minutes

Antonyms

Directions: Each question contains a word printed in capital letters, followed by five answer choices. Choose the answer choice that contains the word or phrase most nearly OPPOSITE in meaning to the word in capital letters.

1. PRAGMATIC :

   A. reticent
   B. quixotic
   C. lavish
   D. practical
   E. hopeful

2. COGENT :

   A. unintelligent
   B. culpable
   C. thoughtful
   D. unconvincing
   E. mysterious

3. OBDURATE :

   A. persuadable
   B. gullible
   C. litigious
   D. manageable
   E. stubborn

4. EBULLIENT :

   A. stoic
   B. stationary
   C. stern
   D. turgid
   E. static

5. GARRULOUS :

   A. trepidatious
   B. decorious
   C. irksome
   D. gregarious
   E. taciturn

6. ENERVATE :

   A. disabuse
   B. strengthen
   C. maximize
   D. maltreat
   E. articulate

7. MANUMIT :

   A. enslave
   B. indemnify
   C. ostracize
   D. simplify
   E. delete

8. ADUMBRATE :

- A. to cease
- B. to blandish
- C. to foreshadow
- D. to make explicit
- E. to loosen

9. PANEGYRIC :

- A. assertion
- B. elegy
- C. dirge
- D. dissertation
- E. obloquy

Analogies

Directions: In each question, there is an initial pair of words or phrases that are related in some manner. Select the answer choice containing the lettered pair that best expresses a relationship similar to the initial pair.

10. ECLIPSE : OVERSHADOW ::

- A. set : rise
- B. outstrip : flail
- C. debauch : debase
- D. overcome : outstretch
- E. pervert : correct

11. EMPHATIC : INSIST ::

- A. contentious : argue
- B. absorbed : engrossed
- C. raucous : mitigate
- D. delusional : rage
- E. intentional : forget

12. ASTRONOMER : STARS ::

- A. account : financial records
- B. librarian : books
- C. historian : past
- D. police officer : laws
- E. magician : tricks

13. INOCULATE : DISEASE ::

- A. defraud : conspirator
- B. detest : agitator
- C. delight : friend
- D. defend : enemy
- E. defame : title

14. HALCYON : PEACEFUL ::

- A. tectonic : magnetic
- B. tempestuous : placid
- C. surreptitious : clandestine
- D. boisterous : rueful
- E. terrifying : relaxing

15. DESOLATE : VERDANT ::

- A. destitute : opulent
- B. rococo : ornate
- C. astringent : severe
- D. tropical : humid
- E. technical : detailed

16. HARBINGER : PRESAGE ::

- A. computer : calculates
- B. television : broadcasts
- C. liaison : interrogates
- D. messenger : relates
- E. broker : absconds

17. ASSEVERATE : AVER ::

- A. beseech : request
- B. reject : install
- C. answer : reply
- D. enrage : mollify
- E. approach : accost

289

Sentence Completions

Directions: Each sentence below contains one or two blanks, with each blank corresponding to an omitted word. Find the answer choice that has the word or set or words that best fits the meaning of the sentence as a whole.

18. Mr. Thomas had, in his local community, earned the reputation as being somewhat of a miser, but a review of his financial records revealed he was actually a _____.

    A. maverick
    B. hooligan
    C. maestro
    D. spendthrift
    E. micro-manager

19. Recent demographic shifts in the population of Country X have resulted in many traditional political alliances becoming _____ as nascent political parties _____ large swathes of the electoral landscape.

    A. obsolete..secure
    B. dislodged..provide
    C. unhinged..procure
    D. solvent..release
    E. elusive..gain

20. Many see the attempt to sway public _____, though ostensibly a process of popular persuasion, to be _____ since it has been undertaken employing questionable pretences.

    A. consent..disreputable
    B. opinion..undemocratic
    C. disfavor..impractical
    D. ill-will..treacherous
    E. disinterest..crude

21. The _____ feuds between rival factions of the company's board destroyed the effectiveness of the company's leadership.

    A. fatalistic
    B. infernal
    C. hegemonic
    D. internecine
    E. flagging

22. Unlike his most recent predecessor, the newly elected mayor did not appoint friends and associates to high posts in the city government, but eschewed such _____ in favor of a _____-based appointment criteria.

    A. nepotism..value
    B. cronyism..merit
    C. favoritism..work
    D. jingoism..resumé
    E. recidivism..experience

23. Though customarily marked by deliberate and _____ prose, the author's most recent correspondence was convoluted and _____.

    A. terse..tiresome
    B. genuine..superfluous
    C. acidic..prosaic
    D. urbane..ubiquitous
    E. succinc..prolix

Reading Comprehension

Directions: Questions follow each passage. After reading the passage, determine the best answer for each question based on the passage's content.

Passage 1

Line The existence and novelty of the domain Archaean has demanded many long-standing hypotheses in biology to be reconfigured. The most basic challenge
(5) that the discovery of Archaeans presented to biologists was classification. Prior to the discovery of the existence of Archaeans, life was classified into five kingdoms: Animalia, Plantae, Fungi, Proto-
(10) zoa, and Bacteria. But Archaeans, being such a biological novelty, did not readily submit to this system of classification. In fact, an innovation of biological classification was needed to properly place
(15) Archaeans in the panorama of life. Previously, kingdom had been the most general biological designation, but to properly include the Archaeans a new biological classification, the domain, was
(20) formulated. Now kingdoms are classified as a sub-group of a particular domain. Thus, domain has become the most general biological designation for life.

A second arena in which Archaeans
(25) have challenged accepted hypotheses and broadened biological horizons is in the realm of environmental extremes. It was generally accepted not more than a few decades ago that no life could exist in
(30) temperatures much hotter than 60 degrees centigrade. This limit was set because it was thought that the molecular integrity of vital cellular components could not be maintained beyond such
(35) temperatures. The thermal capacity of

cellular life, it was believed, was a fixture across all biological organisms. Archaeans, in recent decades, have repeatedly demonstrated that the previously
(40) maintained thermal threshold for life was far too low. So-called extremophilic Archaeans have been discovered to thrive in temperatures as high as 160 degrees centigrade. Such discoveries have
(45) required a broadening of biology's conceptions concerning what environments are hospitable to life.

24. This passage could best be titled

    A. "Biological Designations in Transformation."
    B. "The Archaean Diversity of Life."
    C. "The Archaean Challenge to Biological Paradigms."
    D. "Discovering Thermophilic Archaeans."
    E. "Classifying Thermophiles."

25. The passage implies that extremophilic Archaeans

    I. are able to maintain molecular integrity of cellular components past the formerly accepted thermal threshold of life.

    II. have been known to exist in moderate environments for some years, but their extremophilic properties have only recently been discovered.

    III. are able to live and thrive in temperatures as hot as 150 degrees centigrade.

    A. I only

    B. II only

    C. III only

    D. I and II only

    E. I and III only

26. The passage states that a kingdom is

    A. a sub-group within a domain.

    B. the most general biological designation.

    C. composed of sub-groups of domains.

    D. a newly formulated biological classification.

    E. an Archaean domain.

27. It can be inferred from the passage that the phrase "thermal threshold" in line 40 is

    A. the critical point temperature at which the metabolic pathways of extremophiles become functional.

    B. the temperature at which the molecular integrity of cellular components of an organism are compromised.

    C. the thermal capacity of extremophiles.

    D. an environmental extremity indicator.

    E. a biological constant across all of nature.

Passage 2

Line   Theoretical Economics faces considerable challenges in developing reliable models for public choice scenarios. These scenarios involve aggregating individual
(5)   preferences into a public choice outcome. An election in a democratic society is a well-considered example of a public choice scenario. Formulating helpful and insightful models of political elections is
(10)   a perpetual issue in politico-economic discourse.

    Many public-choice election scenario models begin with the individual as the basic building block of the aggregate
(15)   outcome. On this methodology, the primary issue is determining a proper decision-matrix for the individual in the society under consideration. The decision-matrix is a theoretical construct
(20)   which—when given the appropriate input for a particular situation—outputs the choice of a rational individual in the specified situation. The integrity of the decision-matrix is the central concern of
(25)   the model-maker. If the decision-matrix appropriately produces the choices of individuals in specific situations, then the aggregate model will be useable. However, if the decision-matrix inadequately
(30)   reflects the decision-making process of individuals, the aggregate model will be unreliable.

    Decision-matrices are often constructed on the assumption that individu-
(35)   als are rational in decision-making and that they predicate decisions upon self-interest. Furthermore, self-interest is generally construed to mean selfish interests. A serious flaw in such a
(40)   constructional is its disallowal of altruistic motivation in the decision-

matrix. It can easily be empirically verified that human choice is not predominated by altruism, but such
(45) verification does not warrant the complete exclusion of altruism from decision-matrices. Therefore, altruistic motivators should be possible inputs for any decision-matrix schema that attempts
(50) to model human preference determination.

28. The intent of the author in writing this passage is to

A. offer a radical critique of contemporary Theoretical Economics.
B. explain the basic mechanisms of modeling public choice scenarios.
C. contrast two competing views on decision-matrix construction.
D. explain why in public choice scenarios decision-matrices should include altruistic motivators.
E. criticize the assumption that society is composed of aggregates of rational decision-makers.

29. What is a common assumption of decision-matrix construction that the author does not dispute?

A. Self-interest should be construed as selfish interest.
B. Altruism is a basic motivator of human preference.
C. Individuals are rational in decision-making.
D. Altruism is an irrational predicate.
E. Inputs should be expanded to include self-interest motivators.

30. The second paragraph in the passage

A. elaborates on the issues introduced in the first paragraph.
B. presents views in contrast to those introduced in the first paragraph.
C. presents the thesis of the passage.
D. argues for the validity of the thesis of the passage.
E. describes the intellectual issues pertaining to the thesis of the passage.

Answers and Explanations

As before, the following notes are intended to show you one way in which the correct answer can be determined. Try to concern yourself with the methods used to arrive at the right answer, and not focus all your attention on whether you got the question right or wrong.

Quantitative

1. **B** The area of a parallelogram is base times height (like with a triangle). The obvious base to choose is $\overline{ED}$ and then attempt to find its height, or $\overline{AE}$. The triangle is a 45-45-90 triangle, and since the hypotenuse is $2\sqrt{2}$, the other two sides are 2. So the height is 2 and the base is 5, which makes the area 10, or (B).

2. **B** Here, you just need to be careful and work through the problem step by step.

   $$\&(2) = [2 - (2 - 1)](2 + 2) = (2 - 1)(4) = (1)(4) = 4,$$

   and now plug this result in:

   $$\begin{aligned} \&(\&(2)) = \&(4) &= [4 - (4 - 1)](4 + 2) \\ &= (4 - 3)(6) \\ &= (1)(6) \\ &= 6 \end{aligned}$$

   Choice (B) is the answer.

3. **C** You can solve this one quickly if you realize that the stock price increased and that it did so more than 10 percent. If you do not see this right off the bat, you can always just work the equation for percentage change to get the answer:

   $$\left(\frac{5}{40}\right)(100\%) = \left(\frac{1}{8}\right)(100\%) = 12.5\%$$

   The answer is (C).

4. B You need to have an equation that has only the variables a and c in it. If you multiply both sides of $4a + 3d = 18$ by two we get $8a + 6d = 36$. You can subtract this from the other equation to eliminate the d variable; $(3c + 6d = 24) - (8a + 6d = 36)$ yields $3c - 8a = -12$. Now you only need to solve for a:

$$3c - 8a = -12 \rightarrow 8a = 3c + 12 \rightarrow a = \frac{3}{8}c + \frac{3}{2}, \text{ which is (B).}$$

5. D The extinction rate is the solid line, and its highest value is its highest peak. The highest peak is in the early Paleozoic era approximately 560 million years ago.

6. B The extinction rate and the number of families have the same value when the two lines cross. You are looking, then, for the era in which the lines cross the most number of times. They do so four times in the Paleozoic era, which is more than any other, making (B) the answer.

7. E You can eliminate the odd number right off the bat, because a number has to be even in order to be divisible by 6. Now you just have to go through the remaining choices one by one:

1,024: Digits sum to 7, which is not a multiple of 3.

1,506: Digits sum to 12, which is a multiple of 3 but not 9.

1,632: Digits sum to 12, and so same as previous.

1,764: Digits sum to 18, which is a multiple of 3 and 9. For 6, the digits must sum to a multiple of 3 and the original number must be even.

8. D The mean is $\dfrac{10 + 10 + 15 + 7 + 12 + 18}{6} = \dfrac{72}{6} = 12$, and so $a = 12$. The mode is 10, and so $b = 10$. As for the median, order the numbers least to greatest {7, 10, 10, 12, 15, 18}. Since you have an even number of numbers, the median is the average of the two middle numbers. Thus, the median is 11, so $c = 11$. The range is simply the greatest number minus the least, which equals 11, so $d = 11$. So, $a > b < c = d$, which is (D).

9. **C** To begin with, you know that the sides of square *B* are equal to 4 since its area is 16. If you can find the length of the non-hypotenuse sides of triangle *A*, then you could find the answer. Since you know the hypotenuse you can use the Pythagorean theorem to find the other sides of the triangle; $a^2 + b^2 = \left(\sqrt{72}\right)^2 \rightarrow 2a^2 = 72 \rightarrow a^2 = 36 \rightarrow a = 6$. The length of the triangle side that *B* and *C* share is 6, which means that one of the sides of square *C* is 2 (since the *B* side is 4). Therefore, the area of *C* is 4, or (C).

10. **B** Eye the graph to see which of the four options changed little from its 1970 average to its 1990 average. Looking closely, you can see that the average production of corn in County Y was the same in 1970 and 1990. Thus, the percentage change is 0. That must be the smallest, so the answer is (B).

11. **C** First note that the graph is given in terms of bushels per acre. Reading the graph then, County Y in 1980 produced 15 bushels of corn per acre. Thus, 10 acres on average would produce 150 bushels, so (C) is correct.

12. **D** In 1980 County Y produced 15 bushels of corn per acre on average, and it produced 10 bushels of wheat on average. Thus, the ratio is 15:10, or 3:2, which is answer choice (D).

13. **C** It is best to write the possibilities out and count them up. In the ones column the possibilities are: 2, 4, 6. In the tens, the possibilities are: 22, 24, 26, 42, 44, 46, 62, 64, 66. That exhausts the possibilities. You get 12 when you count them up, so (C) is the answer.

14. **C** First, the sum of the interior angles of an *n*-sided polygon is $(n - 2)(180)$, which makes the sum of the interior angles of a 5-sided polygon 540 degrees. You can find the sum of $a + d$ by summing the two equations $a + b = 160$ and $d - b = 30$. The end result is $a + d = 190$. The remaining angles must sum to 350 for the sum of the interior angles to be 540. The answer, then, is (C).

15. **B** The sum of a set of consecutive integers is the average times the number of terms. The average is $\dfrac{55 + 15}{2} = 35$. The number of terms is (remember, it is inclusive) $55 - 15 + 1 = 41$. Now you just have to multiply these together. Their product is 1,435, or (B).

296

16. **D** The circumference of the circle is $2\pi \approx 6.28$. The perimeter of the square is just 4 times the length of the side, which is equal to 6. Column A is greater.

17. **B** Here you just need to work through simplifying each fraction.

Column A	**Column B**
$\dfrac{\left(\dfrac{1}{3}\right)\left(\dfrac{1}{4}\right)}{\left(\dfrac{2}{3}\right)\left(\dfrac{2}{4}\right)} = \dfrac{\dfrac{1}{12}}{\dfrac{4}{12}}$	$\dfrac{\left(\dfrac{2}{3}\right)\left(\dfrac{1}{5}\right)}{\left(\dfrac{2}{5}\right)\left(\dfrac{1}{3}\right)} = \dfrac{\dfrac{2}{15}}{\dfrac{2}{15}}$
$= \dfrac{1}{12}\,\dfrac{12}{4} = \dfrac{1}{4}$	$= \dfrac{2}{15}\,\dfrac{15}{2} = \dfrac{2}{2} = 1$

As you can see, Column B is greater.

18. **A** Use the information given about the line segments to write down equations that might be helpful in comparing the two columns. $\overline{AB} = \overline{CD}$ yields: $r + s = s + 3t \rightarrow r = 3t$. You can plug this directly into $\overline{BC} = 2t + 3r = 2t + 3(3t) = 11t$. You can infer that both r and t are positive numbers since they only differ by a multiple of three and at least one of them has to be positive since $\overline{BC}$, a distance, is positive. Column A is greater.

19. **D** To begin, you need to solve the inequality for x, $-2x > 2 \rightarrow x < -1$. You know x is less than -1. What does that tell you about x^2? Not much, certainly nothing definite in relation to 2 since x could be -1.1 or it could be -10. Thus, (D) is correct.

20. **D** The circumference of the circle has to be something around $7\pi \approx 22$. The perimeter of the rectangle, on the other hand, is not definite. The sides could be 2 and 12, and so the perimeter would be 28, or the sides could be 4 and 6 and the perimeter would be 20. In one instance Column A is greater and in the other Column B is greater.

21. **B** The first thing to do is determine the value of z. The 1-digit even integers are 2, 4, 6, and 8. The square root of z is also an integer. That is only true of 4. Thus, z equals 4. Four squared is 16, and three times 4 is 12. Thus, Column B is greater.

22. B Five percent simple annual interest means that after one year's time, 5 percent of interest will have accrued. After eight months (which is two thirds of a year) three fourths of the interest will have accrued. You need to multiply the 16,000 times 5 percent times three fourths, which is $(16,000)(0.05)\left(\dfrac{2}{3}\right) = 533.33$. Column B is greater, so the answer is (B).

23. C You know that $\dfrac{a}{b} = \dfrac{3}{4} \rightarrow a = \dfrac{3}{4}b$, and that the area of a sector is the sector angle measure divided by 360 times πr^2. For Column A, the area of sector 1 is.

$$\left(\dfrac{a}{360}\right)(\pi r^2) = \left(\dfrac{3}{4}\right)\left(\dfrac{b}{360}\right)(\pi r^2)$$

For Column B, you need the area of the sector 2 times 0.75, which is

$$(0.75)\left(\dfrac{b}{360}\right)(\pi r^2) = \left(\dfrac{3}{4}\right)\left(\dfrac{b}{360}\right)(\pi r^2)$$

Column A and B are equal and (C) is the answer.

24. C Remember the factors of a number multiply to give that number and the multiples of a number are that number times the integers. For Column A, begin by checking to see if 120 is evenly divisible by 24 because that would clearly make 24 the greatest common factor. Five times 24 gives 120 and so 24 is the greatest common factor. For Column B, if the number does not quickly come to mind then, write out multiples of each to find the least common multiple. The LCM is 24 so the answer is again (C).

25. D Column A is equivalent to $m^2 + 2mn + n^2$ and Column B is equivalent to $m^2 + mn - 2n^2$. You have to compare these two expressions. Since the first term in each is the same, you can eliminate them from consideration. If n equals zero then both expressions are zero and so equal, but if n is non-zero then there certainly are situations when the two expressions are unequal. Thus, the answer is (D).

26. C First solve the equation to see if you can glean any useful information about the relationship of x and y:

$$x^2 - 4y^2 + 7 = 7 \rightarrow x^2 = 4y^2 \rightarrow x = 2y$$

If $x = 2y$, then side b is equal to side c. This means that we can eliminate c^2 and b^2 from the columns, and all we are left with is a^2 in each. Ergo, the answer is (C).

298

27. B The number of integers from D to C is simply $C - D$, but since it is inclusive we must include D and so add one, $C - D + 1$. Now you just need to see if we can manipulate Column B so that you can compare it to Column A.

$$\frac{C^2 - CD + 2C}{4C - 3C} = \frac{C(C - D + 2)}{C} = C - D + 2$$

You can now directly compare Column A and B, and Column B is greater since they share the C minus D term but Column B is $+2$.

28. C You might suspect (D) here, but look closely at the number set. The only way that y and $y + 3$ could have the two intervening numbers in the set is if they are all consecutive integers:

$$(x + 4) = (y) + 1$$
$$(z) = (y) + 2$$

Solve for x and z in terms of y:

$$x = y + 1 - 4 = y - 3$$
$$z = y + 2$$

So, Column A, $z - 5$, must equal $(y + 2) - 5$, or $y - 3$. Since $x = y - 3$, both columns are equal, and the correct answer is (C).

Verbal

Antonyms

1. B To be *pragmatic* is to focus on the practical. The opposite of this is something like *idealistic*. Looking through the answer choices, (B), *quixotic*, fits the pre-guess. If you are unfamiliar with this term, pick up a copy of Cervantes' literary classic *Don Quixote*.

2. D A *cogent* argument is compelling and well-constructed. You are looking for the opposite of this. *Unintelligent* might attract you, but *unconvincing* is much nearer the mark.

3. A To be *obdurate* about an issue is to stubbornly maintain your position. *Flexible* or *changeable* is a good pre-guess for the antonym. Choice (A) fits the pre-guess well because to be *persuadable* is to be capable of change.

4. A *Ebullient* means to be boiling over with emotion. The opposite of this is *emotionless*. *Stern* approximates our pre-guess, but *stoic* hits it on the head.

5. E   A *garrulous* person is extremely talkative, even inconsiderately so. Thus, you are looking for an adjective that means "not talkative." *Decorious* means to act with decorum, or good manners, and so might seem attractive, but *taciturn* is a better choice. It means "tight-lipped."

6. B   To *enervate* is to weaken the strength of something. The opposite is to make stronger. Looking through the answer choices, (B) obviously jumps out. It is correct.

7. A   To *manumit* someone is to free them from slavery. The antonym is to make someone a slave. *Enslave*, choice (A), clearly fits the pre-guess and it is correct.

8. D   *Adumbrate* means to foreshadow vaguely, and so its opposite would be something like "to clearly state." *To make explicit*, choice (D), fits the pre-guess and is correct.

9. E   A *panegyric* is a speech of effusive praise. You are therefore looking for something like "criticize." *Obloquy* means "abusive or condemnatory language." That certainly is the opposite of *praise*, and so (E) is the answer.

Analogies

10. C   The relationship between the stem words is one of definition, as to *eclipse* is to *overshadow*. Going through the answer choices, to *set* is not to *rise*; to *outstrip* is not to *flail*; to *debauch* is to *debase*; to *overcome* is not necessarily to *outstretch*; to *pervert* is certainly not to *correct*.

11. A   Here the stem relationship is one of degree: To be *emphatic* is to *insist* strongly. Choice (B) might seem appealing here, but be careful because it has the order of degree reversed—to be very *absorbed* is to be *engrossed*. (A) is the correct choice—to be *contentious* is to *argue* excessively.

12. C   An *astronomer* studies the *stars*. That is a good relationship. Applying it to the answer choices, an *accountant* keeps the financial *records*; a *librarian* manages *books*; a *historian* studies *history*; a *police officer* administers the *laws*; and a *magician* performs *tricks*.

13. D   The relationship between the stem pair is that you *inoculate* to protect against a *disease*. Of the answer choices, only (D), you *defend* to protect against an *enemy*, shares this relationship.

300

14. **C** *Halcyon* means peaceful and calm, and so the relationship between the stem words is one of definition—*halcyon* means *peaceful*. Choices (B) and (E) are antonyms not synonyms, and (A) and (D) do not share a necessary relationship. Choice (C) does share a necessary relationship—*surreptitious* means *clandestine*. Choice (B) is there to catch people shopping for words like *peaceful*.

15. **A** The stem words are opposites—a *desolate* place is the opposite of a *verdant* place. Choices (B) and (C) are synonyms and so do not fit the stem relationship, and (D) and (E) do not have a strong relationship (a *tropical* place is often *humid*, a *technical* manual may or may not be *detailed*.) Choice (A) shares the stem relationship—a *destitute* area is the opposite of an *opulent* area.

16. **D** Here, the relationship is again one of definition—a *harbinger* *presages* something (*presage* means to foretell, or portend). A *computer* can *calculate* something; a *television* shows things that have been *broadcast*; a *liaison* does not necessarily *interrogate* someone; a *messenger* *relates* something; and a *broker* does not necessarily *abscond* with something.

17. **A** *Asseverate* means to *aver* or affirm earnestly, and so the stem relationship is to *asseverate* is to *aver* earnestly. Choice (A) shares this relationship—to *beseech* is to *request* earnestly. Do any of the other answer pairs share it? *Approach* and *accost* might, but the order of degree is reversed—to *accost* is to *approach* forcefully.

Sentence Completions

18. **D** The word *but* in the sentence is the key clue. It tells you that the first and second parts of the sentence are in contrast to each other. In the first part we are told that Mr. Thomas had earned the reputation as a *miser*, and so in the second part you should expect to find a strong contrast to this. Which answer choice makes a strong contrast to *miser*? Choice (D), *spendthrift*, which means one who spends money wastefully, fits the bill.

19. **A** Consider the first blank first. *Shifts* in the *demographics* of a country would at least challenge *traditional political alliances* and at most destroy them. Since the sentence speaks of *nascent political parties*, you can infer that the *traditional* ones are at least being challenged. *Solvent* and *elusive* are not good answer choices for the first blank. As the old political parties are being challenged, the new ones then are gaining ground. *Gain* then is a good pre-guess to the second blank. *Provide* does not match this pre-guess. Between *procure* and *secure*, *secure* is the better choice since *procure* intimates buying, and one does not purchase *large swathes of the electoral landscape*.

20. B Begin with a pre-guess on the first blank. What is a word that goes with *public* and "can be persuaded"? *Opinion*. Looking down the first blank answer choices, (B) obviously matches this pre-guess, but (A) and possibly (C) and (D) do as well. The word *ostensibly* clues you to the fact that the second blank is a strong contrast to *process of popular persuasion*. Which of the answer choices matches this conception? *Undemocratic* does. Thus, (B) is a strong candidate for the best answer choice. Reading the other answer choices, (A) is the *reasonable* selection, but (B) is *better* since both answer blanks more specifically fit the logic of the sentence.

21. D You are looking for a word that modifies *feuds between rival factions* of a company. *Internal* is a good pre-guess. *Internecine* means fighting within a group, and so matches the pre-guess. It is the best choice, (D).

22. B The sentence tells us that the first blank can be described as the practice of appointing *friends and associates to high posts*. A good pre-guess would be *favoritism*. Looking at the answer choices, (D) and (E) can definitely be eliminated. Choice (A) also can be eliminated because *nepotism* is showing favor to one's own family, not to *friends and associates*. The second blank is a contrast to the first since the favoritism of the *predecessors* is being *eschewed* in favor of the new way. Both (B) and (C) are contrasts to favoritism, and so you must ask which one better fits the flow of the sentence. *Merit*, based makes more sense than *work*, based, and so (B) is a better choice.

23. E In this sentence, the author's customary style of correspondence is being contrasted with the style in her most recent letter. *Customarily* her style is *deliberate*, but in this letter it is *convoluted*. Therefore, in the first blank, you are looking for a word that pairs well with *deliberate* and contrasts well with *convoluted*. In the second blank, you are looking for a word that pairs well with *convoluted* and contrasts well with *deliberate*. *Genuine*, *acidic*, and *urbane* are not good pairs with *deliberate* or contrasts with *convoluted*. As for the second blank, *tiresome* does not pair as well with *convoluted* as *prolix* does (which means to be wordy). Choice (E) is best.

302

Reading Comprehension

24. **C** A question about the proper title of the passage is looking for the basic point or thrust of the passage. What is the point of this passage? It relates how the discovery and study of the Archaeans has led to the reformulation of central concerns in the field of biology. Choice (A) is too narrow because it excludes the discussion of the extremophiles. Choice (B), although better than (A), is still too narrow. Choice (C) is a good restatement of the thrust of the passage, since reformulation of central concerns in biology is a good approximation of *Challenge to Biological Paradigms*. Choices (D) and (E) are too narrow in that they exclude the classification issues, and notice that the passage discusses extremophiles and not thermophiles. (C)'s the one.

25. **E** On questions of this form you must go through each proposition individually:

> Option I—The passage states that prior to the discovery of extremophiles the thermal threshold was set at 60 degrees centigrade "because it was thought that the molecular integrity of vital cellular components could not be maintained beyond such temperatures." It can be inferred that if extremophiles can live and thrive past 60 degrees centigrade, they can maintain molecular integrity past the previous thermal threshold.

> Option II—The passage does not mention extremophiles existing in moderate environments, so II cannot be inferred from the passage.

> Option III—The passage states that extremophiles can live and thrive at 160 degrees and so it can be inferred that they can live and thrive in temperatures *as hot as 150 degrees*.

Since I and III are inferable, the answer is (E).

26. **A** The passage states that, "kingdoms are classified to be a sub-group of a particular domain" (lines 20–21). Choice (A) states exactly that.

27. **B** The passage uses *thermal threshold* to mean "the temperature at which biological organisms begin to break down due to heat." Which of the answer choices matches this usage? Choice (A) does not, and it uses terms not in the passage. Choice (B) matches up. As for (C), the passage clearly uses the term *thermal threshold* to apply to all kinds of life and not just extremophiles, and so this choice is out. Choice (D) uses terms not in the passage and that should make you skeptical. Choice (E) is tricky because the passage does speak of the former thermal threshold as being thought of as a constant across nature. Yet, the threshold changed when extremophiles were discovered. Choice (B) is unquestionably a strong answer, and (E) is problematic because the threshold has fluctuated. Therefore, (B) is a better choice.

28. D The entire passage culminates in the conclusion of the author in the last sentence of the passage, "Therefore, altruistic motivators should be possible inputs for any decision-matrix schema that attempts to model human preference determination." The passage builds to this conclusion and so the clear intent of the author is to make this point. Which answer choice reflects this intent? Choice (D) does.

29. C To answer this question you have to go to the place in the passage where the assumptions of decision-matrices are discussed (lines 31–37). The passage clearly states that in the construction of decision-matrices it is assumed that individuals are rational in decision-making. The author does not dispute this assumption. That is answer choice (C), and it is correct.

30. A Looking at the structure of the passage, the first paragraph presents the challenge of modeling public choice scenarios, the second paragraph explains the details of a particular methodology for such modeling, and the third paragraph discusses problems with the methodology presented in the third paragraph. Given this basic structure, we can inspect the answer choices to see which best describes the role of the second paragraph. Choice (A) matches the tone and content of our description of the second passage, and it is correct.

Practice Test

3

Quantitative

28 Questions—45 Minutes

General Information

1. The test has 28 questions. If you decide to take this exam under timed conditions, you have 45 minutes to complete the section.

2. All numbers used are real numbers.

3. All angle measurements can be assumed to be positive unless otherwise noted.

4. All figures lie in the same plane unless otherwise noted.

5. Drawings that accompany questions are intended to provide information useful in answering the question. The figures are drawn closely to scale unless otherwise noted.

Directions: For questions 1–14, Column A and Column B will have one quantity each. Your goal is to compare the quantities in each column and choose

    A if the quantity in Column A is greater
    B if the quantity in Column B is greater
    C if the two quantities are equal
    D if the relationship between the two quantities cannot be determined from the information in the problem

On some questions, information about one or both quantities will be given. This information will be centered above the two columns.

Column A   **Column B**

1. $\sqrt{3^2 + 7^2}$ 3^2

2.
$$x + 2y = 9$$
$$x = y$$

$2y$ 6

---

3. x is a positive integer.

$1 - \left(\dfrac{1}{3}\right)^x$ 0.90

4.

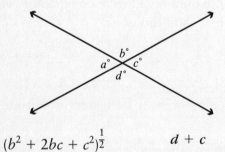

$(b^2 + 2bc + c^2)^{\frac{1}{2}}$ $d + c$

Column A   **Column B**

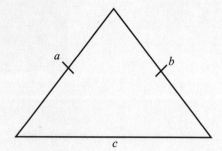

5. The figure above is an isosceles triangle.

c $\sqrt{2b}$

---

6. $b - a > 1$

$x^a x^b$ $\dfrac{x^a}{x^b}$

---

7. $|x| > 1$

$x(x - 1)$ 0

Column A	Column B

8. A certain swim-team is composed of divers, individual swimmers, and relay swimmers, and each member only participates in one event. The team has 50 members, 20 percent of which are divers.

Four times the number of divers	The number of relay racers

9. Kathy drives 20 kilometers due north from town A to town B. Then she drives 30 kilometers due west to town C.

Distance between town A and C in kilometers	40

10. A sock drawer contains 75 socks. There are an equal number of unpaired black, white, and gray socks in the drawer.

The probability of grabbing two gray socks in two attempts	One sixth

Column A	Column B

11.

4^{15}	$4^{11} + 4^{12} + 4^{13} + 4^{14}$

12. Six students compete for first, second, and third place finishes in a ski race.

120	Number of possible outcomes for first, second, and third place

13. C and D are digits and $C > D$.

$$\begin{array}{r} CD \\ -\ DC \\ \hline EF \end{array}$$

$E + F$	9

14. n is a positive integer.

$\dfrac{(n + 1)!}{n! + 1}$	$\dfrac{n! + 1}{(n + 1)!}$

Directions: Select the best answer for each of the following questions.

15.

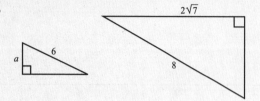

The figures above are similar triangles. What is the value of *a*?

A. $\dfrac{5}{3}$

B. 2

C. 3

D. $\dfrac{9}{2}$

E. 5

Questions 16–17 refer to the following graph.

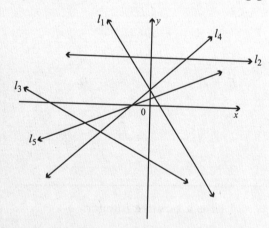

16. Which line has the greatest slope?

A. Line 1
B. Line 2
C. Line 3
D. Line 4
E. Line 5

17. Which two *y*-intercepts could sum to zero?

A. Line 1 and 4
B. Line 1 and 3
C. Line 2 and 3
D. Line 2 and 4
E. Line 4 and 5

18.

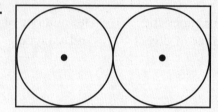

The two circles above have the same radius. Their circumference is 6π each. What is the distance between opposite corners of the rectangle?

A. $\sqrt{160}$

B. $\sqrt{165}$

C. $\sqrt{180}$

D. $\sqrt{210}$

E. $\sqrt{220}$

19. A class has *x* number of students in it. Three students join the class, and the class size increases by 20 percent. How many students are in the class now?

A. 12
B. 15
C. 18
D. 20
E. 21

20. A square has a side of length 4. What is the distance from the center of the square to one of its corners?

A. $\sqrt{2}$

B. $2\sqrt{2}$

C. $4\sqrt{2}$

D. $6\sqrt{2}$

E. $8\sqrt{2}$

21. If 3 pounds of peanuts, which cost 34 cents per pound, are mixed with 5 pounds of cashews, which cost 90 cents per pound, how many cents per pound is the mixture of the two?

A. 67
B. 69
C. 71
D. 73
E. 75

22. A board is 6 feet long, 6 inches wide, and 2 inches tall. What is its surface area in feet squared? (One foot is 12 inches.)

A. $\dfrac{11}{2}$

B. $6\dfrac{1}{2}$

C. 7

D. $\dfrac{49}{6}$

E. 9

Questions 23–25 refers to the following graph.

The Spectrum of Electromagnetic Radiation

Frequency of Radiation, Hz	Energy of Radiation cV	Kinds of Radiation	Wavelength of Radiation, meters
10^{22}	10^7		10^{-13}
10^{21}	10^6	Gamma Rays / X-rays	10^{-12}
10^{20}	10^5		10^{-11}
10^{19}	10^4		10^{-10}
10^{18}	10^3		10^{-9}
10^{17}	10^2		10^{-8}
10^{16}	10	Ultra-violet / Visible	10^{-7}
10^{15}	1		10^{-6}
10^{14}	10^{-1}		10^{-5}
10^{13}	10^{-2}	Micro Waves	10^{-4}
10^{12}	10^{-3}	Infrared	10^{-3}
10^{11}	10^{-4}		10^{-2}
10^{10}	10^{-5}		10^{-1}
10^{9}	10^{-6}		1
10^{8}	10^{-7}		10
10^{7}	10^{-8}	TV, FM	10^2
10^{6}	10^{-9}	Radio	10^3
10^{5}	10^{-10}		10^4
10^{4}	10^{-11}	Standard Broadcast	10^5

23. According to the table, what is the relationship between the frequency and the energy level of electromagnetic radiation?

A. As one increases, the other increases.
B. As one increases, the other decreases.
C. There is no direct relationship.
D. The energy level is twice as much as the frequency level.
E. The frequency level is twice as much as the wavelength level.

24. Which kind of radiation has the shortest wavelength?

A. Gamma Rays
B. X-rays
C. Ultra-violet
D. Infrared
E. Radio

25. If electromagnetic radiation has a frequency of 10^{22}Hz, what kind of radiation is it?

    A. Gamma Rays
    B. X-rays
    C. Ultra-violet
    D. Infrared
    E. Radio

26. If a, b, and c are all positive odd integers, then which of the following must be odd?

    I. $ab - bc$
    II. abc
    III. $c + c^2$

    A. I only
    B. II only
    C. I and II only
    D. I and III only
    E. I, II, and III

27. How many liters of a solution that is 20 percent water by volume must be added to 3 liters of a solution that is 40 percent water by volume to create a solution that is 25 percent water by volume?

    A. 5
    B. 6
    C. 7
    D. 8
    E. 9

28. There are 150 students in math courses at Kronhorst High School: 73 are in geometry, 62 are in algebra, and 52 are in neither. How many students are in both geometry and algebra?

    A. 32
    B. 33
    C. 35
    D. 36
    E. 37

Verbal

30 Questions—30 Minutes

Antonyms

Directions: Each question contains a word printed in capital letters, followed by five answer choices. Choose the answer choice that contains the word or phrase most nearly OPPOSITE in meaning to the word in capital letters.

1. CORROBORATE :

    A. pledge
    B. deny
    C. harbor
    D. detain
    E. affirm

2. INEXACTITUDE :

    A. crude
    B. precise
    C. inexpert
    D. industrious
    E. articulate

3. FOMENT :

   A. quell
   B. agitate
   C. appropriate
   D. estimate
   E. exonerate

4. CALLOW :

   A. picturesque
   B. mature
   C. timid
   D. canny
   E. particular

5. BACCHANALIAN :

   A. petulant
   B. orgiastic
   C. analgesia
   D. pious
   E. shrewd

6. PULCHRITUDE :

   A. ostentatious
   B. elegant
   C. estranged
   D. comedic
   E. uncomely

7. STOLID :

   A. imaginative
   B. sterile
   C. venal
   D. emotional
   E. abrasive

8. PREVARICATE :

   A. speak honestly
   B. speak hastily
   C. speak slowly
   D. speak with vulgarities
   E. speak with pathos

Analogies

Directions: In each question, there is an initial pair of words or phrases that are related in some manner. Select the answer choice containing the lettered pair that best expresses a relationship similar to the initial pair.

9. LONG-WINDED : BREVITY ::

   A. oversized : large
   B. attractive : repulsive
   C. lean : excess
   D. wealthy : money
   E. spent : used

10. LAWYER : COURT ::

    A. actor : play
    B. janitor : school
    C. manager : team
    D. prison : guard
    E. bureaucrat : bureaucracy

11. CANDID : FRANK

    A. sincere : kind
    B. erudite : learned
    C. duplicitous: timorous
    D. pernicious : hopeful
    E. measured : mercurial

12. AUSTERE : DECORATED ::

    A. paltry : exorbitant
    B. offensive : tactful
    C. ingenious : creative
    D. lackluster : ominous
    E. powerful : elusive

PETERSON'S
getting you there

13. PHYSICIAN : HUMAN BODY ::

A. horticulturist : plant
B. coach : player
C. teacher : student
D. veterinarian : cow
E. biologist : evolution

14. CRAVEN : TREPIDATIOUS ::

A. miniscule : minute
B. migratory : transitory
C. ageless : ancient
D. agile : acute
E. exultant : joyful

15. TURGID : BOMBASTIC ::

A. lazy : lethargic
B. rotund : portly
C. bemused : distract
D. catatonic : cataclysmic
E. histrionic : sordid

Sentence Completions

Directions: Each sentence below contains one or two blanks, with each blank corresponding to an omitted word. Find the answer choice that has the word or set or words that best fits the meaning of the sentence as a whole.

16. The demolition crew did not successfully _____ the building since two walls remained intact.

A. raze
B. construct
C. erect
D. incapacitate
E. deactivate

17. The ethicist argued that the person in question was not _____ for the man's injury since it was an accident.

A. culpable
B. attributable
C. capable
D. reasonable
E. actionable

18. The publicity surrounding the mismanagement of the company's capital _____ the company's credibility with investors, but the company remained solvent largely on account of its _____ market share.

A. belabored..steady
B. weakened..evolving
C. aided..climbing
D. lessened..volatile
E. damaged..stable

312

19. Though the official had hoped his speech would calm the citizenry, his assurances did not _____ the crowd's fears concerning the likelihood of the natural disaster recurring.

A. alter
B. assuage
C. increase
D. bolster
E. gauge

20. It is a commonly noted behavior for a younger sibling to _____ the behavior of an older sibling, taking on their mannerisms or sense of style.

A. antagonize
B. ridicule
C. improve
D. emulate
E. vex

21. Since the visitor was unfamiliar with the region's customs he was unaware of the _____ of his actions, and so he was _____ to the fact that he had offended his host.

A. impropriety..oblivious
B. curtness..ignorant
C. blandness..blithe
D. boldness..unaware
E. audacity..blind

22. Though the glass was _____ when bought, years of poor maintenance had rendered it nearly _____, stifling almost all of the sunlight that strained to cross its interior.

A. permeable..dark
B. clear..obscure
C. lucid..obstructed
D. penetrable..impregnable
E. translucent..opaque

23. Historiography, at least of historic personages, in the last century tended toward hagiography, but today _____ distance and a _____ tone are basic requirements of professional history writing.

A. critical..reserved
B. minute..extravagant
C. impartial..subdued
D. holistic..daring
E. even..careful

Reading Comprehension

Directions: Questions follow each passage. After reading the passage, determine the best answer for each question based on the passage's content.

Passage 1

Line The introduction of electronic computers into the field of quantum chemistry in the 1950s had an immediate and ultimately polarizing effect on the discipline.

(5) Quantum chemistry is primarily concerned with solving Schrödinger's Equation—the fundamental equation of the quantum realm—for different theoretical scenarios. The difficulty in

(10) this endeavor is that Schrödinger's Equation does not readily submit to straightforward solutions. Elaborate and extensive calculations are often necessary for solving Schrödinger's Equation,

(15) which explains why the introduction of electronic computing held great promise as a research tool in theoretical quantum chemistry.

As the discipline incorporated the use

(20) of electronic computers, two research methodologies emerged. The first, termed *ab initio*, relied entirely upon the electronic computer to solve the knotty mathematics of Schrödinger's Equation,

(25) and it employed no empirical data save fundamental constants of nature. The second, the so-called semi-empirical method, simplified the computational hurdles by neglecting possibly negligible

(30) components of the calculations and by extensively employing empirical data. The semi-empirical method quickly became very fruitful, but the *ab initio* practitioners were skeptical of this

(35) research because of the possible impor-
tance of the components neglected by the semi-empirical method. Furthermore, the *ab initio* practitioners criticized the semi-empirical method as only able to

(40) sustain the current theoretical paradigm and not able to explore possible inadequacies in the current framework. The semi-empirical practitioners, on the other hand, criticized the *ab initio* methodol-

(45) ogy as overly laborious and ultimately less productive. Since the *ab initio* methodology solved all computational components to Schrödinger's Equation, it demanded considerable amounts of time

(50) and effort, so fewer research projects could be pursued with this methodology.

Ultimately, both methodologies have proved important to quantum chemistry. The semi-empirical method has been

(55) essential for exploring questions within the standard paradigm while the *ab initio* method has probed the boundaries of our understanding of quantum chemistry.

24. The *ab initio* method was criticized for

   I. being too demanding with regard to labor.
  II. its inability to critique the current paradigm.
 III. being a slower producer of new research.

  A. I only
  B. II only
  C. III only
  D. I and II only
  E. I and III only

25. According to the passage, what was the primary methodological challenge in working with Schrödinger's Equation?

  A. The difficulty of correctly applying Schrödenger's Equation in the quantum world
  B. The complexity of the calculations required to solve Schrödinger's Equation
  C. The inability of electronic computers to solve Schrödinger's Equation
  D. The rivalry between the *ab initio* practitioners and the semi-empirical practitioners
  E. The difficulty of obtaining reliable empirical data

26. The semi-empirical method was empirical in that it employed

  A. strictly empirical means in obtaining a result.
  B. the fundamental constants of nature in obtaining a result.
  C. extensive empirical data in obtaining a result.
  D. only empirically verifiable scenarios in modeling quantum outcomes.
  E. restricted amounts of empirical data in obtaining results.

27. The author's intent was to

  A. explain the effects of the introduction of electronic computers on quantum chemistry.
  B. point out the harmfulness of scientific rivalries.
  C. argue that the semi-empirical method was more productive.
  D. illustrate the importance of cooperation in scientific disciplines.
  E. lay out the differences between the *ab initio* and semi-empirical methods.

Passage 2

Line Though nearly fifty years of research has been done since the Khartoum Hospital and Shaheinab excavations in Central Sudan, a coherent and rigorous frame-
(5) work for understanding the Mesolithic-Neolithic (8000 B.C.E.–4000 B.C.E.) transition in the Central Nile has not been achieved. A. J. Arkell, the primary excavator at these sites, developed a
(10) model of cultural evolution based on two basic ceramic typologies—the wavy and dotted line—found at these sites. Predictably, the wavy line type are ceramics whose outer surface are

(15) decorated with wavy lines, while the dotted line ceramics are decorated with the same grooves of the wavy line but with indentions, or dots, further lining the grooves.

(20) Arkell's model designates the wavy line type as markers for Khartoum Mesolithic culture and the dotted line type as markers for Khartoum Neolithic culture. Yet this model became problem-

(25) atic as excavations beyond the Central Nile began to unearth wavy and dotted line pottery across the Sahara-Sahel belt in strata and in sequences inconsistent with Arkell's designations. It appeared a

(30) new model was needed to account for not only chronological development but geographical dispersal as well.

To address these issues, I. Canerva put forth a classification strategy for

(35) Nilotic and Saharan ceramics based on technique. Arkell's model classified by motif, the ceramic's outer decorations, but Canerva focused on the techniques employed, such as method of hardening,

(40) and technologies needed, such as tools, in making the ceramics. This strategy initially promised to provide artifact markers for the cultural evolution from the Nile basin to the western edges of the

(45) Sahara in the Mesolithic-Neolithic. This approach, though, became mired in questions related to determination of technique, as the reverse inference from motif to technique became dubious.

(50) At this point major questions remain unanswered concerning wavy and dotted line ceramics in Mesolithic-Neolithic Nilotic and Saharan regions. Do these ceramic typologies provide any sort of

(55) chronological index for the region? Does their geographical dispersion tell us of possible cultural uniformities across these diverse regions? The answers these to questions about the past hopefully lie

(60) somewhere in the not-too-distant future.

28. The main idea of the passage is

   A. Nilotic and Saharan archaeology has failed to provide an adequate frame-work for understanding the Me-solithic-Neolithic transition.

   B. Arkell and Canerva were incorrect in their respective attempts to system-atize their research.

   C. wavy line ceramics clearly are not the chronological predecessors of dotted line ceramics.

   D. dotted and wavy line pottery has not been successfully incorporated into a larger theory that explains their importance, thus leaving important further research open.

   E. research on Nilotic and Saharan ceramics has matured over the past five decades.

29. Arkell's model was problematic in that

   A. the discovery of wavy and dotted line pottery in the Central Nile conflicted with his findings.

   B. dating discrepancies were discovered within his account.

   C. wavy and dotted line pottery were discovered outside the Central Nile that did not conform to his model.

   D. pottery fragments were discovered outside the Central Nile as far west as the Western Sahara.

   E. ceramics that chronologically pre-ceded the wavy line pottery were discovered in the Central Nile.

30. It can be inferred from the passage that the author would agree with which one of the following?

    A. The work of Arkell and Canerva has been thoroughly debunked.

    B. Future research into Mesolithic-Neolithic Khartoum should be done.

    C. Motif should be considered over technique when researching ceramics.

    D. The material composition of a ceramic is an important clue in archaeological research.

    E. Material culture is more readily studied than non-material culture.

Answers and Explanations

This is the last sample test you will take before moving onto the computer adaptive exams. Hopefully, you have tested out some new strategies and ideas on the previous two tests and are now comfortable with them.

Quantitative

1. B The only way to do a problem like this is to simplify the expressions.

For Column B, $3^2 = 9$.

For Column A, $\sqrt{3^2 + 7^2} = \sqrt{9 + 49} = \sqrt{58} < 8$ since $\sqrt{64} = 8$.

Column B is greater.

2. C To be able to compare $2y$ to 6, you need to solve for y. You can do this by substituting y for x in the first equation. This yields:

$$x + 2y = 9 \rightarrow$$
$$y + 2y = 9 \rightarrow$$
$$3y = 9 \rightarrow$$
$$y = 3$$

This means $2y = 6$. Choice (C) then is the answer.

3. D A good way to attack a problem like this is try a few values for x. At its smallest $x = 1$, and Column A would equal two thirds, or 0.67. If $x = 2$, Column A equals eight ninths, and if $x = 3$, Column A equals twenty-six twenty-sevenths. As you can see, Column A increases as x increases. In the first case, Column B was greater; in the third, Column A was. Thus the answer is (D).

4. A First, simplify the expression in Column A,

$$\left(b^2 + 2bc + c^2\right)^{\frac{1}{2}} = \left[(b+c)^2\right]^{\frac{1}{2}} = b + c.$$

$b + c = 180° > 0.90$

5. D Remember that an isosceles triangle is not necessarily a right triangle. Since the triangle is not a right triangle, you have no way of comparing b with c. Thus, the answer is (D).

6. D Begin by manipulating the exponents to more readily compare the columns:

Column A: $x^a x^b = x^{a+b}$

Column B: $\dfrac{x^a}{x^b} = x^{a-b}$

and you know that $b - a > 1 \rightarrow a - b < -1$. This means that the x in Column B is raised to a negative power, but how much does this tell us about its value in comparison to Column A? $a + b$ could also be negative, which would mean that Column A was also raised to a negative, and a greater negative at that. Or $a + b$ could be positive, which would mean that the x in Column A would be raised to a positive.

In the former case, Column B could be greater, depending on the value of x, and in the latter case, Column A would be greater, again depending on the value of x. As you can see, there are a variety of possible outcomes.

7. A Distribute the x in Column A, which yields $x^2 - x$. You can reason that this difference is greater than zero. x's absolute value is greater than 1, and x^2 is positive and greater than x. Column A, then, is greater.

8. A Twenty percent of 50 is 10, and so there are 10 divers. Four times this number is 40. How many relay racers are there? Since each member only participates in 1 event, and since there are 10 divers, there are 40 members who are either divers or individual swimmers. We know there must be at least 1 individual swimmer, or the team would not be composed of individual swimmers; that means there can at most be 39 relay racers. Thus, Column A is greater.

PETERSON'S
getting you there

9. B Since the directions are due north and due west, the three towns form a right triangle, and we can use the Pythagorean theorem to determine the distance between A and C.

$$c^2 = 400 + 900 = 1{,}300 \rightarrow c = \sqrt{1{,}300} = 10\sqrt{13}$$

The question now becomes, "How do you compare the value of c with 40?" Notice that $\sqrt{13} < \sqrt{16} = 4$ and so ten times the square root of 13 is less than 40. Ergo, Column B is greater.

10. B The probability of the first event, grabbing the first gray sock, is one third. The probability of grabbing the second gray sock is not as straightforward. Now there are only 24 gray socks and still 25 black and white socks. Thus, the probability is something a little bit less than one third. To get the probability of both events occurring, we have to multiply the two probabilities together. One third times something a little smaller than one third is going to be smaller than one sixth, the value in Column B.

11. A Obviously it is going to be difficult to compare these by multiplying out the exponents. There must be another way, and there is $4^{15} = 4 \times 4^{14} = 4^{14} + 4^{14} + 4^{14} + 4^{14}$, which gives us four terms in Column A to compare with four terms in Column B. The terms in Column B are less than all the respective terms in Column A, and so (A) is the answer.

12. C Six students are competing for first place, and so there are six possibilities for first. But since there will always be a first before a second, only five can be second. And since there will be a first and a second before a third, only four can be third. Multiply these together to get the total number of possibilities, $(6)(5)(4) = 120$. The answer is (C). You may recall the formula for these kinds of permutation problems as $P = \dfrac{n!}{(n-c)!}$ where P is the total number of possible outcomes, n is the number of participants, and c is the number of places.

13. C Consider the subtraction in the ones column and tens column, respectively. In the ones, since $C > D$, you have to borrow ten from the tens column. This means $F = D + 10 - C$. As for the tens column, $E = C - 1 - D$ since you borrowed one from the column. Putting these two results together, $E + F = (C - 1 - D) + (D + 10 - C) = 9$. The answer then is (C).

14. D The numerator in Column A might at first blush appear greater, but be careful. If $n = 1$ then $n! + 1 = (n + 1)!$, in which case Column A and B are equal. If n is a large number, though, $n! + 1 < (n + 1)!$, in which case Column A would be greater. Thus the answer is (D).

15. D Since the triangles are similar the ratios of the side lengths are proportional, and you can use this to find a. You do not know the length of the side on the larger triangle that corresponds with side a, and so you need to determine the third side of the larger triangle. Using the Pythagorean theorem, you can determine that the third side is equal to 6. Using similar triangles then,

$$\frac{6}{8} = \frac{a}{6} \rightarrow 36 = 8a \rightarrow a = \frac{36}{8} = \frac{9}{2},$$

which is answer choice (D).

16. D The greatest slope means the line that has the steepest ascent left to right. If a line ascends right to left, then its slope is negative. Line 4, choice (D), has the steepest slope left to right.

17. C Recall that the y-intercept is simply the y-value where a line crosses the y-axis. If the y-intercepts of two lines sum to zero, then they either both must have y-intercepts of zero, or they must have y-intercepts equidistant from the x-axis, one with a positive value and the other a negative value. Line 2 and line 3 cross the y-axis equidistant from the x-axis.

18. C To begin with, since you know the circumference of the circles, you can determine the radius of the circles, which is 3 ($C = 2\pi r$). If the radius is 3, then the height of the rectangle is 6, and the length of the rectangle is 12. The distance between two opposite corners then is the hypotenuse of a right triangle with sides 6 and 12. Using the Pythagorean theorem we can determine the hypotenuse, $\sqrt{36 + 144} = \sqrt{180}$. Choice (C) then is the answer.

19. C Three students constitute a 20-percent increase for the class. This translates mathematically to

$$0.20 = \frac{3}{x} \rightarrow x = \frac{3}{0.20} = 15,$$

which gives you the number of original students. Add 3 to get 18.

Part IV: Three Practice GREs

20. B Drawing a square with a diagonal creates a 45-45-90 triangle, since the diagonal bisects the 90 degree angles. This means that the diagonal is $4\sqrt{2}$. But you are not looking for the length from corner to corner. You are looking for the length from center to corner, which would be half the length of the diagonal, or $2\sqrt{2}$, choice (B).

21. B Three pounds of peanuts at 34 cents/pound costs 102 cents. Five pounds of cashews at 90 cents/pound costs 450 cents. Added together they cost 552 cents, and there are 8 pounds total. 552 cents divided by 8 pounds is 69 cents/pound, or choice (B).

22. D The first thing to do is to convert the measurements in inches into feet. Six inches is a $\frac{1}{2}$ foot. Two inches is a $\frac{1}{6}$ foot. The surface area of a three-dimensional rectangle is the sum of areas of the sides.

Top and bottom:

$$2\left(6\cdot\frac{1}{2}\right) = 6,$$

two ends:

$$2\left(\frac{1}{6}\cdot\frac{1}{2}\right) = \frac{1}{6},$$

two sides:

$$2\left(\frac{1}{6}\cdot 6\right) = 2$$

The sum of these is choice (D).

23. A Looking at the frequency column, the frequency increases as you ascend the column. The same thing is true for the energy level column—as you ascend the column the energy level increases. Thus, (A) is the answer. If you want further confirmation of this—simply pick a certain frequency and read the energy level at that frequency. Then pick another frequency and read the energy level at that frequency. If the frequency increased—then so did the energy and vice versa.

322

24. A On this question, you have to be careful. Notice that the wavelengths get shorter as they ascend the column (e.g., 10^{-13} meters is shorter than 10^5 meters). This means that the shortest wavelengths are at the top of the column. Which kind of radiation corresponds to this part of the column? Choice (A), gamma rays, is correct.

25. A First find 10^{22} Hz on the frequency column on the far left. Then slide over to see which kind of radiation this is. It is gamma rays, choice (A).

26. B On a problem like this, you have to go through the three choices and determine which must be odd as follows:

> Option I—Is not odd since the two products are even and an even minus an even is even.

> Option II—Is odd since an odd times an odd is even and an even times an odd is odd.

> Option III—Is even since an odd squared is odd and an odd plus an odd is even.

So only option II is odd, which is answer choice (B). If all that seemed a bit confusing, just assign odd values to the three variables, plug them in, and see if the results are odd or even.

27. E There is a helpful formula for a problem of balancing weaker and stronger solutions, (amount of weaker solution) times (percentage difference of desired and weaker solution) = (amount of stronger solution) times (percentage difference of stronger and desired solution). In this situation, the formula reads, $n(25 - 20) = 3(40 - 25) \rightarrow 5n = 45 \rightarrow n = 9$. Therefore, (E) is the answer.

28. E There is a formula for neither or both problems like this, $G_1 + G_2 + Neither + Both = Total$. You can use this equation or reason your way through this problem. If 52 students are in neither class, then 98 students are in algebra or geometry. This means that 25 are in algebra but not geometry and 36 are in geometry but not algebra. So, there are 73 in geometry and 36 of them are not in algebra, which means that 37 of those in geometry are in algebra. You can obtain the same result using the formula.

Verbal

Antonyms

1. **B** To *corroborate* someone's claim is to back it up or validate it, so you are looking for a word that means something like "not support." Scanning the answer choices, only (B) fits the pre-guess.

2. **B** *Inexactitude* is the opposite of exactitude, or being exact, so you are looking for a word that means exact. *Precise*, choice (B), certainly means exact, and none of the other answer choices do.

3. **A** To *foment* means to incite, and so its antonym would be something like "un-incite." Not a real word, but a fine pre-guess since it puts you on the right path. Answer choice (A), *quell*, matches this pre-guess.

4. **B** *Callow* has a negative-sounding connotation, and so the answer will have a positive-sounding connotation. You can, at least, eliminate choice (C), *timid*, on these grounds. *Callow* means immature. Choice (B), *mature*, then, is a good antonym.

5. **D** *Bacchanalian* derives from Bacchus, the Greek god of wine. It means "unbridled revelry." The opposite is something like sobriety, or a tame activity. Of the answer choices, *pious* best approximates this pre-guess.

6. **E** *Pulchritude* means beauty. This word was used in the first part of the book, so hopefully you remembered it.

7. **D** To be *stolid* is to lack emotion. Thus, the antonym here is something like "emotional." Choice (D) is exactly that.

8. **A** If you do not know the definition of *prevaricate*, you might guess that it has a negative-sounding connotation, and so the answer would be positive. Choices (A) and (E) are the strong positives. *Prevaricate* means to lie, and so (A) is the correct answer.

Analogies

9. **C** Someone who is *long-winded* lacks *brevity*. Choices (B) and (C) appear to be possibilities. *Attractive* is the opposite of *repulsive*. Something *lean* lacks *excess*. Choice (C) is the better of the two choices.

10. **E** A *lawyer* is an officer of the *court*, or a *lawyer* works in the *court*. An *actor* acts in a *play*, but a *play* is an activity whereas a *court* is a location or part of a system. A *janitor* might work at a *school*. A *manager* manages a *team*, a *prison* has *guards*, and a *bureaucrat* works in a *bureaucracy*.

11. **B** The relationship between the stem pair is one of definition; to be *candid* is to be *frank*. Which of the answer choices shares this relationship? Only (B)—to be *erudite* is to be *learned*. Choice (A) might have seemed appealing but realize that a *sincere* person might be *kind* or he or she might be sincerely unkind.

12. **B** Here, the stem relationship is of lack or negation—to be *austere* is to not be *decorated*. In a similar fashion, to be *offensive* is to not be *tactful*. None of the other stem pairs share the relationship of negation.

13. **A** *Physician* studies/cares for the *human body*. In the same way, a *horticulturist* studies/cares for a *plant*. But it is also true that *veterinarians* study/care for *cows*. And certainly *biologists* study *evolution*. But notice that *biologists* do not care for *evolution*. Also notice that a *cow* is a specific kind of animal that a *veterinarian* cares for while *human body* and *plant* are general terms. So, (A) is the best choice.

14. **B** *Craven* means "cowardly" and "completely subdued by fear." *Trepidatious* means "to be apprehensive or fearful." Thus—*craven* is an extreme of *trepidatiousness*. This is a relationship of degree. Only choice (E) shares this relationship of degree—*exultant* is an extreme of *joyfulness*. Choice (A) is not as strong a choice because *miniscule* and *minute* both mean very small, and so there is no difference in degree. The same is true for *migratory* and *transitory*, choice (B). As for (C), *ageless* means without age while *ancient* means to by very old. They do not have a relationship of degree.

15. **B** If you do not know the definition of either of these words, you can eliminate some of the answer pairs that have a weak relationship. *Catatonic* and *cataclysmic* do not have a necessary relationship, nor do *histrionic* (to be overly theatrical) and *sordid*. That leaves (A), (B), and (C). *Turgid* actually means pompous or *bombastic*, and so the stem relationship is one of definition. To be *turgid* is to be *bombastic*. Is to be *lazy* to be *lethargic*? Maybe. To be *rotund* is to be *portly*. And to *bemuse* is to *bewilder*, not to *distract*.

325

PETERSON'S
getting you there

Sentence Completions

16. A What does a *successful demolition* crew do? It demolishes buildings, and so you are looking for a word like *demolish*. Which of the answer choices fits this pre-guess? Certainly not *construct* or *erect*. *Incapacitate* and *deactivate* do not fit the context. *Raze* means to destroy completely, so it completes the sentence well.

17. A Begin with a pre-guess. Something like *punishable/responsible* works, since it is generally thought that if something is an accident then one is not fully punishable/responsible. Looking down the list, *culpable* matches our pre-guess. Reading it back into the sentence, it works well.

18. E Remember to do a two blank sentence one blank at a time. The first blank is clearly a negative term since *publicity surrounding mismanagement* would hurt a *company's credibility*. Thus, we can eliminate choice (C), *aided. Belabored*, choice (A), also does not fit with the notion of hurt. On the second blank, we can infer that it must be a positive since it is on its account that the company *remained solvent*. This eliminates (D) and (B) also, since *evolving* is a more neutral than positive term.

19. B The *though* at the beginning of the sentence clues you into the fact that the official's hopes were not achieved. Thus, his assurances must not have had their desired effect. Assurances are meant to *calm*, and that is a good pre-guess. Looking at the answer choices, *assuage*, choice (B), is the only choice that matches the pre-guess.

20. D The sentence structure indicates that the word in the blank is described by the *younger sibling . . . taking on mannerisms . . .* What are the younger siblings doing? They are *copying* their older siblings. Which answer choice matches with copy? *Emulate*, choice (D), means to copy, and it is the best answer choice.

21. A Start with the first blank here. Since the visitor was *unfamiliar with the region's customs* and you know that he *offended his host*, you should suspect that his actions were culturally improper. Looking at the answer choices, we can eliminate (C). Moving to the second blank, since he was *unaware* of his poor *actions*, it makes sense that he did not realize he had *offended his hosts. Unaware* does not fit the context, and *blind* does not fit as well as *oblivious* or *ignorant*. That leaves choices (A) and

(B). Reading both back into the sentence, (A) works better. *Curtness* does not capture the idea of culture improperness like *impropriety* does.

22. E The second blank is quite approachable since you know that it means "allowing no light through" or something like that. Which answer choices fit this? *Opaque*, choice (E), really is the only good fit. *Translucent* works well in the first blank, and so (E) is the best choice.

23. A Here the sentence is contrasting the way that history was written in the past with the professional standards of history writing today. In the past, the sentence reads, *historiography . . . tended to hagiography*. In this usage, hagiography means overly sympathetic and full of praise. Thus, *today's requirements* should be in strong contrast to this. With this in mind, which of the answer choices is a good modifier for *tone* in the second blank? *Reserved* and *careful* are good choices. Looking at the first blank, *even*, choice (E), does not fit with distance, while *critical* does fit well. Therefore, choice (A) is the best choice.

Reading Comprehension

24. E The passage reads, "The semi-empirical practitioners . . . criticized the *ab initio* methodology as overly laborious and ultimately less productive." That is I and III. II, on the other hand, is actually a criticism of the semi-empirical method.

25. B The second half of the first paragraph clearly explains that the major hurdle in working with Schrödinger's Equation was that it was difficult to solve. If you have been keeping track of the flow of ideas in the passage, it will be easy to locate the pertinent part of the text and answer the question. Choice (B) is correct.

26. C Lines 27–31 read, ". . . the so-called semi-empirical method, simplified the computational hurdles by neglecting possibly negligible components of the calculations and by extensively employed empirical data." Thus, it was empirical in that it employed extensive empirical data in obtaining a result, which is choice (C).

27. A A question about the author's intent will include both the main idea of the passage and the author's tone in expressing the main idea. What was the main idea of the passage? The introduction of electronic computers produced a bifurcation in methodologies in quantum chemistry. What was the author's tone in

327

expressing this idea? Primarily explanatory as opposed to argumentative. Which answer choice captures both of these elements? Choice (A) does. All the other answer choices are either wrong in tone or wrong in content.

28. **D** You should read with this question in mind, because questions like this are standard. The passage discusses the inadequacies of current theories of wavy and dotted line pottery in the Mesolithic-Neolithic transition, and points to the need for further research in this area. The answer should include both of these aspects. Choice (A) includes the former but not the latter. Choices (B) and (C) are too specific, while choice (E) is too general. Only choice (D) contains both aspects of the passage, the shortcomings of contemporary theories and the need for more research.

29. **C** The passage clearly states that Arkell's model was problematized by the discovery of wavy and dotted line pottery outside of the Central Nile in strata and progressions that conflicted with his account. That is answer choice (C).

30. **B** On inference questions like this, you have to bear down and read through each answer choice and compare it with what you know of the author through reading the passage. In choice (A), the word *thoroughly* sounds extreme in comparison to the tone of the passage and so should give you caution. Choice (B) sounds like something the author would recommend. As for (C), the author never makes any specific methodological suggestions of this kind. Choice (D) might be something that the author would agree with but the author never mentions composition in the passage, and the same could be said for choice (E) and material vs. non-material culture. Choice (B) is best.

Chapter
8

Closing Remarks

Congratulations! You have just read through a mountain of GRE-related information! Consider yourself an expert on a subject, but don't go bragging about it at social functions because it's not likely to impress people. Believe me; I speak from experience.

If you have studied all the strategies and techniques, learned the formats for each section, and practiced on the sample questions, then you should feel pretty good about your chances on the real test. There's only so much preparation you can do, and if you've finished this book, you've done more than most people taking the test. Be confident about your chances on the real test, because at the very least, this book has shown you what to expect on the GRE. You would be surprised at how people's scores improve when a test leaves the realm of "mysterious, unexpected exam" and becomes "just another standardized test."

That's all the GRE is, really. By now, you should realize that the GRE says nothing about your potential as a graduate student or your abilities as a scholar. It's little more than a hoop you must pass through to get into graduate school, testing you in subjects that have a bearing on higher education in only the vaguest, most general sense. If you do well on the test, then you're a good standardized test-taker, nothing more.

I would wish you luck on the GRE, but if you've read this book, then you will have made your own luck. Your GRE score will reflect it.

PART V

Appendix

PART V

About the CAT

How to Apply for the GRE

The best way to learn all the relevant facts about the GRE is to go on line to the official GRE Web site, www.gre.org. There, you will find a list of testing centers in your area, registration information, stuff about score reporting, and scads of other GRE-related trivia. If you don't want to go on line because you don't like computers, you should keep in mind that it's a computer-based test you are about to take. It's time to start familiarizing yourself. There is a phone number to call during business hours, 609-771-7670, but the recorded voice there will harangue you to use the Web site. You can eventually get a person, but it normally takes a while.

If you do want to speak to a person, a better approach is to call someone at a local testing center. Since you may potentially give them your money, they are often more amenable to answering any questions you might have.

The GRE CAT Interface

The three simulated screen shots on pages 333, 335, and 336 show the GRE CAT interface for the Analytical Writing sections, the Quantitative section, and the Verbal section. Let's first examine the features of the interface that are common to all exam sections.

The CAT Title Bar

A dark title bar will appear across the top of the computer screen at all times during all test sections. (You cannot hide this bar.) The CAT title bar displays three items:

- **Left corner:** The time remaining for the current section (hours and minutes)

- **Middle:** The name of the test (GRE) and current section number

- **Right corner:** The current question number and total number of questions in the current section

332

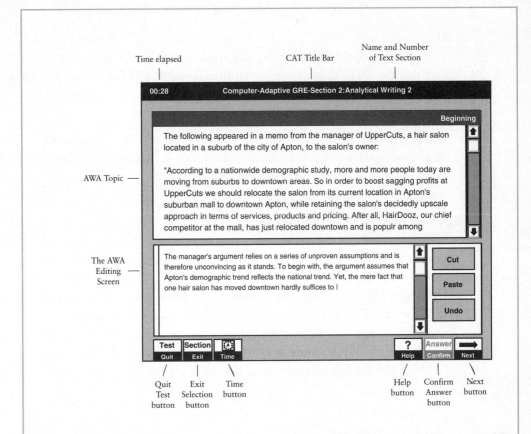

The CAT Toolbar

A series of six buttons appear in a toolbar across the bottom of the computer screen at all times during all test sections. (You cannot hide the toolbar.) Here's a description of each button's function:

QUIT TEST

Click on this button to stop the test and cancel your scores for the *entire* test. (Partial score cancellation is not allowed in any event.) If you click here, a dialog box will appear on the screen, asking you to confirm this operation. Stay away from this button unless you're absolutely sure you wish your GRE score for the day to vaporize and you're willing to throw away your GRE registration fee.

EXIT SECTION

Click on this button if you finish the section before the allotted time expires and wish to proceed immediately to the next section. A dialog box will appear on the screen asking you to confirm this operation. Stay away from this button unless you've already answered every question in the current section and don't feel you need a breather before starting the next one!

TIME

Click on this button to display the time remaining to the nearest *second*. By default, the time remaining is displayed (in the upper left corner) in hours and minutes, but not to the nearest second.

HELP

Click on this button to access the directions for the current question type (for example, Data Sufficiency or Sentence Completion), as well as the general test directions and the instructions for using the toolbar items.

NEXT and CONFIRM ANSWER

Click on the NEXT button when you're finished with the current question. When you click on NEXT, the current question will remain on the screen until you click on CONFIRM ANSWER. Until you confirm, you can change your answer as often as you wish (by clicking on a different oval). But once you confirm, the question disappears forever and the next one appears in its place. Whenever the NEXT button is enabled (appearing dark gray), the CONFIRM ANSWER button is disabled (appearing light gray), and vice versa.

The Analytical Writing Screen

As illustrated in the screen shot on page 333, the Analytical Writing prompt appears at the top of your screen, and your essay response appears below it as you type your response. (The screen in the figure includes the first several lines of a response.) Notice that you have to scroll down to read the entire topic and question. You compose your essays using the CAT word processor. (Just ahead, you'll look closely at its features and limitations.)

The Quantitative and Verbal Screens

To respond to multiple-choice questions, click on one of the ovals to the left of the answer choices. You can't use the keyboard to select answers. Notice that the answer choices are *not* lettered; you'll click on blank ovals.

334

In the sample questions throughout this book, the answer choices were lettered for easy reference to corresponding explanations.

Split screens. For some multiple-choice questions, the screen splits either horizontally or vertically.

Reading Comprehension: The screen splits vertically. The left side displays the passage; the right side displays the question and answer choices.

Quantitative questions that include figures: The screen splits horizontally. The figures appears at the top; the question and answer choices appear at the bottom.

Vertical Scrolling. For some multiple-choice questions, you'll have to scroll up and down (using the vertical scroll bar) to view all the material that pertains to the current question.

Reading Comprehension: Passages are too long for you to see on the screen in their entirety; you'll need to scroll.

Quantitative questions that include figures: Some figures—especially charts and graphs—won't fit on the screen in their entirety; you might need to scroll.

01:06	Computer-Adaptive GRE-Section 3:Quantitative	21 of 37

Richard began driving from home on a trip averaging 30 miles per hour. How many miles per hour must Carla drive on average to catch up to him in exactly 3 hours if she leaves 30 minutes after Richard?

- 35
- 55
- 39
- 40
- 60

Test	Section	[⟳]		?	Answer	➡
Quit	Exit	Time		Help	Confirm	Next

PETERSON'S
getting you there

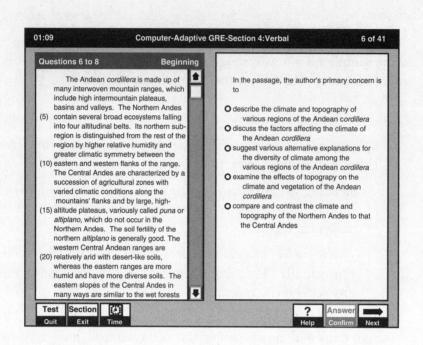

Questions 6 to 8   **Beginning**

The Andean *cordillera* is made up of many interwoven mountain ranges, which include high intermountain plateaus, basins and valleys. The Northern Andes
(5) contain several broad ecosystems falling into four altitudinal belts. Its northern sub-region is distinguished from the rest of the region by higher relative humidity and greater climatic symmetry between the
(10) eastern and western flanks of the range. The Central Andes are characterized by a succession of agricultural zones with varied climatic conditions along the mountains' flanks and by large, high-
(15) altitude plateaus, variously called *puna* or *altiplano*, which do not occur in the Northern Andes. The soil fertility of the northern *altiplano* is generally good. The western Central Andean ranges are
(20) relatively arid with desert-like soils, whereas the eastern ranges are more humid and have more diverse soils. The eastern slopes of the Central Andes in many ways are similar to the wet forests

In the passage, the author's primary concern is to

○ describe the climate and topography of various regions of the Andean *cordillera*
○ discuss the factors affecting the climate of the Andean *cordillera*
○ suggest various alternative explanations for the diversity of climate among the various regions of the Andean *cordillera*
○ examine the effects of topograpy on the climate and vegetation of the Andean *cordillera*
○ compare and contrast the climate and topography of the Northern Andes to that the Central Andes

Test | Section | [⟳]
Quit | Exit | Time

? | Answer | ➡
Help | Confirm | Next

The CAT's Word Processor

During the two GRE essays section, you'll use the simple word processor built into the CAT system. While the word processor includes some features standard in programs like Word and WordPerfect, it also lacks many of these programs' features.

Keyboard Commands for Navigation and Editing

Here are the navigational and editing keys available in the CAT word processor:

- **Backspace** removes the character to the left of the cursor.
- **Delete** removes the character to the right of the cursor.
- **Home** moves the cursor to the beginning of the line.
- **End** moves the cursor to the end of the line.
- **Arrow Keys** move the cursor up, down, left, or right.
- **Enter** inserts a paragraph break (starts a new line).
- **Page Up** moves the cursor up one page (screen).
- **Page Down** moves the cursor down one page (screen).

Certain often-used features of standard word processing programs are not available in the CAT word processor. For example, no keyboard commands are available for:

- TAB—disabled (does not function)

- Beginning/end of paragraph (not available)

- Beginning/end of document (not available)

- No key combinations (using the CTRL, ALT, or SHIFT key) or other so-called "macros" are available for editing functions. (You'll use your mouse for cutting and pasting text.)

Mouse-Driven Navigation and Editing Functions

Just as with other word processors, to navigate the editing screen you can simply point the cursor to the position at which you wish to begin typing, then click. The CAT word processor also includes mouse-driven CUT, PASTE, and UNDO.

Selecting text you wish to cut. You select text the same way as with standard word processing programs: either (1) hold down your mouse button while sweeping the I-beam on the screen over the desired text, or (2) hold down the SHIFT key and use the navigation keys to select text.

The CUT Button. If you wish to delete text but want to save it to a temporary clipboard for pasting elsewhere, select that text (see above) then click on the CUT button. Cutting text is not the same as deleting it. When you delete text (using the DELETE key), you cannot paste it elsewhere in your document (but see UNDO below).

The PASTE button. If you wish to move text from one position to another, select and cut the text, then reposition your cursor where you want the text to go and click on the PASTE button.

The UNDO button. Click on this button to undo the most recent delete, cut, or paste that you performed.

Limitations of CUT and UNDO. The following mouse-driven features are not available:

- DRAG-AND-DROP cut-and-paste (not available)

- COPY (not available; to copy you need to cut, then paste, in the same spot)

- MULTIPLE UNDO (the CAT word processor stores *only your most recent* delete, cut, or paste, or keyboard entry.)

PETERSON'S
getting you there

The vertical scroll bar. Once you key in ten lines or so, you'll have to scroll to view your entire response. A vertical scroll bar also appears to the right of the AWA prompt. Be sure to scroll all the way down to make sure you've read the entire prompt.

Spell-checking, grammar-checking, fonts, attributes, hyphenation. The CAT word processor does not include a spell-checker or grammar-checker, nor does it allow you to choose typeface or point size. Neither manual nor automatic hyphenation is available. Attributes such as bold, italics, and underlining are not available.

> As for words that you would otherwise italicize or underline (such as titles or non-English words), it's okay to leave them as is. The readers understand the limitations of the CAT word processor.

Note

The GRE CAT Test-Taking Experience

When you take a test as important as the GRE, it's a good idea to minimize test anxiety by knowing exactly what to expect on exam day—aside from the timed test itself. Let's walk you through the various pre-test and post-test procedures and describe the physical testing environment.

When You Arrive at the Test Center

Here's what you can expect when you arrive at the test center:

- The supervisor will show you a roster, which includes the names of test-takers scheduled for that day, and will ask you to initial the roster next to your name, and indicate on the roster your arrival time.

- The supervisor will ask you to read a two-page list of testing procedures and rules. (I'll cover all these rules in the pages immediately ahead.)

- The supervisor will give you a "Nondisclosure Statement." You're to read the printed statement, then *write* the statement (in the space provided on the form) and sign it. In the statement, you agree to the testing policies and rules, and you agree not to reproduce or disclose any of the actual test questions. The supervisor will not permit you to enter the exam room until you've written and signed the statement.

- You'll probably have to sit in a waiting room until the supervisor calls your name. A 5- to 10-minute wait beyond your scheduled testing time is not uncommon. (Taking the GRE is like going to the dentist—in more than one respect!)

- The supervisor will check your photo identification. (You won't be permitted to take the test unless you have one acceptable form of photo identification with you.)

- The test center will provide a secure locker (free of charge) for stowing your personal belongings during the test.

- To help ensure that nobody else takes any part of the exam in your place, the supervisor will take a photograph of you.

- The supervisor might give you some rudimentary tips about managing your time during the exam. Just ignore the supervisor's tips, because they might not be good advice for you!

- Before you enter the testing room, you must remove everything from your pockets except your photo I.D. and locker key.

- The supervisor will provide you with several pieces of scratch paper (stapled together), along with two pencils. These are the only items you'll have in hand as you enter the testing room.

Testing Procedures and Rules

- If you want to exit the testing room for any reason, you must raise your hand and wait for the supervisor to come in and escort you from the room. (You won't be able to pause the testing clock for any reason.)

- No guests are allowed in the waiting room during your test.

- No food or drink is allowed in the testing room.

- No hats are allowed.

- You must sign out whenever you exit the testing room.

- You must sign in whenever you re-enter the testing room (the supervisor will ask to see your photo I.D. each time).

- If you need more scratch paper during the exam, just raise your hand and ask for it. The supervisor will happily replace your bundle with a fresh one.

- The supervisor will replace your tired pencils with fresh, sharp ones upon your request anytime during the exam (just raise your hand).

What You Should Know about the CAT Testing Environment

- Individual testing stations are like library carrels; they're separated by half-walls.

- The height of your chair's seat will be adjustable and the chair will swivel. Chairs at most testing centers have arms.

- Computer monitors are generally of the 15-inch variety. You can adjust contrast. If you notice any flickering, ask the supervisor to move you to another station. (You won't be able to tell if you monitor has color capability, because the GRE is strictly a black-and-white affair.)

> You can't change the size of the font on the screen, unless you specifically request before the exam begins that a special ZOOMTEXT function be made available to you.

Alert!

- If your mouse has two buttons, you can use either button to click your way through the exam (both buttons serve the same function). Don't expect that nifty wheel between buttons for easy scrolling, because you're not going to get it. For all you gamers and laptop users, trackballs are available, but only if you request one before you begin the test.

- Testing rooms are not soundproof. During your test, you might hear talking and other noise from outside the room.

- Expect the supervisor to escort other test-takers in and out of the room during your test. Do your best to ignore this potential distraction.

- If the testing room is busy, expect to hear lots of mouse-clicking during your test. Because the room is otherwise fairly quiet, the incessant mouse-clicking can become annoying!

- Earplugs are available upon request.

- Expect anything in terms of room temperature, so dress in layers.

- You'll be under continual audio and video surveillance. To guard against cheating, and to record any irregularities or problems in the testing room as they occur, the room is continually audiotaped and videotaped. (Look for the cameras or two-way mirrors, then smile and wave!)

Before You Begin the Test—The Computer Tutorial

Okay, the supervisor has just escorted you into the inner sanctum and to your station, and has wished you luck. (Some supervisors have been known to encourage test-takers to "have fun!") Before you begin the test, the CAT System will lead you through a tutorial which includes five sections (each section steps you through a series of "screens"):

1. How to use the mouse (6 screens)

2. How to select and change an answer (6 screens)

3. How to scroll the screen display up and down (6 screens)

4. How to use the toolbars (21 screens); here you'll learn how to:

   - Quit the test.

   - Exit the current section.

   - Access the directions.

   - Confirm your response and move to the next question.

5. How to use the AWA word processor features (14 screens)

Here's what you need to know about the CAT tutorial:

- You won't be able to skip any section or any screen during the tutorial.

- As you progress, the system requires that you demonstrate competency in using the mouse, selecting and confirming answer choices, and accessing the directions. So you can't begin taking the actual test unless you've shown that you know how to use the system. (Don't worry: no test-taker has ever flunked the CAT system competency test.)

- At the end of each tutorial section (series of screens), you can repeat that section, at your option. But once you leave a section you can't return to it.

Alert!

Don't choose to repeat any tutorial section. Why not? If you do, you'll be forced to step through the entire sequence of screens in that section again (an aggravating time-waster, especially for the 21-screen section!)

- The Analytical Writing section of the tutorial allows you to practice using the word processor.

- If you carefully read all the information presented to you, expect to spend about 20 minutes on the tutorial.

On test day, you'll already know how the CAT system works. So step through the tutorial as quickly as you can, reading as little as possible. You can easily dispense with the tutorial in 5–10 minutes this way. Remember: The less time you spend with the tutorial, the less fatigued you'll be during the exam itself.

Tip

Post-Test GRE CAT Procedures

Okay, it's been about 4 hours since you first entered the testing center, and you've just completed the second of two multiple-choice GRE sections. You may think you've finished the CAT, but the CAT has not quite finished with you yet! There are a few more hoops to jump through before you're done.

1. **Respond to a brief questionnaire.** The CAT will impose on you a brief questionnaire (presented in a series of screens) about your test-taking experience (believe it or not, these questions are multiple-choice, just like the exam itself). The questionnaire might ask you, for example:

   - Whether your supervisor was knowledgeable and helpful

   - Whether the testing environment was comfortable

   - How long you waited after you arrived at the testing site to begin the test

   - Whether you were distracted by noise during your exam

2. **Cancel your test, at your option.** The most important question you'll answer while seated at your testing station is this next one. The CAT will ask you to choose whether to:

   - Cancel your scores (no scores are recorded; partial cancellation is not provided for) *or* see your scores immediately.

If you click on the CANCEL SCORES button, the CAT will then give you yet another 5 minutes to think over your decision. So you really have 10 minutes altogether to make up your mind.

Alert!

Once you elect to see your scores, you can no longer cancel them—ever! So you should take a few minutes to think it over. The CAT gives you 5 minutes to choose. If you haven't decided within 5 minutes, the CAT will automatically show you your scores (and you forfeit your option to cancel).

3. **View and record your scores.** If you elect to see your scores, you should write them down on your scratch paper. When you leave the testing room, the supervisor will allow you to transcribe them onto another sheet of paper (one that you can take home with you), so that you don't have to memorize them.

4. **Direct your scores to the schools of your choice.** Once you've elected to see your scores, the CAT will ask you to select the schools you wish to receive your score report (the CAT provides a complete list of schools).

Tip

You can select as many as five schools at this time—without incurring an additional fee. This is your last chance for a freebie, so you should take full advantage of it. Be sure to compile your list of five schools before exam day.

Before You Leave the Testing Center

Upon exiting the testing room for the final time, the following will happen:

1. The supervisor will collect your pencils and scratch paper, and will count the number of sheets of paper to make sure you aren't trying to sneak out with any. (Then, if you're lucky, you'll be allowed to watch while the supervisor ceremoniously rips up your scratch paper and drops it in the trash basket!)

2. The supervisor will remind you to collect your belongings from your locker (if you used one), and turn in your locker key.

3. The supervisor will provide you with an ETS pamphlet that explains how to interpret your test scores. (You can take this home with you.)

Note

The supervisor might also provide you with a postcard-sized invitation to "blow the whistle" on anybody you suspect of cheating on the exam (the invitation ends with the assurance: "Confidentiality guaranteed").

PETERSON'S
getting you there

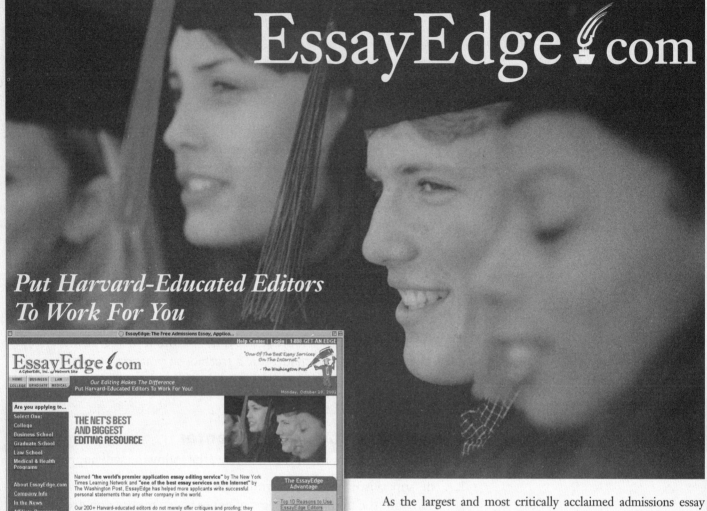